How to Publish High-Quality Research

How to Publish High-Quality Research

Jeff Joireman
Paul A. M. Van Lange

AMERICAN PSYCHOLOGICAL ASSOCIATION
WASHINGTON, DC

Published by
American Psychological Association
750 First Street, NE
Washington, DC 20002
www.apa.org

To order
APA Order Department
P.O. Box 92984
Washington, DC 20090-2984
Tel: (800) 374-2721; Direct: (202) 336-5510
Fax: (202) 336-5502; TDD/TTY: (202) 336-6123
Online: www.apa.org/pubs/books
E-mail: order@apa.org

In the U.K., Europe, Africa, and the Middle East, copies may be ordered from
American Psychological Association
3 Henrietta Street
Covent Garden, London
WC2E 8LU England

Typeset in Meridien by Circle Graphics, Inc., Columbia, MD

Printer: Maple Press, York, PA
Cover Designer: Berg Design, Albany, NY

The opinions and statements published are the responsibility of the authors, and such opinions and statements do not necessarily represent the policies of the American Psychological Association.

Library of Congress Cataloging-in-Publication Data

Joireman, Jeff.
  How to publish high-quality research / Jeff Joireman and Paul A. M. Van Lange.
    pages cm
  Includes bibliographical references and index.
  ISBN 978-1-4338-1861-5 — ISBN 1-4338-1861-2 1. Psychology—Authorship. 2. Psychology—Research. 3. Scholarly publishing. I. Lange, Paul A. M. van. II. Title.

  BF76.8.J65 2015
  808.06′615—dc23
                                        2014022533

British Library Cataloguing-in-Publication Data

A CIP record is available from the British Library.

Printed in the United States of America
First Edition

http://dx.doi.org/10.1037/14525-000

For Len, Mike, and Paul, whose mentoring over the years made this book possible
—Jeff Joireman

In memory of Willem and Hal, for their generosity and wisdom
—Paul A. M. Van Lange

Contents

III

Acknowledgments

This book would never have been accomplished without the support and encouragement of our colleagues, family, and friends, and we would like to acknowledge their many contributions. First, we would like to thank Maureen Adams for her support and enthusiasm, which were essential for starting the project, and Tyler Aune, our editor, who provided exceptional insights and guidance as we revised the book. We also thank the two anonymous reviewers, who helped us to significantly improve the book. Finally, we are also deeply indebted to each of the authors whose articles we discuss in Part II of the book. They all responded quickly and enthusiastically, shared carefully considered insights in a timely fashion, and expressed support and enthusiasm for the project. Indeed, their consistent support made this large undertaking possible and inspired us to keep pushing onward, especially when the goal of completing the book seemed so far off in the distance. We hope they enjoy the fruits of their insights.

Each of us would also like to extend special thanks to those within our respective circles. Jeff would like to thank Darrel Muehling and the rest of the Marketing Department at Washington State University for giving him room to write, even as a number of valuable projects were put on hold. He would also like to thank a number of people who provided input on various parts of the book, including Dominique Braxton, Brian Gillespie, Ioannis Kareklas, Sky King, Richie Liu, Mark Mulder, Adrienne Muldrow, U.N. Umesh, and Manja Zidansek. Finally, he would like to thank his wife, Esther, for her continual encouragement and feedback on various chapters, and Trevor and Joshua, for understanding why dad could not always attend every event.

Paul would like to thank all colleagues and students at the Vrije Universiteit, as well as other universities, for reflections and discussions about the various issues that are covered in this book. He also would like to thank his family, Wilma, Dion, and Sera, for understanding why late e-mails from the state of Washington can be urgent.

How to Publish
High-Quality
Research

Introduction

Goals and Organization of the Book

M ost dedicated scientists are driven by their scientific curiosity—their quest for knowledge and understanding of facts, phenomena, and principles. And most social and behavioral scientists are deeply interested in understanding human cognition, emotion, and behavior. But as scientists, we are also challenged to make a contribution and impact our fields. This challenge can be triggered by various motives, including wanting to make a difference; gain tenure or promotion; have a lasting impact on a field (or fields); support departmental or university goals; or at the broadest level, advance science.

Despite such lofty goals, it is not always easy to make a significant contribution to one's field. For example, in social and consumer psychology, our primary fields, the base rates for accepting manuscripts in top-tier journals are low, typically less than 20%, and reviewers tend to emphasize a manuscript's limitations a bit more than its strengths. Thus, all too often, when the reviews arrive, authors—of any rank—

http://dx.doi.org/10.1037/14525-001
How to Publish High-Quality Research, by J. Joireman and P. A. M. Van Lange

are somewhere in between slightly-to-exceptionally disappointed, frustrated, and occasionally angry as well.

At this point, a flurry of questions often races through a researcher's mind: "I worked so hard on this. Why didn't the reviewers recognize my efforts?" or "Most people I talked to seemed to like my paper. Why didn't the reviewers find my paper interesting?" These reactions are only human, and we readily admit to having raised the same questions ourselves. But if a researcher truly aspires to make a significant contribution, it is imperative to ask oneself a number of additional questions: "Why wasn't my contribution strong enough? What constitutes a significant contribution? And how can I optimize my chances of publishing high-quality research capable of making a lasting impact on my field?"

A quick look at an array of high-quality and heavily cited articles within any discipline suggests that there are, in the end, many ways to publish high-quality research and ultimately impact one's field. Some articles advance a theory, others review the literature, and others introduce a new way to study a phenomenon. Take a closer look, however, and a central theme will emerge: Regardless of the route taken, high-quality research capable of impacting one's field makes a significant contribution by filling a meaningful gap in our understanding of a phenomenon. From this perspective, the key challenge facing researchers hoping to publish high-quality research is to uncover the various ways one can "make a contribution" and "fill a meaningful gap" in the literature.

Qualities and Pillars Supporting High-Quality Research

With this as a backdrop, the primary goal of this book is to offer a framework and set of tools that can help readers make a contribution, fill a gap, publish high-quality research, and have an impact. The fundamental assumption underlying this book is that the probability of publishing high-quality research is a function of three types of quality: (a) the quality of the ideas (and theoretical framework) at the heart of the manuscript; (b) the quality of the methods and empirical findings supporting those ideas; and (c) the quality of the initial submission, revision, and one's promotion activities, such as sharing one's work with colleagues and the media (i.e., the 3Qs). If any of the 3Qs is low, the likelihood of eventually publishing in a top-tier journal and having a significant impact is also low. Accordingly, the goal of this book is to help readers understand how to maximize the 3Qs.

FIGURE 1

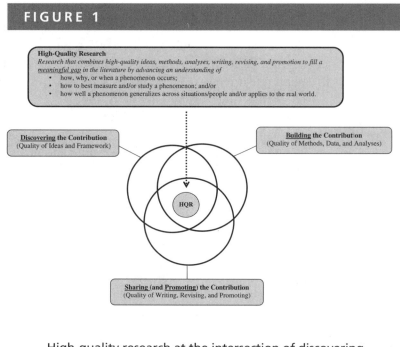

High-quality research at the intersection of discovering, building, and sharing.

In Figure 1, we conceptualize the 3Qs in terms of three key "pillars" supporting high-quality research: (a) discovering the contribution (which deals with the quality of the ideas and theoretical framework), (b) building the contribution (which deals with the quality of the methods and analyses), and (c) sharing the contribution (which deals with the quality of the initial submission, effectiveness in dealing with the revision process, and quality of one's promotion activities).

As can be seen, high-quality research lives at the intersection of discovering, building, and sharing and can be defined as research that combines high-quality ideas, methods, analyses, writing, revising, and promotion to fill a meaningful gap in the literature by advancing an understanding of (a) how, why, or when a phenomenon occurs; (b) how to best measure and/or study a phenomenon; and/or (c) how well a phenomenon generalizes across situations/people or applies to the real world. Of course, it is not necessary to achieve each of these goals in a single paper or line of research. Indeed, the approach one takes will depend largely on one's specialization and orientation. Applied psychologists, for example, are likely to be mostly interested in understanding real-world applications, whereas neuroscientists aiming to develop animal models may be more interested in precisely how, why, or when a phenomenon occurs. Accordingly, the definition of high-quality research we offer is able to accommodate multiple approaches and interests. Indeed, our definition underscores our original claim that there are many different ways to make a significant contribution and that the essential feature of high-quality research is its contribution, or ability to fill a meaningful gap in the literature.

Throughout this book, we take a careful look at the three essential pillars that support high-quality research. To be more precise, we offer an integrative framework for publishing high-quality research that addresses key questions raised by researchers at each stage of the process, as shown in Figure 2. For example, how do I locate and identify good ideas that "make a contribution"? How do I frame those ideas and position my contribution? How do I design research that makes a contribution? How do I get reviewers interested in my ideas? How do I navigate the review process? How do I translate publication into impact? And what are effective ways to promote my work? Of course, these questions serve only as salient examples; as we explore in detail throughout this book, researchers must address many more questions at each stage of the process.

Intended Audience

The book's intended audience includes graduate students, advisors, instructors, and professors at all ranks. To begin, it is no secret that many graduate students struggle as they try to find a way to make their mark on their field. Our hope is that this book will help graduate students recognize, early on, the different ways that they can make a contribution to their chosen field and to proceed systematically toward that end. The book is also written to help advisors and instructors in their efforts to mentor graduate students. Mentoring and teaching is hard work. Graduate students, especially early on, may have difficulty independently formulating novel research questions that have the potential to make significant contributions. They may bring the advisor or instructor a partially formed research idea based on one or two previous studies, but they fail to see how the proposed study fits within the broader picture and, most important, how the proposed study fills a meaningful gap in the literature. From our perspective, as advisors (and some years ago, as graduate students), this book can also potentially serve as a useful framework for advisor—mentee discussions of how to publish high-quality research. Finally, we hope the book can help even experienced scholars strengthen their research and ultimately publish

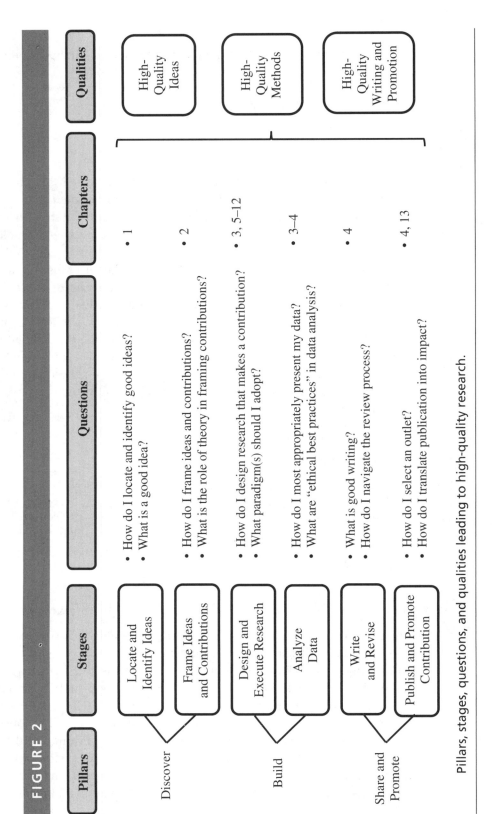

FIGURE 2

Pillars	Stages	Questions	Chapters	Qualities
Discover	Locate and Identify Ideas	• How do I locate and identify good ideas? • What is a good idea?	• 1	High-Quality Ideas
	Frame Ideas and Contributions	• How do I frame ideas and contributions? • What is the role of theory in framing contributions?	• 2	
Build	Design and Execute Research	• How do I design research that makes a contribution? • What paradigm(s) should I adopt?	• 3, 5–12	High-Quality Methods
	Analyze Data	• How do I most appropriately present my data? • What are "ethical best practices" in data analysis?	• 3–4	
Share and Promote	Write and Revise	• What is good writing? • How do I navigate the review process?	• 4	High-Quality Writing and Promotion
	Publish and Promote Contribution	• How do I select an outlet? • How do I translate publication into impact?	• 4, 13	

Pillars, stages, questions, and qualities leading to high-quality research.

high-quality papers that advance their careers, disciplines, and most broadly, science.

Preparing the Book

Preparing this book was a real pleasure. We both started this project enthusiastic about research and walked away more excited than ever about the variety of important theoretical and practical questions being addressed, often with very creative methods, across a variety of fields within psychology and marketing.

Preparing this book was also a bit of a challenge. Most notably, selecting a limited number of papers to illustrate the eight publication paradigms discussed in Part II repeatedly posed a dilemma, as it was unfortunately impossible to discuss all the high-quality publications we would have liked. However, we sought to highlight a variety of different topics that would be of interest to a wide range of scholars, and we hope readers will find that the examples help shed light on the underlying paradigms for publishing high-quality research and how their own work fits within these paradigms.

Organization of the Book

This book is divided into three major sections. The three sections correspond to (a) several key foundations for research, (b) eight paradigms for publishing high-quality research, and (c) reflections on the process of publishing.

FOUNDATIONS FOR HIGH-QUALITY RESEARCH

In Part I, we consider four basic foundations for high-quality research. In Chapter 1, we discuss strategies for discovering and developing novel and thought-provoking questions. Drawing on insights from leading scholars in our fields, we reveal 16 sources of inspiration that can lead researchers to identify engaging and important research questions. In Chapter 2, we define theory, explain why it is important for developing high-quality research, and outline a framework for evaluating theories known as TAPAS (Van Lange, 2013). The TAPAS system argues that researchers should use truth, abstraction, progress, and applicability as standards for evaluating theories. Building on good ideas and strong theory, in Chapter 3, we subsequently discuss the importance of conducting research and analyzing data in accordance with high ethical standards. In this chapter, it will be clear that we believe striving for high-quality and high-impact research cannot be separated from sound ethical research principles and that these principles always need to be respected in the pursuit of making a significant contribution. In Chapter 4, we provide detailed advice on how to submit a strong initial manuscript and successfully navigate the revision process, drawing on our experience as authors, reviewers, and editors. Checklists are included to help researchers work through the initial submission and revision process.

PARADIGMS FOR PUBLISHING HIGH-QUALITY RESEARCH

With these issues laid as a foundation, in Part II of the book, we outline eight powerful paradigms for publishing high-quality research. To help readers appreciate the paradigms "in action," in each of these chapters we describe six articles that illustrate the paradigm. Here, we highlight how the authors came up with and fine-tuned their research question(s), developed their theory and hypotheses, and empirically tested their hypotheses. As we prepared each illustration, we also asked the authors for their advice on publishing high-quality and high-impact research. A brief overview of the paradigms is provided next.

Paradigm 1: Bridge Disciplines

Bridging disciplines involves drawing on the human, theoretical, methodological, and/or empirical resources of a related discipline to shed new light on one's own discipline, contribute new insights to a related discipline, and consequently advance progress in both disciplines. In Chapter 5, we illustrate the bridging paradigm with papers (a) using an evolutionary social psychological framework to understand the motives that encourage "green" consumption behaviors (Griskevicius, Tyber, & Van den Bergh, 2010), (b) exploring the potential of subliminal priming to impact consumer preferences (Karremans, Stroebe, & Claus, 2006), (c) testing the hypothesis that social exclusion motivates consumers to spend money strategically to reestablish social connection (Mead, Baumeister, Stillman, Rawn, & Vohs, 2011), (d) using terror management theory to understand what motivates people to connect to brands (Rindfleisch, Burroughs, & Wong, 2009), (e) exploring if and why people stigmatize materialistic people and pursuits (Van Boven, Campbell, & Gilovich, 2010), and (f) drawing on ego-depletion theory to understand impulsive buying (Vohs & Faber, 2007).

Paradigm 2: Conduct a Meta-Analysis

Meta-analysis allows researchers to compute an average effect size across a collection of studies and evaluate how methodological and theoretically relevant variables moderate the effect size. In Chapter 6, we illustrate the meta-analysis paradigm with papers summarizing research on (a) the theory of planned behavior's ability to predict condom use (Albarracín, Johnson, Fishbein, & Muellerleile, 2001), (b) the consequences of workplace harassment from the victim's perspective (Bowling & Beehr, 2006), (c) the predictive validity of the Implicit Association Test (Greenwald, Poehlman, Uhlmann, & Banaji, 2009), (d) the strength model of self-control (Hagger, Wood, Stiff, & Chatzisarantis, 2010), (e) a cascading model of emotional intelligence as a predictor of job performance (Joseph & Newman, 2010), and (f) the individual and organizational consequences of engaging in organizational citizenship behaviors (N. P. Podsakoff, Whiting, Podsakoff, & Blume, 2009).

Paradigm 3: Launch a Paradigm Shift: Challenging Existing Assumptions and Testing Competing Theories

The bridging and meta-analysis paradigms both focus on finding similarities and structure across potentially disparate domains. Complementing these paradigms, researchers often find it valuable to launch paradigm shifts by "pushing the boundaries" of existing theory and challenging existing (theoretical and/or common-sense) assumptions. In Chapter 7, we focus on how researchers can create paradigm shifts by testing competing theories and challenging existing assumptions. The articles used in this chapter illustrate the paradigm-shifting paradigm by (a) testing competing theories on how concern with the well-being of others and self-control interact to predict forgiveness in social dilemmas (Balliet, Li, & Joireman, 2011); (b) challenging the assumption that insincere flattery does not work (E. Chan & Sengupta, 2010); (c) demonstrating that counter to many lay theories, spending money on others leads to greater happiness than spending money on the self (Dunn, Aknin, & Norton, 2008); (d) highlighting that customers do not always seek revenge following failed service recoveries (Joireman, Grégoire, Devezer, & Tripp, 2013); (e) showing that although high-status influence sources are typically assumed to be more effective, low-status consumers can sometimes significantly influence the consumption patterns of other consumers (Shalev & Morwitz, 2012); and (f) establishing that generosity, rather than a strict tit-for-tat (eye-for-an-eye) strategy, is the most effective way to promote cooperation in situations characterized by negative noise, where one's actual level of cooperation is occasionally lower than one's intended cooperation because of factors outside one's control (Van Lange, Ouwerkerk, & Tazelaar, 2002).

Paradigm 4: Combine Mediators and Moderators: Mediated Moderation, Moderated Mediation

Regardless of the domain, once researchers establish a basic effect (or relationship), they are often interested in understanding why the effect occurs (mediation) and identifying conditions under which the effect is stronger or weaker (moderation). Identifying mediators and moderators helps contribute to the refinement of theory by articulating underlying mechanisms and boundary conditions for an effect. Recently, researchers have begun to combine mediation and moderation in the same paper, which allows for a test of mediated moderation (i.e., what mediates the key interaction?) and moderated mediation (i.e., is the indirect/mediated effect of interest moderated by a third variable?). In Chapter 8, we illustrate mediated moderation with three papers exploring (a) whether the interaction between frequency of sex and insecure attachment on relationship satisfaction is mediated by expectations of partner availability (Little, McNulty, & Russell, 2010), (b) whether the interaction between a political candidate's gender and power-seeking intentions on voter support is mediated by feelings of moral outrage (Okimoto & Brescoll, 2010), and (c) whether the interaction between brand biography (underdog vs. top dog) and consumer characteristics (e.g., underdog disposition, culture) is mediated via identification with the underdog brand (Paharia, Keinan, Avery, & Schor, 2011). Following these mediated moderation illustrations, we illustrate moderated mediation with studies showing that (a) actual/ideal self-discrepancy moderates the impact of exposure to thin media models on social comparison processes, as well as the relationship between social comparison and negative psychological outcomes (e.g., depression and reduced self-esteem; Bessenoff, 2006); (b) good intentions predict plans to exercise, but plans to exercise only translate into behavior when self-efficacy is high (Luszczynska et al., 2010); and (c) strong exercise and dental hygiene intentions "catalyze" action plans into action (Wiedemann, Schüz, Sniehotta, Scholz, & Schwarzer, 2009).

Paradigm 5: Develop a New Tool to Assess Individual Differences

Scholars in various disciplines have long been interested in developing tools, often consisting of self-report scales, to measure new individual differences. In Chapter 9, we provide an overview of the scale-development paradigm and then illustrate this paradigm with papers that have developed scales to measure (a) *grit*, defined as "perseverance and passion toward long-term goals" (Duckworth, Peterson, Matthews, & Kelly, 2007, p. 1087); (b) need for cognitive closure (Webster & Kruglanski, 1994); (c) the tendency to be a tightwad (who has trouble spending money) versus a spendthrift (who can easily spend money; Rick, Cryder, & Lowenstein, 2008); (d) compulsive buying tendencies (Ridgway, Kuhar-Kinney, & Monroe, 2008); (e) brand engagement in the self-concept, defined as the "propensity to include important brands as a part of how [people] view themselves" (Sprott, Czellar, & Spangenberg, 2009, p. 92); and (f) consideration of future consequences (Strathman, Gleicher, Boninger, & Edwards, 1994).

Paradigm 6: Introduce an Innovative New Method

Innovative methods represent any novel, intriguing, or cutting-edge independent variable, data collection method, or data analytic technique that, briefly put, makes readers say, "I wish I had thought about that." In Chapter 10, we illustrate these types of methods by highlighting six papers exploring (a) whether women purchase sexier clothing when they are ovulating (Durante, Griskevicius, Hill, Perilloux, & Li, 2011); (b) how much people would "pay" for an attractive mate (Li, Bailey, Kenrick, & Linsenmeier, 2002); (c) whether eating Thanksgiving dinner can reduce impulse buying (Mishra & Mishra, 2010); (d) if women exposed to social identity threat show increased cortisol responses, indicative of stress (Townsend, Major, Gangi, & Mendes, 2011); (e) whether men who are exposed to sexy stimuli, including lingerie, are more likely to desire immediate gratification (Van den Bergh, Dewitte, & Warlop, 2008); and (f) the relatively subtle ways in which people can demonstrate concern for another person's broader desires (social mindfulness; Van Doesum, Van Lange, & Van Lange, 2013).

Paradigm 7: Venture Into the Real World

Complementing the innovative method paradigm, in Chapter 11, we consider the benefits of conducting research in the real world, which helps establish the generalizability and practical implications of one's findings. The six articles we highlight to illustrate the real-world paradigm draw on a variety of creative methods, using interventions, confederates, and behavioral coding to show that (a) consumers respond more favorably to a product when an attractive member of the opposite sex touches the product (Argo, Dahl, & Morales, 2008), (b) cooperation can be enhanced when subtle cues suggesting that one is being watched are placed in the environment (Bateson, Nettle, & Roberts, 2006), (c) health behaviors can be promoted by linking unhealthy behaviors with "dissociative reference groups" (i.e., groups one does not necessarily dislike but would prefer to not be associated with; Berger & Rand, 2008), (d) exposure to violent media (videogames and films) reduces prosocial behavior (Bushman & Anderson, 2009), (e) winter weather reduces financial risk taking among people with seasonal affective disorder (Kramer & Weber, 2012), and

(f) thinking about money reduces the amount of time spent socializing with others (Mogilner, 2010).

Paradigm 8: Explore the Role of Culture

The final paradigm chapter focuses on how researchers can enhance the impact of their research by "exploring the role of culture." The major focus is on the benefits of, and methodological issues involved in, cross-cultural psychology. The six illustrations chosen for Chapter 12 represent an incredible range of creative approaches researchers are using to study cross-cultural differences, including papers exploring (a) cross-cultural differences in the tendency to punish cooperators (and noncooperators) in public goods dilemmas (Herrmann, Thöni, & Gächter, 2008); (b) a culture × personality × situation (CuPS) model of face, dignity, and honor cultures (Leung & Cohen, 2011); (c) how differences in the built environment (e.g., density and complexity of buildings) between cultures shapes basic perceptual processes (Miyamoto, Nisbett, & Masuda, 2006); (d) cultural differences in responses to brand extensions (Monga & John, 2007); (e) how regional differences in disease prevalence around the world shaped cultural variation in sociosexual orientation, extraversion, and openness to experience (Schaller & Murray, 2008); and (f) cultural differences in willingness to accept a free gift from a casual acquaintance (Shen, Wan, & Wyer, 2011).

Integrating Paradigms

In preparing this book, we aimed to select papers that nicely illustrated each paradigm. As readers will see, many of the papers used as a primary illustration for one paradigm also illustrate one or more of the other paradigms. Although we did not consciously choose to highlight such "multiple paradigm papers," it turns out that most, if not all, of the papers we have highlighted fall into that category. This fact underscores a broader conclusion for readers interested in publishing high-quality research: Although your project may emphasize one paradigm over another, integrating multiple paradigms can increase the likelihood that your paper will receive significant attention.

Interdisciplinary Perspectives

Given our backgrounds, the illustrations selected for the book focus heavily on social psychology and consumer behavior. With that said, generating ideas, theory building and ethics, the eight publication paradigms, and elements of high-quality writing apply to most, if not all, scholars. Moreover, as we selected the illustrations, we endeavored to put together a collection of articles with broad appeal to a variety of

EXHIBIT 1

Relevance of Paradigm Illustrations to Various Psychological Disciplines Beyond Social and Consumer Psychology

Applied Psychology	Entire chapter devoted to conducting research in real-world settings, and many other featured articles are conducted in applied settings.
Behavioral Economics	Temporal discounting, impulsive buying, compulsive buying, pain of paying, brand identification and willingness to pay, cooperation and trust
Clinical Psychology	Compulsive buying, self-control, forgiveness, aggression, persistence toward goals, social exclusion, stress from stereotyping
Cognitive Psychology	Priming, need for cognitive closure, self-brand connections, implicit versus explicit attitudes, risk aversion, temporal discounting
Cultural Psychology	Entire chapter devoted to exploring how culture shapes thoughts and behavior
Developmental Psychology	Attachment theory, trust, self-control, social exclusion, body esteem
Evolutionary Psychology	Human cooperation and reputation, costly signaling theory, competitive altruism, ovulation and consumer behavior, status and green consumerism, sex differences in mating strategies
Health Psychology	Ego depletion, self-control, persistence toward goals, healthy eating, stress and cortisol responses, condom use, psychological well-being
(Social) Neuroscience	Biological basis of altruism and cooperation, processing of reward and punishment, fiscal responsibility and the "pain of paying," hormonal responses to threat and challenges
Organizational Psychology	Trust, cooperation, reputation, organizational citizenship behavior, implicit and explicit attitudes, workplace harassment, stereotyping
Personality Psychology	Entire chapter devoted to developing individual differences scales, and many illustrations of personality as a moderator across a wide range of settings
Quantitative Psychology	Meta-analysis, scale development, mediated moderation, moderated mediation, novel experimental methods

disciplines. Indeed, as we summarize in Exhibit 1, the content covered in the highlighted articles spans a large range of topics of interest to at least 12 related disciplines.

PROCESS MODEL FOR PUBLISHING HIGH-QUALITY RESEARCH

In the final part of the book, we wrap up the book's insights. In Chapter 13, we develop and discuss an integrative process model for publishing high-quality research that emerged on the basis of the combined wisdom of the authors we interviewed. The process model is a flowchart articulating the various stages of the research process leading to high-quality research capable of having a significant impact. The model starts by highlighting how a researcher's goals and objectives are key drivers of the entire process. On the basis of the insights of the authors we interviewed, researchers are encouraged to pick a topic of genuine interest; recognize that there are multiple routes to a quality publication; avoid chasing the "dragon of impact" (Griskevicius, Tybur, & Van den Bergh, 2010; Chapter 5); and strive for perfection, integrity, and transparency. Scholars then must prepare mentally for the research process (e.g., think big, attend to real-world problems) and prepare academically (e.g., by reading broadly and continually learning new methods). This mental and academic preparation, in turn, enhances several critical skills, including one's ability to ask compelling questions, to be aware of theory and research, and to attain a "methodological bandwidth" (Leung & Cohen, 2011; Chapter 12, this volume). These skills then support the ability to execute high-quality research and ultimately publish (and promote) the contribution by writing a strong initial submission; successfully navigating the revision process; and promoting the work following publication, for example, through news releases and sharing one's work within the broader "community of scholars." Our hope is that the model will be useful for both emerging scholars looking for a systematic approach to establishing a meaningful line of research and mentors considering how to best train students to publish high-quality research.

In Chapter 14, we reflect on the book's key themes and discuss the importance of collaborating and persisting in the research process. Research is a stimulating endeavor, but it can also be a challenging process. As we discuss in this chapter, often what makes or breaks one's ability to publish in top-tier outlets is assembling a top-notch research team, conviction in one's ideas, and Grit or determination to persist in the face of challenges and obstacles (Duckworth, Peterson, Matthews, & Kelly, 2007; Chapter 9). Our hope is that the tools, strategies, and processes outlined in this book will help readers initiate, execute, and publish research that helps them reach new heights in their research careers.

DEVELOPING IDEAS, DESIGNING STUDIES, AND WRITING MANUSCRIPTS

Discovering High-Quality Ideas
The Many Roads to Rome

1

Overview

In the Introduction to this volume, we defined *high-quality research* as research that combines high-quality ideas, methods, analyses, writing, revising, and promotion to fill a meaningful gap in the literature by advancing an understanding of (a) how, why, or when a phenomenon occurs; (b) how to best measure and/or study a phenomenon; and/or (c) how well a phenomenon generalizes across situations and people and/or applies to the real world. In this chapter, we consider the many different ways researchers discover, identify, and develop high-quality ideas. By the end of the chapter, it should be clear that there are "many roads to Rome." Good ideas come from many sources, and yet all possess a common feature. At the end of the day, quality ideas pose questions that readers feel compelled to answer. Ideas offer a paradox, a puzzle, a mystery, or a problem that needs to be solved. Ideas are the bait that gets readers to bite, and once hooked, readers want answers. In our

http://dx.doi.org/10.1037/14525-002
How to Publish High-Quality Research, by J. Joireman and P. A. M. Van Lange

experience, this "bait and hook" nearly always occurs in the very beginning of a manuscript, often as early as the first several paragraphs (for a discussion of how to write effective opening paragraphs, see Chapter 4).

Of course, knowing where ideas should be placed in a manuscript is important. But knowing where they come from is even more important. And as many readers will likely know, discovering good ideas can sometimes be quite challenging. Oftentimes, of course, profitable ideas come from reading the literature. We would not disagree, but given time to reflect, many experienced researchers would add that reading is only part of the equation. Indeed, as we illustrate in this chapter, ideas come not only from reading the literature but also from an intuition, a hunch, a curiosity, an observation, a personal interaction, or the need to solve an immediate and practical problem (see also Fiske, 2004). Given this, some might suggest that researchers searching for good ideas can simply abandon the literature and "shoot from the hip." A closer inspection, however, suggests that this approach would ultimately lack power. Indeed, even when the idea seems to originate from a more casual, atheoretical approach, it is clear that the ability to recognize these good ideas is strongly grounded, at least at an implicit level, in the researcher's knowledge of the relevant theory and research. In other words, when traced back to its origins, an idea that first appears as a hunch or an intuition usually has its roots in a researcher's knowledge of a certain literature. Directly applying the relevant theory and research may occur later, but we would argue that even "intuitions" and "hunches" that an idea is worth pursuing are typically well grounded in the researcher's training.

To gain greater insight into the idea-generating stage, we asked the authors of the articles we discuss in Part II of this book to share the origin of their project and their advice for others hoping to publish high-quality research. As shown in Table 1.1, the highlighted authors provided at least 16 different strategies a researcher can use to identify high-quality ideas. For purposes of discussion, we have organized the strategies into eight broader styles, though a close inspection of any article will likely reveal that the authors have used multiple styles to identify their questions. Complementing Table 1.1, Exhibit 1.1 lists several examples of questions a researcher might ask using each of the eight styles.

Styles and Strategies for Identifying High-Quality Ideas

The majority of strategies for identifying and motivating research questions can readily be found in the first few paragraphs of any journal article. Other sources of inspiration, however, are more tacit and more

TABLE 1.1

Styles and Action Strategies for Generating High-Quality Ideas

Style	Action strategy	Object
Interactive	Interact	with colleagues
	Read	across disciplines
Observant	Draw on	personal, social, or historical observations
	Observe	a real-world phenomenon
Societal	Address	a real-world problem
	Generalize	theory to a societal problem
Integrative	Merge	disciplines
	Organize	a literature
Challenging	Challenge	intuition, common sense, or assumptions
	Test	competing theories (or reverse an effect)
Inquisitive	Resolve	a paradox
	Understand	a mechanism
Creative	Develop	new methods
	Introduce	a new model
Comparative	Compare	cultures
	Explore	boundary conditions

Note. Based on coding of interviewed authors' responses to the question *How did you hope to make a contribution?*

EXHIBIT 1.1

Questions Useful for Generating High-Quality Research Ideas by Style

1. Interactive: How do my colleagues in different disciplines approach this problem? What ideas can I gather by reading other disciplines that can help me better understand my own research?
2. Observant: What interesting and important phenomena am I observing in my own life or the world at large? Is there a serious, real-world problem that needs to be better understood?
3. Societal: How might theory and research be applied to a real-world problem? What study could make a real contribution to understanding this societal issue—and perhaps even help resolve it?
4. Integrative: What new insights could we gain by drawing on fields outside our own? How might a variety of disciplines be integrated to help bring order to disparate (but related) literatures?
5. Challenging: Is conventional wisdom correct? Under what circumstances might it not hold? Are the hypotheses advanced by a given theory correct? Is there an alternative logic or theory that would suggest opposing hypotheses?
6. Inquisitive: We know this phenomenon occurs, but why? How can we understand this puzzling paradox?
7. Creative: How can we develop better methods to gain greater insight into this problem? Can I offer a novel theoretical framework to bring order to this area?
8. Comparative: Do these findings generalize across situations and cultures? What might be some boundary conditions that would eliminate or even reverse this effect?

likely to be "lurking behind the scenes." In particular, it is rarely the case that authors will reveal (in the manuscript) that a direct personal experience, a social encounter with colleagues, or a reading of the literature was the genesis for their project. However, sit down with any author and it is not uncommon to find that many good research ideas sprung from these very experiences (see also Fiske, 2004). In what follows, we discuss a variety of styles and strategies researchers use to identify high-quality ideas.

INTERACTIVE STYLE

According to many of the scholars we interviewed, interacting with colleagues both within and outside one's discipline is a fertile source of high-quality ideas. We call this approach the *interactive style*. A particularly fascinating example of the "interacting with colleagues" strategy is the research by Melissa Bateson, Daniel Nettle, and Gilbert Roberts (2006), highlighted in Chapter 11. To briefly summarize, Bateson and her colleagues found that when they posted a picture of a pair of eyes above the "honesty box" in the department's break room, people were more likely to pay for their coffee, tea, milk, and condiments than when they posted a picture of flowers above the honesty box. How did Bateson and her colleagues come up with such a great idea? The answer may surprise you. Although their research is clearly grounded in the literature on how rewards, punishment, and reputational concerns impact cooperation in social dilemmas, the original inspiration for conducting the study came not from reading that literature per se but from the very practical need to solve a real-world problem. In short, Bateson was losing money. As Bateson explained, she was in charge of buying the coffee, tea, milk, etc., for the department, and people were not paying for all the beverages they enjoyed. Bateson needed a solution. As she spoke to her colleagues, the group realized that the failure to cooperate in the break room could be framed as a social dilemma. As such, Bateson and her colleagues reasoned that it should be possible to increase donations to the honesty box by drawing on theory and research demonstrating that rewards and punishments (even indirectly administered) could increase cooperation levels. And so, the idea was born.

Many of the authors we interviewed also suggested reading broadly both within and across disciplines. Often, this approach offers researchers a new theoretical or methodological lens through which to approach their research. This strategy also can result in paradigm-shifting integrative reviews of a literature, or several literatures to be precise. An excellent example is Taylor and Brown's (1988) article titled, "Illusion and Well-Being: Offering a Social Psychological Perspective on Mental Health." In their article, the authors' primary aim was to "weave a theoretical context for thinking about mental health" (p. 193). The authors drew on literatures in social, clinical, cognitive, personality, developmental, educational, and motivational psychology to show that mental health is often promoted by systematic cognitive biases (e.g., unrealistically positive views of the self and perceptions of personal control). Because so many of the problems our world faces require an interdisciplinary approach, reading across disciplines is an essential strategy for producing high-quality research capable of having an impact (on multiple fields).

OBSERVANT STYLE

Another approach for identifying high-quality ideas is what we refer to as the *observant style*. Using the observant style, a researcher draws on personal, social, or historical observations as the starting point for an interesting idea or set of questions. For example, Barnhart and Peñaloza (2013) recently published a study exploring how older adults negotiate their identity via the consumption process. Through qualitative interviews, the authors documented the value in viewing older adults' consumption through the lens of an "elderly consumption ensemble" made up of the older adult consumer, family members, and caregivers who interact, navigate, and negotiate the older consumer's identity (e.g., as old vs. young). Illustrating the use of personal experience, Barnhart reported that the idea for the research came from her professional experience selling emergency services to elderly consumers and her experience with older family members.

Shared social experiences can also serve as a valuable basis for interesting and important research questions. As an example, noting the heavy media coverage of the 9/11 attacks on New York City and the war in Iraq, Silver and her colleagues set out to explore how exposure to such disturbing images impacts posttraumatic stress symptoms and physical health (e.g., Silver et al., 2013). Consistent with the authors' hypothesis, exposure to these troubling images increased stress and reduced physical health.

Finally, researchers can also generate excellent ideas by drawing on historical traditions. Historical traditions (and quotes) are often useful as a starting point because they can represent long-held assumptions that may (surprisingly) have never been tested directly. Condon, Desbordes, Miller, and DeSteno (2013), for example, tested (and supported) the Buddhist teaching that meditation enhances compassion.

SOCIETAL STYLE

Closely related to the observant style is the *societal style*. In the societal style, the researcher is specifically interested in understanding or solving a real-world social problem or testing the applicability of a theory to a real-world phenomenon. For example, Wolke, Copeland, Angold, and Costello (2013) were interested in determining the long-term impacts of one of society's most pressing concerns, bullying. Drawing on longitudinal data, Wolke and colleagues found that relative to children not involved in bullying, children involved in bullying showed poorer health, financial, and social outcomes and an increased likelihood of risky and illegal behavior.

In another paper illustrating the societal style, Tangney, Stuewig, and Martinez (2014) were interested in understanding arrest recidivism. Drawing on past theory and research, Tangney and her colleagues predicted that incarcerated felons would be less likely to reoffend after release when they experienced more guilt and less shame (assessed at intake). Results showed that guilt was directly associated with lower recidivism, and shame indirectly increased recidivism through externalization of blame (i.e., shame was positively associated with externalization, and externalization was positively related to recidivism).

INTEGRATIVE STYLE

A fourth style is the *integrative style*. Here, researchers may be motivated to merge two or more disciplines to gain insight into a problem, or organize a literature—for example, via meta-analysis. Taylor and Brown's (1988) paper, reviewed earlier, serves as an obvious example of this style (in addition to reading across disciplines). Another interesting example is work by Calogero (2013), who merged insights from system-justification and self-objectification theories to understand how women's self-objectification can interfere with their inclination to engage in feminist-based social activism (e.g., signing a petition supporting women's rights). In another example, Balliet, Mulder, and Van Lange (2011) used meta-analysis in an effort to bring order to the large literature testing the effects of reward and punishment on cooperation in social dilemmas (situations involving a conflict between short-term self-interest and long-term collective interest).

CHALLENGING STYLE

Another approach to generating research ideas is the *challenging style*, motivated by a desire to challenge intuition or commonly held assumptions or to test competing theories. For example, Grant (2013) called into question the assumption that extraverts were naturally better leaders, demonstrating instead that "ambiverts" (who are in between the two extremes and can switch between extraversion and introversion) make better leaders. In another study, S. K. Nelson, Kushlev, English, Dunn, and Lyubomirsky (2013) mounted a "defense of parenthood," challenging recent media accounts that "paint a dismal picture of parenting" (p. 3) and providing evidence counter to that proposition. Finally, Asplund, Fougnie, Zughni, Martin, and Marois (2014) tested competing theories regarding whether attention and awareness are allocated in a more discrete or graded manner.

INQUISITIVE STYLE

Another style that often motivates research questions is what we refer to as the *inquisitive style*. Although all research is, by definition, inquisitive, these strategies are particularly useful for understanding *why* a phenomenon works the way it does (i.e., the mechanism responsible for an established effect) or in resolving a paradox. As an example of the former, Jaremka et al. (2013) noted that although research had established a link between loneliness and poor health, the mechanism responsible for this link was not understood. To address this gap, the authors conducted two studies demonstrating that lonely people have more adverse reactions to stress, which in turn promotes less favorable health outcomes.

The inquisitive style is also used when a researcher is interested in trying to resolve an enigma or a paradox. Dahl et al. (2013), for example, were interested in understanding what could account for infants' "puzzling shift" from nonavoidance of heights to aversion to heights. Surprisingly, neither falls nor depth perception had been shown to explain the shift, leaving something of an enigma. Through a series of two studies, the authors were able to resolve the enigma by showing that wariness of heights emerged as a child engaged in and had the perception of self-movement.

CREATIVE STYLE

Researchers can also adopt a *creative style* by developing new methods or introducing a new model to explain a phenomenon. For example, Park and colleagues (2014) were interested in finding a way to study the effects of cognitive engagement on cognitive functioning in older adults. Prior to Park et al.'s paper, research had established a correlation between engagement and cognitive functioning, but little work had shown that engagement caused an improvement in cognitive functioning. The authors creatively addressed this problem by designing the "Synapse Project" in which older adults were engaged in cognitively challenging activities over a 14-week period (i.e., learning complex digital photography skills, quilting skills, or both). Compared with nonengaged control conditions (socializing, and routine activities not requiring new learning), the engaged conditions saw significant improvements in their (episodic) memory.

Another way authors can use the creative approach is to develop a new theoretical model to understand a phenomenon. In one recent study, for example, Wayne, Casper, Matthews, and Allen (2013) were motivated to develop a model to understand the impact of family-supportive organizational practices on employees' commitment to the organization. Consistent with their model, Wayne and colleagues found that family-supportive organizational practices reduced work-to-family conflict, which encouraged the employee's partner to form more favorable attitudes toward the employee's work and express higher commitment to the partner's firm, which in turn increased the employee's own commitment to the firm.

COMPARATIVE STYLE

Finally, researchers interested in studying whether a phenomenon generalizes across situations could adopt the *comparative style* by comparing cultures or identifying boundary conditions. Oishi and Diener (2014), for example, recently reported a large cross-national study designed to assess the relationship between gross domestic product, religiosity, meaning in life, and suicide rates. Drawing on data from a 2007 Gallup poll of 132 nations, Oishi and Diener showed that poorer nations were more likely to report being religious, which predicted higher reported meaning in life, which consequently predicted lower suicide rates.

The comparative style is also used when researchers are interested in establishing factors that might moderate a relationship between two variables and/or identify boundary conditions for an effect. As an example, W. K. Chan and Wan (2012) were interested in whether supervisor support might buffer the tendency for work stress and fatigue to reduce an employee's service quality and customer satisfaction. Across two studies, the researchers showed that although work stress always led employees to feel fatigued, fatigue only reduced employee service quality and customer satisfaction when supervisor support was low; when supervisor support was high, fatigue no longer reduced service quality or customer satisfaction.

Conclusion

In sum, various goals and activities lead researchers to discover high-quality ideas, and often researchers use a mix of these styles. As we will explore in more detail, many of these "styles" and "action strategies" can be directly linked to one of the eight "paradigms for publishing high-quality research" covered in the second part of this book (i.e., bridging disciplines, meta-analysis, launching a paradigm shift, understanding mediators and moderators, developing a scale, introducing novel new methods, venturing into the real world, and exploring the role of culture). Regardless of the source of inspiration, or the style or paradigm adopted, it is always important to keep in mind the key goal underlying high-quality research: namely, one must strive to fill a meaningful gap in the literature. Readers must be convinced not only that the researcher has an interesting idea and related question but also that answering that question will fundamentally advance an understanding of an important theoretical and/or societal issue.

Developing and Testing Theories

Truth, Abstraction, Progress, and Applicability as Standards (TAPAS)

2

As we noted at the outset of this book, the vast majority of manuscripts fail to get published in top-tier journals and have a significant impact either because they fail to offer a significant contribution or because the authors have failed to articulate that contribution. Although these failures can be due to poor design, execution, or data, more often than not, the key reason a manuscript fails to make a contribution is that it fails to fill a meaningful gap in the literature. And more often than not, failure to fill a meaningful gap in the literature is due to a failure to articulate and validly test a meaningful hypothesis derived from theory.

In this chapter, we encourage readers to "mind the gap" by prioritizing theory development and testing in their research. We begin by discussing what theory is and what it is not. We next review why theory is important. We then outline a system for evaluating theories based on the idea of truth, abstraction, progression and applicability as standards (TAPAS; Van Lange, 2013). We end by considering how the paradigms in this book can help researchers meet these standards.

http://dx.doi.org/10.1037/14525-003
How to Publish High-Quality Research, by J. Joireman and P. A. M. Van Lange
Copyright © 2015 by the American Psychological Association. All rights reserved.

What Theory Is and Is Not

Scholars have long debated what theory is and how it develops. A review of this vast literature is beyond the scope of this chapter. Readers interested in recent discussions can consult Van Lange, Kruglanski, and Higgins's (2012) *Handbook of Theories of Social Psychology* and a special issue of the journal *Personality and Social Psychology Review* (2004, Vol. 8, Issue 2). For our purposes, we offer a general definition that can help guide our discussion of the link between theory and the eight publication paradigms outlined in this book.

So, how might *theory* be defined? Recently, Van Lange (2013) suggested that theories can be viewed in terms of truth, abstraction, progress, and applicability. In this TAPAS framework, discussed in detail later in the chapter, theory ideally is aimed at addressing the "how and why" of particular events and phenomena to help us find the underlying "truth," beyond surface appearances. Theory helps us see the coherent structures in seemingly chaotic environments and make inroads into previously uncharted domains, thus affording progress in the way we understand the world around us. Because it elucidates the causal mechanisms that produce manifest effects, theory points to ways of intervening in phenomena and changing the course of events; hence, theory is of essential pragmatic value and constitutes an indispensable tool for application (Van Lange, 2013, p. 40).

Similarly, Sutton and Staw (1995) noted that

theory is the answer to queries of *why*. Theory is about the connections among phenomena, a story about why acts, events, structure, and thoughts occur. Theory emphasizes the nature of causal relationships, identifying what comes first as well as the timing of such events. Strong theory, in our view, delves into underlying processes so as to understand the systematic reasons for a particular occurrence or nonoccurrence . . . it may have implications that run counter to our common sense. (p. 378)

Taken together, these perspectives suggest that a theory may minimally be defined as a set of interrelated propositions (or principles) concerning how, why, or when a phenomenon or a set of phenomena occurs (Mandler & Kessen, 1959, p. 159; Shaw & Costanzo, 1982, p. 4).

Another way of understanding what theory is, is to consider "what theory is not." In their article by the same title, Sutton and Staw (1995) illustrated five common strategies authors mistakenly use in place of rigorous theory development—to summarize: (1) references to past work are not theory, because listing references does not explain *why* certain variables are interconnected; (2) reviewing past empirical evidence (data) is not theory, as "data describe *which* [italics in original] empirical patterns were observed and theory explains *why* [italics in original] empirical patterns were observed or are expected to be observed" (p. 374); (3a) offering and defining a long list of variables or constructs is not theory, (3b) testing the relative strength of different predictors is not theory, and (3c) testing a causal model (by itself) is not theory (though structural modeling is certainly a valuable tool for evaluating how reasonable a well-articulated theory matches the data); (4) similarly, though valuable, diagrams are not theory; rather, diagrams should be considered "stage props rather than the performance itself" (p. 376); and finally, (5) hypotheses and predictions are not theory; rather, they are *"crucial bridges* [italics added] between theory and data, making explicit how the variables and relationships that follow from a logical argument will be operationalized" (p. 376). Readers interested in specific examples of these misconceptions can consult Sutton and Staw.

THEORY VERSUS HYPOTHESES: AN ILLUSTRATION

One of the more common mistakes researchers make is to confuse hypotheses with theory. As such, in this section, we next illustrate the distinction between theory and hypotheses. This is not always an easy distinction to make, but we believe the current example can serve as a useful model for researchers.

Theory

One novel theoretical model, developed recently and highlighted in this book is the *strength model of self-control* (e.g., Baumeister, Bratslavsky, Muraven, & Tice, 1998; Hagger, Wood, Stiff, & Chatzisarantis, 2010). The strength model proposes that self-control operates like a muscle and that people possess a limited amount of self-control resources. As a result, when people exercise their self-control resources in one domain, their ability to exercise self-control in a subsequent domain diminishes (i.e., they become "ego depleted"). The model also assumes that just as a muscle can be strengthened over time, people can build up their self-control resources through distributed self-control exercises. In other words, the strength model is a theory about how self-control works.

Hypothesis

Research has tested a wide range of hypotheses derived from this theory (e.g., Hagger et al., 2010; see also Chapter 6, this volume). As an example, consider one of the experiments reported in Baumeister, Bratslavsky, Muraven, and Tice's (1998) original research (Experiment 3). In this experiment, participants were asked to watch a humorous or sad video. Participants in the control condition were instructed to let their emotions flow freely while watching the video (an initial task requiring no self-regulation); participants in the ego-depletion condition were instructed to suppress their emotions (an initial task requiring self-regulation). After watching the video, participants were given the task of solving anagrams because the authors assumed that this task would require "some degree of self-regulation" (p. 1259). As the authors noted, "the prediction [hypothesis] was that participants who had tried to control their emotional responses to the videotape would suffer from ego depletion, and as a result, would perform more poorly at anagrams" (p. 1259). Results confirmed that prediction, supporting the theory.

DISTINGUISHING BETWEEN THEORIES, MODELS, PRINCIPLES, AND HYPOTHESES

The preceding example illustrates the difference between theory (how self-control works, like a muscle) and hypotheses (specific predictions, operationalized with relevant independent and dependent variables) derived from the theory. Although the distinction in this case seems clear-cut, we do not mean to imply that the distinctions between theory, models, principles, and hypotheses are always obvious—indeed, for a particular model or theory, this can be a topic of hot scientific debate. Clearly, theories may differ in their generality, precision, and origins. And like individual scientists, areas of research, fields, and disciplines might differ in terms of the criteria that must be met to call a theory a theory, a model a model, and so on. Moreover, theories and disciplines are continually changing over time, and what was once yesterday's set of principles may have evolved into today's grand theory. For example, Kelley and Thibaut were exceptionally careful scientists who wrote a very influential book on interdependence (Thibaut & Kelley, 1959), which integrated social exchange insights and conceptual tools derived from game theory to help understand questions revolving around power, leadership, negotiation, coalition formation, trust, cooperation, communication, and coordination. Almost 20 years later, they felt that their ideas had been given the cumulative and systematic treatment to warrant describing their logic and ideas as a theory, namely, interdependence theory (Kelley & Thibaut, 1978), which then was further developed and enriched by Kelley and other interdependence scholars (Kelley et al., 2003; for a historical overview, see Van Lange, 2012). Finally, it is worth noting that the vast majority of social psychological theories tend to be "middle range" (Merton, 1949, p. 5) "works in progress" and "intermediate to minor working hypotheses" rather than grand theoretical edifices (see Pinker, 2002, p. 241; Van Lange, 2006, p. 8).

Why Theory Is Important

Having defined theory, we now consider why theory is important for filling meaningful gaps in the literature. In short, theory is important for at least three reasons. First, by focusing on broad, abstract principles, theories allow researchers to organize disparate and sometimes loosely connected empirical findings into an overall explanatory framework. This helps researchers, often from different disciplines, see connections between findings that otherwise might not be connected and form broader principles that can be tested in future research. Second, and relatedly, theories are tools for communication that transcend idiosyncratic methods, measures, statistical procedures, and the like. Finally, theories allow researchers to address the most fundamental scientific questions, namely, the "how" and "why" of different phenomena. For example, one might observe that exposure to violent video games increases aggression. This is important, of course, but the more interesting and fundamental question is why and how this occurs (e.g., by activating hostile cognitions or scripts; e.g., Anderson & Bushman, 2001).

Evaluating Theories: TAPAS

Whatever definition of a theory one adopts, it is important to ascertain what constitutes a good theory. Though numerous constructs have been advanced to outline various qualifications, standards, and criteria for theoretical "goodness," there is a fair amount of consensus on at least the following: Theories are believed to be better if they have greater explanatory power; are more suitable to empirical tests and modeling; are more "logical" in that they demonstrate coherence and internal consistency; and are capable of explaining more (phenomena) with less (by way of assumptions), reflecting the criterion of parsimony or Occam's razor (e.g., Fiske, 2004; Higgins, 2004). Subsequently, Kruglanski (2006) outlined the relevance of truth, abstraction, and progress in evaluating theories. And more recently, building on these insights, a TAPAS framework was advanced, which conceptualizes the evaluation of theories in terms of four broad regulatory ideals: namely, truth (including testability), abstraction, progress, and applicability (Van Lange, 2013).

A theory that "stands the test of time" meets at least four inter-related ideals. First, the theory is testable and deals with *truth*. That is, it leads to hypotheses that receive empirical support through carefully conducted research. Indeed, the entire logic of experimental design is to eliminate (or prove invalid) possible alternative interpretations of empirical facts. Critical experiments are designed to set apart competing theories and decide which one appears more valid—and is better supported by the available evidence—than its competitors. Of course, truth can be striven for but never securely attained, as alternative accounts of the same data are always possible in the future even if they may not be apparent in the present. Nevertheless, a good theory not only is testable but also stands up to empirical testing, over time.

Second, a theory that "stands the test of time" is *abstract* in the sense that the particulars (e.g., phenomena, events) are described in terms of the general (concepts, assumptions, principles). Although a particular phenomenon may be interesting in and of itself, one needs a theory to understand the psychological principles that underlie the phenomenon— the same principles that underlie other seemingly disparate phenomena as well. It is the higher level of abstraction (aggregation) that a theory should pursue, to transcend particular observations and link them at a deeper (i.e., more abstract) level to other observations. Thus, theories focus on the heart of the matter in terms of understanding and insight, as it deals with essential causal mechanisms underlying observed effects.

Third, a strong theory makes *progress*. In other words, the theory is expected to make a contribution beyond what was previously known; it should improve or expand our understanding of a given realm of phenomena; it should relate to and build on past theories, replacing inaccurate principles with accurate principles or complementing a predecessor theory with new principles (e.g., new causal variables, moderators, mediators) that had not previously been identified. Moreover, it often inspires new ways of thinking, because it serves as a tool for researchers to see connections and relationships that would not have been evident on the basis of data alone (Shaw & Costanzo, 1982). Finally, a theory is often an inspiration for new research questions, along with new tools, methodologies, and paradigms (Fiedler, 2004; Fiske, 2004). As such, theories function both as bridges to the past (the past findings a theory accounts for), to the future (future research and findings inspired by the theory), and between related disciplines. Because the implications of a theory inspire new predictions that in turn inspire new research to test them, a theory is the driving force behind new empirical discoveries about what the world is and how it works, resulting in progress from new discoveries (Higgins, 2004).

Finally, a good theory is *applicable*. That is, it speaks to many events and issues in everyday life and affords interventions aimed at addressing real-world problems. Just as scientific progress is closely linked to the quest for truth, a theory's applicability is closely linked to the precept of abstraction. In other words, the more abstract the theory, the greater its empirical content (Popper, 1935/1959) and the broader the range of situations to which it applies. Of course, theoretical breadth in and of itself is not tantamount to application, and an appreciable measure of ingenuity is needed to translate a theory's implications into specific procedures and interventions of practical value. In fact, despite the intimate relation between theory and application, the two have been often juxtaposed with each other and are often viewed as fundamentally disparate (i.e., theory vs. practice). Theory has been often associated with logic, deduction, and knowledge ("knowing"), whereas application has been often associated with intuition, induction, and implementation ("doing"). Perhaps Kurt Lewin's (1936) famous dictum, "There is nothing so practical as a good theory," received so much attention because it was surprising in light of the general tendency to view application as the very antithesis of theorizing.

Evaluating the Theories in This Book on the Basis of TAPAS

In Part II of this book, we highlight classic research that has clearly made a lasting impact and more recent research with strong potential to make a lasting impact. One common theme running through many of the highlighted articles is the fundamental role of a meaningful theoretical framework. The strength model of self-control (Baumeister et al., 1998; Hagger et al., 2010; Muraven, Tice, & Baumeister, 1998) serves as just one example of a theory that has been highly fruitful. Its tenants are strongly supported by a recent large-scale meta-analysis (truth), its basic premises are very general (abstract), it sheds important new light on a fundamental topic within psychology (progress), and it has been applied across a wide range of different settings (application). Although this is just one example, we think you will agree that many of the other theories highlighted in this book also stand up well in light of the TAPAS model.

How the Publication Paradigms Support TAPAS

The eight paradigms for publishing high quality research described in this book also support the TAPAS system. Each paradigm, for example, allows researchers to better understand the truth of a theory, and each allows a researcher to make progress with a theory. In their own ways, each paradigm also allows researchers to test the applicability of a given theory across domains and, hence, evaluate how abstract the theory can be. *Bridging disciplines*, for example, involves using a theory developed in one discipline to shed new light on phenomena in other disciplines. *Meta-analysis* not only allows one to examine truth but may also reveal an overall trend in a given domain and identify possible moderators of that effect size, thus allowing researchers to determine the abstractness of a theory and how far the theory applies. And *challenging assumptions* is a critical component of the iterative search for truth, as it may identify boundary conditions for an effect or alternative mediating processes to explain a causal path. Indeed, an assumption in the TAPAS framework is that the four ideals can help advance science through an iterative process, whereby bridging disciplines might open new avenues of research and help develop "the bigger picture"; meta-analyses might uncover critical moderators (and perhaps a serious quest for reevaluation); and challenging assumptions can uncover uncharted territories, perspectives, and ideas that lead to important innovations in theory (or application thereof) or even complete paradigm shifts in thinking. Indeed, a theory is never finished.

Conclusion

Quality theory development is a key to filling meaningful gaps in the literature, and filling meaningful gaps in the literature is essential for publishing high-quality research. In this chapter, we have considered what theory is and what theory is not, and we have highlighted the TAPAS system for evaluating theories, emphasizing its iterative nature and how the eight publication paradigms help support and inform the TAPAS system. Hand in hand with good theory development are quality methods for testing those theories, and one vital component of a quality method is its adherence to well-established ethical principles, a topic to which we turn next.

Ethical Guidelines for Data Collection and Analysis

A Cornerstone for Conducting High-Quality Research

3

I f research is to be of high quality, and if it is to have a significant impact, it is vital that the work (data collection, analysis, publication) be done in accordance with high ethical standards. Unfortunately, as we have witnessed over the past several years, one possible—and unsavory—side effect of the pressure to publish can be engagement in unethical research practices. High-profile cases in social psychology and marketing, for example, have revealed instances in which scholars have either completely fabricated their data or "cleaned" their data files by deleting cases that did not fit their hypothesis. Further from the spotlight, researchers from all walks of life routinely face difficult decisions about how to collect, analyze, and report their results. These issues have forced academic societies and editorial boards to reconsider how to best encourage ethical research practices. Some issues are black-and-white, whereas others exist in a gray zone. For example, it would be hard to find many scholars who believe that it is justifiable to prevent participants from terminating their involvement in a study when they choose.

http://dx.doi.org/10.1037/14525-004
How to Publish High-Quality Research, by J. Joireman and P. A. M. Van Lange

And nobody would regard data fabrication as appropriate. On the other hand, researchers could disagree over data screening (i.e., "cleansing") techniques. Some might argue that screening out certain observations is appropriate, whereas others might argue that dropping data is never appropriate. And there may also be a fair amount of disagreement about the criteria for excluding certain observations.

In this chapter, we first consider why conducting research in an ethical manner is so important. We next discuss the American Psychological Association's (APA's) standards for ethical research. Finally, we examine and make recommendations for resolving key ethical dilemmas facing researchers at the data analysis and reporting stage.

Reasons for Conducting Research in an Ethical Manner

Broadly speaking, the decision to conduct research in an ethical manner has implications for at least four constituencies: science in general (and the scientific discipline in particular), society, research participants, and other researchers. As the reader will see, we pull no punches in this section, as the implications for each constituency are significant.

First, from a basic scientific perspective, the publication of flawed data hampers the ability of a field as a whole to advance. It undermines the most important goal of science: the accumulation of accurate, replicable knowledge. Our published literature—empirical articles, and further down the line, review articles, textbooks, widely read popular books—is more likely to contain "knowledge" that is biased and not replicable. And it has the disadvantage that researchers may fruitlessly expend significant time and other scarce resources attempting to replicate or build on a publication that is based on fabricated data. Needless to say, this wastes the researcher's time and potentially prevents her or him from pursuing more valuable lines of inquiry.

Second, from a broader scientific perspective (application), the usefulness of our disciplines rests on the quality of data we produce. The quality of the data we produce, in turn, has important implications for our ability to help solve the challenges we face as a society. Needless to say, interventions or policy recommendations based on psychological research will be misguided at best, and harmful at worst, if those recommendations are based on flawed data. In addition, the public and policymakers are likely to disregard scientists' recommendations if they believe the field's research is based on questionable data. In sum, unethical research practices undermine our ability to contribute meaningful solutions to pressing societal problems.

Third, unethical research practices can have short-term and/or long-term negative impacts on participants. Classic examples include the failure to provide penicillin to African Americans in the Tuskegee trials and the debate following Milgram's obedience studies. Additional examples include feelings of inadequacy left unresolved because of a researcher's failure to engage in an appropriate debriefing or because of the disclosure of private information. In addition, unethical treatment of participants can in turn lead future groups of participants to be less trusting of research and potentially less cooperative, further undermining the quality of our data. For example, when the same people participate in studies over time (e.g., respondents recruited via Amazon's Mechanical Turk service), the repeated use of some forms of deception may make participants somewhat suspicious about the transparency or honesty of the instructions. Providing bogus feedback about performance on a particular test, even though this may be useful for a single experiment, can to some degree make participants suspicious about a new test or about the feedback they receive in a future experiment. In that sense, it may be important to keep in mind the longer term impact of using deception in experimental procedures.

Fourth, when researchers engage in unethical research practices, they can seriously jeopardize the careers and/or reputations of coauthors and graduate students working under their guidance, as well as those of a graduate student's faculty advisor. Although coauthors, a graduate student, or an advisor may be innocent, a retracted publication or an ethics investigation is likely to be uncomfortable at best and career ending at worst. In short, unethical research practices have a significant negative impact on one's colleagues, mentees, and mentors.

Of course, unethical research practices have important implications for the researcher in question. Researchers who do their best to follow the best practices for ethical research can be assured that the knowledge has been obtained using acceptable methods and research practices, whereas researchers who engage in unethical research practices will, at best, worry that they may someday be exposed as a fraud and, at worst, actually be exposed as a fraud.

Established Ethical Principles and Standards for Research and Publication

Certain principles concerning ethics in research are well-established but nevertheless worth reviewing. In this section, we summarize the most relevant parts of APA's (2010) *Ethical Principles of Psychologists and*

Code of Conduct[1] (hereinafter the *Ethics Code*). APA's *Ethics Code* consists of a preamble outlining its goals, a set of five general principles that are aspirational in nature, and a list of 10 standards that represent obligations for psychologists.

The five general principles aim to "guide and inspire psychologists to toward the very highest ethical ideals of the profession" (p. 3). The principles are (a) beneficence and nonmaleficence (striving to benefit and not harm those with whom psychologists work), (b) fidelity and responsibility (establishing relationships characterized by trust, acting professionally, and accepting responsibility for one's actions), (c) integrity (promoting honesty in research, teaching, and practice of psychology), (d) justice (ensuring that all people are able to access and benefit from the contributions of psychology equally), and (e) respect for people's rights and dignity (respecting people's right to privacy, confidentiality, and self-determination, and respecting differences based on culture, age, gender, sexual orientation, socioeconomic status, ethnicity, etc.).

Of the 10 ethical standards articulated in the *Ethics Code*, the most relevant of which, for our purposes, is Standard 8 (Research and Publication), which consists of 15 subsections (8.1–8.15). These standards cover the entire research process including gaining institutional review board (IRB) approval, obtaining informed consent, appropriate use of incentives, use of deception, debriefing, care of animals, reporting results, plagiarism, publication credit, using duplicate data, sharing data following publication, and appropriate actions of reviewers. The 15 subsections of Standard 8 are reproduced, in their entirety, in Exhibit 3.1.

Emerging Ethical Dilemmas in Data Analysis and Reporting

Although some ethical standards are likely to endure over a long period of time, many are not fixed in stone but are continually changing. Broadly speaking, ethical norms are currently evolving toward fuller, more complete and transparent presentations of all steps taken, analyses done (regardless of the results), changes in statistical approaches, and even writing (e.g., the precision in describing the sample or measurements). In recent years, we have seen ever-greater international, federal, and disciplinary expectations of data sharing. Given the often lengthy delay from proposal to publication, researchers are well-advised to expect and plan for changes in ethical norms ahead of time in initial proposals and IRB

---

[1]Readers can access the full APA *Ethics Code* at http://www.apa.org/ethics/code/index.aspx

EXHIBIT 3.1

American Psychological Association's Ethics Standard 8: Research and Publication

8.01 Institutional Approval

When institutional approval is required, psychologists provide accurate information about their research proposals and obtain approval prior to conducting the research. They conduct the research in accordance with the approved research protocol.

8.02 Informed Consent to Research

(a) When obtaining informed consent as required in Standard 3.10, Informed Consent, psychologists inform participants about (1) the purpose of the research, expected duration, and procedures; (2) their right to decline to participate and to withdraw from the research once participation has begun; (3) the foreseeable consequences of declining or withdrawing; (4) reasonably foreseeable factors that may be expected to influence their willingness to participate such as potential risks, discomfort, or adverse effects; (5) any prospective research benefits; (6) limits of confidentiality; (7) incentives for participation; and (8) whom to contact for questions about the research and research participants' rights. They provide opportunity for the prospective participants to ask questions and receive answers. (See also Standards 8.03, Informed Consent for Recording Voices and Images in Research; 8.05, Dispensing With Informed Consent for Research; and 8.07, Deception in Research.)

(b) Psychologists conducting intervention research involving the use of experimental treatments clarify to participants at the outset of the research (1) the experimental nature of the treatment; (2) the services that will or will not be available to the control group(s) if appropriate; (3) the means by which assignment to treatment and control groups will be made; (4) available treatment alternatives if an individual does not wish to participate in the research or wishes to withdraw once a study has begun; and (5) compensation for or monetary costs of participating including, if appropriate, whether reimbursement from the participant or a third-party payor will be sought. (See also Standard 8.02a, Informed Consent to Research.)

8.03 Informed Consent for Recording Voices and Images in Research

Psychologists obtain informed consent from research participants prior to recording their voices or images for data collection unless (1) the research consists solely of naturalistic observations in public places, and it is not anticipated that the recording will be used in a manner that could cause personal identification or harm, or (2) the research design includes deception, and consent for the use of the recording is obtained during debriefing. (See also Standard 8.07, Deception in Research.)

8.04 Client/Patient, Student, and Subordinate Research Participants

(a) When psychologists conduct research with clients/patients, students, or subordinates as participants, psychologists take steps to protect the prospective participants from adverse consequences of declining or withdrawing from participation.

(b) When research participation is a course requirement or an opportunity for extra credit, the prospective participant is given the choice of equitable alternative activities.

8.05 Dispensing With Informed Consent for Research

Psychologists may dispense with informed consent only (1) where research would not reasonably be assumed to create distress or harm and involves (a) the study of normal educational practices, curricula, or classroom management methods conducted in educational

(*continued*)

EXHIBIT 3.1 (*Continued*)

settings; (b) only anonymous questionnaires, naturalistic observations, or archival research for which disclosure of responses would not place participants at risk of criminal or civil liability or damage their financial standing, employability, or reputation, and confidentiality is protected; or (c) the study of factors related to job or organization effectiveness conducted in organizational settings for which there is no risk to participants' employability, and confidentiality is protected or (2) where otherwise permitted by law or federal or institutional regulations.

8.06 Offering Inducements for Research Participation

(a) Psychologists make reasonable efforts to avoid offering excessive or inappropriate financial or other inducements for research participation when such inducements are likely to coerce participation.
(b) When offering professional services as an inducement for research participation, psychologists clarify the nature of the services, as well as the risks, obligations, and limitations. (See also Standard 6.05, Barter With Clients/Patients.)

8.07 Deception in Research

(a) Psychologists do not conduct a study involving deception unless they have determined that the use of deceptive techniques is justified by the study's significant prospective scientific, educational, or applied value and that effective nondeceptive alternative procedures are not feasible.
(b) Psychologists do not deceive prospective participants about research that is reasonably expected to cause physical pain or severe emotional distress.
(c) Psychologists explain any deception that is an integral feature of the design and conduct of an experiment to participants as early as is feasible, preferably at the conclusion of their participation, but no later than at the conclusion of the data collection, and permit participants to withdraw their data. (See also Standard 8.08, Debriefing.)

8.08 Debriefing

(a) Psychologists provide a prompt opportunity for participants to obtain appropriate information about the nature, results, and conclusions of the research, and they take reasonable steps to correct any misconceptions that participants may have of which the psychologists are aware.
(b) If scientific or humane values justify delaying or withholding this information, psychologists take reasonable measures to reduce the risk of harm.
(c) When psychologists become aware that research procedures have harmed a participant, they take reasonable steps to minimize the harm.

8.09 Humane Care and Use of Animals in Research

(a) Psychologists acquire, care for, use, and dispose of animals in compliance with current federal, state, and local laws and regulations, and with professional standards.
(b) Psychologists trained in research methods and experienced in the care of laboratory animals supervise all procedures involving animals and are responsible for ensuring appropriate consideration of their comfort, health, and humane treatment.
(c) Psychologists ensure that all individuals under their supervision who are using animals have received instruction in research methods and in the care, maintenance, and handling of the species being used, to the extent appropriate to their role. (See also Standard 2.05, Delegation of Work to Others.)
(d) Psychologists make reasonable efforts to minimize the discomfort, infection, illness, and pain of animal subjects.

EXHIBIT 3.1 (*Continued*)

(e) Psychologists use a procedure subjecting animals to pain, stress, or privation only when an alternative procedure is unavailable and the goal is justified by its prospective scientific, educational, or applied value.

(f) Psychologists perform surgical procedures under appropriate anesthesia and follow techniques to avoid infection and minimize pain during and after surgery.

(g) When it is appropriate that an animal's life be terminated, psychologists proceed rapidly, with an effort to minimize pain and in accordance with accepted procedures.

8.10 Reporting Research Results

(a) Psychologists do not fabricate data. (See also Standard 5.01a, Avoidance of False or Deceptive Statements.)

(b) If psychologists discover significant errors in their published data, they take reasonable steps to correct such errors in a correction, retraction, erratum, or other appropriate publication means.

8.11 Plagiarism

Psychologists do not present portions of another's work or data as their own, even if the other work or data source is cited occasionally.

8.12 Publication Credit

(a) Psychologists take responsibility and credit, including authorship credit, only for work they have actually performed or to which they have substantially contributed. (See also Standard 8.12b, Publication Credit.)

(b) Principal authorship and other publication credits accurately reflect the relative scientific or professional contributions of the individuals involved, regardless of their relative status. Mere possession of an institutional position, such as department chair, does not justify authorship credit. Minor contributions to the research or to the writing for publications are acknowledged appropriately, such as in footnotes or in an introductory statement.

(c) Except under exceptional circumstances, a student is listed as principal author on any multiple-authored article that is substantially based on the student's doctoral dissertation. Faculty advisors discuss publication credit with students as early as feasible and throughout the research and publication process as appropriate. (See also Standard 8.12b, Publication Credit.)

8.13 Duplicate Publication of Data

Psychologists do not publish, as original data, data that have been previously published. This does not preclude republishing data when they are accompanied by proper acknowledgment.

8.14 Sharing Research Data for Verification

(a) After research results are published, psychologists do not withhold the data on which their conclusions are based from other competent professionals who seek to verify the substantive claims through reanalysis and who intend to use such data only for that purpose, provided that the confidentiality of the participants can be protected and unless legal rights concerning proprietary data preclude their release. This does not preclude psychologists from requiring that such individuals or groups be responsible for costs associated with the provision of such information.

(b) Psychologists who request data from other psychologists to verify the substantive claims through reanalysis may use shared data only for the declared purpose. Requesting psychologists obtain prior written agreement for all other uses of the data.

(*continued*)

EXHIBIT 3.1 (*Continued*)

8.15 Reviewers

Psychologists who review material submitted for presentation, publication, grant, or research proposal review respect the confidentiality of and the proprietary rights in such information of those who submitted it.

Note. From *Ethical Principles of Psychologists and Code of Conduct*, by the American Psychological Association, 2010. Retrieved from http://www.apa.org/ethics/code/index.aspx. Copyright 2010 by the American Psychological Association. Regarding Standard 8.12: Readers interested in computing an author's relative contribution, based on publication record and order of authorship, will find Aziz and Rozing's (2013) recent article thought provoking. In that article, the authors introduced and validated what they referred to as the profit index (p-index) to estimate the extent to which an author profits from the contributions of other coauthors. Readers should note, however, that one assumption of the p-index, based on the biomedical research tradition, is that first and last authors have contributed the most to an article, and those closer to the middle of the list have contributed the least.

applications. You do not want to put in all the hard work described in this book, only to find you cannot get published because you did not plan for future changes in data-sharing expectations. Given the evolution of ethical norms in psychology and other disciplines, we provide tentative answers to some ethical challenges within the discipline that are directly relevant to the pursuit of high quality.

Today, researchers are grappling with a set of complex ethical dilemmas revolving around how they analyze and report their data and the extent to which they should be required to share that data with other interested scholars. These dilemmas deal with three related questions. First, how much of the actual data that was collected should be presented? Second, is data screening acceptable, and if so, where does one draw the line between acceptable data screening and misleading screening? Third, should authors of published articles be required to share the original data? What might be acceptable reasons for not sharing all of the data? And should journals adopt a policy regarding data sharing?

From our perspective, these are not easy questions to answer. With this in mind, in the current section, we highlight some of the fundamental questions researchers should consider when deciding how to analyze and report their data. These questions provide a glimpse into the emerging and complicated dilemmas researchers face when deciding how to report their data. In the next section, we offer several recommendations that may help address this array of questions.

One persistent question facing researchers is how much of the original data to publish. Here, we define *data* broadly to encompass multiple studies, conditions, and variables, rather than individual observations (which we address subsequently). For example, if a researcher conducts three studies on a similar issue, is it justifiable to publish only the ones with findings that are significant? As another example, if a researcher runs a study with four conditions but finds that the "best story" can be told by dropping two of those conditions, is this acceptable? Finally, if statistically controlling for a covariate reduces one's primary finding to a nonsignificant level, should the researcher (a) simply not report the covariate, in the interests of publishing the main finding; (b) report the covariate adjusted results; or (c) rerun the study in an effort to eliminate the confound introduced by the covariate?

Once researchers decide on the studies, conditions, and variables to analyze, they face another ethical question: namely, which observations should one report? Should an outlier be dropped if it transforms a marginally significant finding into a significant finding? Should participants be dropped if it appears that they were not paying attention? How does one best determine whether participants were paying attention? Does a long string of 4s (the midpoint) indicate that the participant was not paying attention or simply holds a consistently neutral attitude?

Relatedly, researchers must determine how to best analyze their data, which raises a host of additional questions. For example, if a median split reveals a significant effect and treating the data as continuous does not, can the researcher use the median split? If results are only significant after transformation, does a researcher have an obligation to report the nontransformed results as well? If Tukey post hoc tests are not quite significant, while Newman-Keuls tests are, can the researcher use the latter, even though the latter are less conservative?

Recommendations on Data Analytic Issues

We assume there is little debate over the basic ethical principles regarding the treatment of participants, data fabrication, and practices such as plagiarism of work by others. Rather, the largely unresolved questions are within the realm of *data analysis*, broadly defined as decisions concerning which studies, conditions, and observations to report (see Simmons, Nelson, & Simonsohn, 2011). Accordingly, in this section, we outline recommendations on the latter. To set the context, we consider how the pressure to "tell a good (and perfect) story" can sometimes create ethical dilemmas for researchers.

Across various fields and disciplines, the scientific community has a tendency to appreciate contributions that provide evidence that is novel, consistent, and strong. Depending on the scope and mission of a journal, this sometimes means a multiple-study approach, with up to five or six studies. In other circumstances, the focus is on truly groundbreaking studies, sometimes even a single study that tells a "new story" that is interesting to a broader audience. There are different approaches to telling a good story that yield publications in the highest impact journals in our fields. Although these approaches are excellent, they do tend to have negative side effects.

Simply put, an overemphasis on telling a good story, rather than testing a meaningful and theoretically driven hypothesis, may make it tempting to ignore data that "don't work" and adopt "data cleansing" procedures that selectively exclude cases in order to arrive at a significant (and perfect) set of findings. Another drawback of the current publication climate is a stronger appreciation of statistically significant findings than of null findings, yielding the well-known publication bias, with an overestimation of published articles that report significant differences. Another problem is that other researchers working in the same domain may toil away fruitlessly on the same project, unaware that a null finding (or several) already exists. And, of course, we have already detailed the social and personal costs of misleading data analysis procedures.

Given this dilemma, it is important to ask: How does one balance the high standards required by journals with the desire to conduct data analysis in an ethical manner? Of course, the answers are complex, but there are some very general recommendations that may well serve as useful guides for us. In Exhibit 3.2, we summarize seven such recommendations.

One key suggestion follows from the overall goal of a study, as this often defines what is appropriate or not. Broadly speaking, we may conduct research in an effort to (a) test questionnaires, instructions, and experimental procedures (pilot research); (b) examine relationships, causal or correlational, among variables in an exploratory manner, often in an attempt to inform oneself about a broad array of relationships and to help develop or select hypotheses to be tested in subsequent research (exploratory research); or (c) test specific hypotheses that are derived from theory, often in combination with past research by themselves or colleagues (hypothesis-testing research). Defining the goal of a study, often as part of a project of more studies, is important because for one type of research (e.g., exploratory research), it is often more appropriate to focus on those variables that have yielded significant effects and can inform hypotheses to be tested in subsequent research. In hypothesis-testing research, by comparison, it is more important to provide information about all variables that have been collected, thereby providing a "balanced" overview of the degree of support for a particular hypothesis.

Another important cornerstone in science is transparency. As noted earlier, it is possible that scientists in a particular field, or in tradition of particular area of research, have somewhat different views about data-cleansing procedures. It is important, especially for hypothesis-testing research, to be transparent in reporting why some data were not included in the reporting of the data analysis. There may be good reasons for doing so, but the essential point is that researchers should

---

EXHIBIT 3.2

Recommendations on Maintaining Integrity During Data Analysis

---

1. Think carefully about the primary goals of your study and the conditions and variables you want to include in your study. Collecting a large number of "exploratory conditions" or "potentially relevant variables" may be helpful for pilot testing and exploratory research, but for hypothesis testing, this approach may make it more likely that you will find yourself facing a conflict between reporting all of the data versus selectively focusing on or reporting data that tell a good story.
2. Be transparent (in terms of your methods and data analytic procedures) so that reviewers, editors, and ultimately readers can evaluate the quality of the data, and the conclusions, in light of the evidence presented.
3. Familiarize yourself with appropriate and acceptable data-screening procedures and have a clear set or data-screening criteria (and reasoning) in place before you begin analyzing data. In our view, Tabachnick and Fidell (2012) and Judd, McClelland, and Ryan (2009) offer particularly well-written chapters on data screening. This will make it less likely that you use the *p*-value on a key finding to drive the decision about whether to drop or retain certain observations.
4. Analyze data "in public," for example, with graduate students or coauthors, and openly discuss your feelings about the ethics of taking certain approaches to the data analysis. This puts you on record as recognizing potential ethical conflicts.
5. Be open and honest with your coauthors and the review team about the steps you have taken to "reduce the data." Although this runs the risk of being penalized, we believe that many conscientious reviewers respect such openness, and editors and reviewers will increasingly become open to such admissions (or should, in our opinion). Report results before and after "data screening," which allows the reader to decide whether the decision to drop any relevant observations had a meaningful impact on the conclusions.
6. If you are a graduate student (or faculty member) who suspects research misconduct, find a (fellow) faculty member you trust to discuss the situation, or when present, share your observations with an ethics officer. Most universities have in place strong safeguards for reporting such unethical activity and protecting the reporter from negative repercussions.
7. Trust your gut. If you have any sense, however slight, that the approach you are taking could be construed as wrong, it is probably an important sign that something is wrong and that you should discuss it with a colleague. Restated, whenever you perceive an ethical dilemma, pursue transparency.

---

inform readers (and before that, the reviewers and editors) about the procedures used for excluding some participants from the data analysis. Moreover, it is conceivable that under some circumstances, it makes sense to report only some of the conditions, rather than all of the conditions. The goal is to be transparent, so that reviewers, editors, and ultimately readers can evaluate the quality of the data, and the conclusions, in light of the evidence presented.

In addition to these two broad suggestions, we suggest five additional data analytic recommendations. In short, researchers should have a well-reasoned strategy for data screening; analyze their data "in public" so that ethical dilemmas can be discussed openly; freely discuss with coauthors (and reviewers) the steps taken to reduce the data; find a trusted colleague with whom to discuss suspected research misconduct; and "trust your gut" and realize that if something feels wrong, it is probably a good sign that a potential problem could arise.

Conclusion

As should be clear from the current chapter, our view is that high-quality research cannot be separated from sound ethical research principles. In this chapter, we have reviewed well-recognized ethical principles, considered a number of the core ethical dilemmas confronting today's researchers, and made a number of recommendations for resolving those dilemmas.

As we also hope we have made clear—as authors, reviewers, and editors—that we recognize that pressure to publish a "sexy" story in high-impact outlets is strong and growing, and data analysis issues are not always straightforward. Yet at the end of the day, resolving these issues is crucial for our ability to offer insights that improve the human condition. Indeed, one of the most exciting developments we have seen over the past decade has been the dissemination of high-quality psychological research into the public domain. Media regularly carry interesting stories about psychological insights that can directly benefit the public. Needless to say, our ability to continue disseminating our insights, improving lives, and shaping public policy rests on the integrity of our research. Beyond these more lofty goals, integrity in research carries significant benefits for one's collaborators and, ultimately, the individual researcher as well. Thus, whether the goal is scientific, societal, social, or even personal benefit, conducting research in an ethical manner is a key foundation for high-quality research.

Writing and Revising 4

s we noted at the outset of the book, the probability of publishing high-quality research in top-tier journals is a joint function of the quality of the ideas and the framing, methods and findings, initial submission and revision, and promotion activities. In this chapter, we provide detailed advice for enhancing the quality of initial submissions and revisions. We begin by considering some broad guiding principles that shape an author's attitude and approach to writing. Next, we offer general and specific tips for writing effectively and successfully navigating the revision process. Checklists for effective writing and revising are provided in Appendixes 4.1 and 4.2, respectively.

http://dx.doi.org/10.1037/14525-005
How to Publish High-Quality Research, by J. Joireman and P. A. M. Van Lange
Copyright © 2015 by the American Psychological Association. All rights
reserved.

Guiding Principles for Writing

Whether writing an initial manuscript or preparing a revision, a researcher must strive for perfection, objectively reflect on the quality of his or her writing (i.e., never fool oneself into believing that great ideas will naturally trump mediocre writing), and seriously consider and respond to suggestions from outside sources (friendly peers, editors, and anonymous reviewers).

STRIVE FOR PERFECTION

As writers, we like to think we strive for perfection. A perfect title. A perfect quote. A perfect opening example. Perfect organization. Perfect sentences. Perfect phrases. Perfect words. Perfect transitions. Perfect formatting. Perfect references. And perfect tables and figures. We methodically revise individual sentences to eliminate widows and orphans from our papers; we lose sleep over unsightly paragraphs that end with one or two words on the last line; and we spend hours and often days striking words or phrases in an effort to cut a paper down to its bare bones so we end up with nothing more and nothing less than is necessary to convey the paper's contribution in a compelling and completely understandable manner. When readers are done with our papers, we want them to feel like there is no space wasted, that every sentence is necessary and meaningful, and that the contribution-to-length ratio is accordingly very high.

Once we have "dotted all the i's and crossed all the t's," we ship the paper out for review and quickly learn that, despite our heroic efforts on the first draft, we are not perfect. In fact, over the years, Paul and I have had distinct pleasure of learning—at least 150 times—that we are not perfect. Our idea is not unique. It is not clear. It is not theoretically driven. The method is fatally flawed. The data are not compelling. The analyses are wrong. The implications are trivial. And (yes), we even left out a reference (or two). Not a good day for a perfectionist.

Despite the bad news, there is often a silver lining within the reviews: An opportunity to revise and resubmit. An opportunity to make the paper better. An opportunity to publish research in a top-tier journal. At the same time, the editor notes that it is a "risky revision"; it will take "substantial theoretical, methodological, and analytic work"; and "even if you do submit a substantial revision, it is not certain that the manuscript will be accepted." The only solution? Make the revision even better than the initial submission, as we detail in this chapter.

If you strive for perfection at each stage of the process, you will have gone a long way toward making a significant contribution to the field that is worthy of publication in the field's top journals. Striving for perfection, of course, is not a guarantee, but it is an approach that in our experience will tip the scales in your favor.

OBJECTIVELY REFLECT ON THE QUALITY OF YOUR WRITING

Too often, as authors (in general), we fool ourselves into believing that we have done all we can to effectively communicate with our readers, when in fact we have stopped well short of the bar necessary to achieve success. We put on our rose-colored glasses for a number of reasons: We think we don't have time to revise our manuscripts (yet again) because we are under so much pressure to publish or perish, we are too busy dealing with the other competing demands of academic life, we are insecure about our writing and are unwilling to accept feedback for improvement that suggests we are imperfect; we lack drive or discipline, or we have never really been taught how to write well. Whatever the reason, to become successful writers, we must overcome these barriers and adopt as objective a perspective as possible on our writing. Sometimes our writing is *not* stellar, but we will never see that until we are able to step outside ourselves and objectively reflect on the quality of our writing.

GATHER, CONSIDER, AND RESPOND TO FEEDBACK FROM OUTSIDERS BEFORE SUBMITTING

Despite our best efforts at objectively reflecting on our own writing, our writing will still have flaws. As such, it is important to actively gather, seriously consider, and effectively respond to feedback from outsiders about our writing before submitting the initial draft. During the initial stages of manuscript preparation (i.e., prior to submission), it can be helpful to ask peers who are both familiar and unfamiliar with your topic to read and provide suggestions for revisions. Although a friendly presubmission peer review can be nice to read, it is not always the most helpful in preparing you for the review process. A better strategy may be to seek more objective feedback from likely critics and to ask your peers to be "brutally honest" in their assessment of the manuscript.

General Tips on Writing the Initial Submission

In this section, we provide more detailed advice on writing the key sections of the manuscript from the Introduction through the Discussion. Just as there are many roads to making a contribution, there are many different ways to write, and each author has his or her own unique style. However, there are also some fundamental strategies that cut across these styles that can contribute to good writing. Thus, before diving into the individual sections of a manuscript, we offer a number of general tips that apply to all sections of the manuscript.

LEAD YOUR READER BY THE HAND

Our first piece of advice is to always lead your reader by the hand. To be an effective writer, you must capture your readers from the outset with an intriguing quote, a real-world example, or compelling statistics, and you must never let them go. In a very real sense, you are leading your readers on what you believe will be an exciting and thought-provoking journey. Unfortunately, exciting journeys are often fraught with potential disasters. An unexpected slip here, a fatal fall there, and the journey is over. Needless to say, as an author, you do not want the journey to end badly, so you must do everything you can to ensure a safe journey throughout your manuscript. To accomplish this, you must lead your reader by the hand.

THINK CAREFULLY ABOUT THE ORGANIZATION OF YOUR PAPER

Several tools can help you lead your readers by the hand. To begin, before writing, it is useful to think carefully about the organization of your paper and its various subsections. For example, think hard about the order in which you plan to discuss a series of arguments in the Introduction; a series of instructions and/or tasks in the Method section; a series of findings in the Results section; and a series of implications, and strengths and limitations, in the Discussion section. In the Introduction, for example, you will likely want to start with the big picture and discuss the more obvious or general principles before diving into the subtleties, such as moderators or mediators. In the Method section, a good rule of thumb is to present the method in the order in which the study was run. In the Results section, it is beneficial to start with manipulation checks or simple correlations before moving on to the primary results; ancillary results that are interesting, but not central to the paper, should be located at the end of the results. Finally, the Discussion section should recap your results, outline your theoretical and practical implications, and consider limitations and future directions.

PROVIDE OVERVIEWS

Beyond good organization, it is very useful to provide overviews of where your paper is headed. These overviews can provide a vision of the entire paper, the set of experiments contained in the paper, or the different elements of a given section (e.g., the general discussion). Though reviewers and editors occasionally suggest deleting such overviews (e.g., to save space), more often than not, these overviews serve an important role within the manuscript. Specifically, well-placed overviews give readers a general framework on which to hang the paper and a travel guide, as it were, to navigate your paper. An overview can also contribute to a feeling of perceptual fluency (Topolinski & Strack, 2009), as the reader has a vague sense that they've "heard this before." Though readers enjoy the occasional surprise, more often than not, readers dislike uncertainty, and this uncertainty can be greatly reduced through the use of good overviews. Later in the chapter, we provide specific examples of how such overviews can be effectively incorporated into the opening paragraphs of the Introduction.

USE EFFECTIVE TRANSITIONS

In addition to occasional overviews, another tool that can help you lead your reader by the hand is to use effective transitions. Just as ladders spanning a crevasse help climbers continue their climb, transitions within your manuscript help readers continue their journey through your paper unimpeded. This is vitally important, as an unimpeded journey through your paper contributes to a positive feeling of "flow" (Csikszentmihalyi, 1998) and significantly reduces a reader's tendency to "raise red flags." Often, we suspect, readers may not even be aware that ineffective (or absent) transitions are raising red flags. Rather, readers are simply aware that "something just isn't right" with the manuscript. These readers may not be able to put their finger on the source, but believe us, reviewers will find a reason to reject your manuscript if this uneasy feeling surfaces too often for comfort. Every paper, of course, will raise red flags (i.e., questions, concerns, etc.), but the red flags that are raised should never be due to something that you, as a writer, can easily control (and avoid). So, pay careful attention to transitions. Make sure there is a logical connection between the end of one paragraph and the beginning of another paragraph, between different sections of the Introduction, Method, Results, and Discussion, and between different studies in a multistudy paper (as we discuss in more detail next).

USE STRAIGHTFORWARD LANGUAGE

A fourth way you can lead your reader by the hand is to use straightforward language. At its core, effective scientific writing is not about dazzling your audience with complex sentences or fancy wordplay. Rather, it is about communicating clearly and effectively with your audience. As advisors, one of the most common pieces of advice we give graduate students, after reviewing their preliminary drafts, is to "be more direct" and to "say what you mean." Don't make your readers guess at what you mean, and don't make your readers work harder than they need to in order to understand your point. It is your job, as a writer, to do the heavy lifting before a reviewer gets ahold of your paper. If you anticipate that future time orientation will be related to higher levels of self-control, say that. Don't say that you think that time orientation will be related to self-control. If you think that consumers from collectivist cultures will be more positively impacted by ads featuring families, whereas consumers from individualist cultures will be more positively impacted by ads featuring individuals, say that. Don't say that you think cultural orientation and ad type will combine in an interactive fashion. Long story short: Use straightforward language to make it absolutely clear what you mean.

MAKE SURE EACH SENTENCE ADDS VALUE

On a related note, it is also important that you make sure that each sentence adds value to the overall story. There are many things you might consider saying in a manuscript, and many of those things could be marginally interesting (or tangentially related to your paper). At the end of the day, however, the only things that should make the final cut are those that add value to the manuscript. A brutal assessment of value, and the subsequent trimming of unnecessary fat, has three important benefits. First, it helps avoid any unnecessary and distracting sideshows that could raise red flags (or "speed bumps") that disrupt the flow of the paper. Second, eliminating distractions focuses your reader's attention on the most important parts of your manuscript. Why dilute a good story with marginally relevant or valueless sentences? Finally, all else being equal, a focused and "compact" manuscript gives the reader the sense that your paper offers a very high contribution-to-length ratio, a criterion that will both explicitly (and implicitly) influence the editorial team's decision to accept or reject your manuscript.

USE (SOME) REDUNDANCY

At the risk of appearing to contradict our previous point, our next piece of advice is to use (some) redundancy. In our experience, many young scientific writers seem to want to avoid redundancy at all costs. Redundancy is boring. It is unimaginative. Redundancy was forbidden in grade school! Indeed, all of these arguments hold some weight, but when used appropriately, redundancy can contribute to a smoother paper and, consequently, a feeling of perceptual fluency and flow, metacognitive experiences that, as we have noted, can enhance the probability of acceptance. One particularly useful application of redundancy is to introduce (even quite broadly) your overall hypotheses and later come back around and reinforce them (for more on this approach, see the section Opening Paragraphs of the Introduction in this chapter). The use of redundancy is also critical when it comes to discussing constructs. If your independent variable is ego depletion, for instance, use that term consistently throughout your manuscript. Don't refer to it as ego depletion, regulatory depletion, and resource depletion. Although many readers may be able to follow you, the introduction of various terms for the same construct often leads to confusion (and frustration) among readers. Say what you mean. Be direct. And don't make the reader work harder than necessary to understand your point.

Specific Tips on Key Sections of the Manuscript

Having provided some general tips on writing, we turn now to more specific tips that apply to particular sections of a manuscript. As shown in Figure 4.1, one useful way of thinking about the paper is as an hourglass. The hourglass approach starts broad with the opening of the Introduction, narrows down to detailed treatment of methods and results, and then broadens back out as the author conveys the implications of the research and the conclusions of the researchers.

OPENING PARAGRAPHS OF THE INTRODUCTION

The first paragraphs of a manuscript's Introduction are critical to the paper's success, for it is in these paragraphs that you orient readers to your topic, convince them of its importance, get them interested in your central questions, help them appreciate significant gaps in the literature, and highlight (at a broad level) how you will address those gaps (i.e., how your manuscript will make a contribution). The first few paragraphs can also afford you an opportunity to prime readers with your key hypotheses and perhaps your major findings. If you fail to do these things, you will have raised a significant barrier to publication. Reviewers may quickly lose interest, become frustrated, and begin thinking of a number of reasons for rejecting your manuscript. However, if you craft the first few paragraphs effectively, you will have gone a long way toward getting reviewers and other readers on board with your idea and eventually accepting and citing your paper. Three common and effective approaches to the opening paragraphs include the three-paragraph, two-paragraph, and one-paragraph opener.

FIGURE 4.1

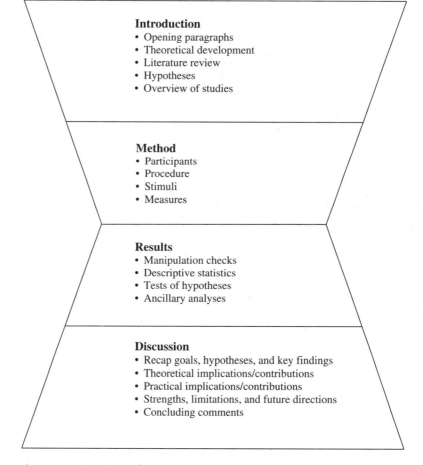

Introduction
- Opening paragraphs
- Theoretical development
- Literature review
- Hypotheses
- Overview of studies

Method
- Participants
- Procedure
- Stimuli
- Measures

Results
- Manipulation checks
- Descriptive statistics
- Tests of hypotheses
- Ancillary analyses

Discussion
- Recap goals, hypotheses, and key findings
- Theoretical implications/contributions
- Practical implications/contributions
- Strengths, limitations, and future directions
- Concluding comments

Hourglass organization of paper.

Three-Paragraph Opener

One particularly effective approach, in our experience, is a three-paragraph opener. Using this approach, the first paragraph introduces the problem in a compelling fashion. This can be done by (a) citing (up-to-date and reliable) statistics on the problem at hand (e.g., Joireman, Kees, & Sprott, 2010), (b) describing a real or hypothetical narrative related to the problem (Balliet & Joireman, 2010), (c) directly demonstrating (with empirical evidence) that the behavior in question is an important one (e.g., Balliet, Li, & Joireman, 2011; Joireman, Van Lange, & Van Vugt, 2004), or (d) framing the problem in the context of broader questions that have long interested psychologists and marketing researchers (e.g., Joireman, Lasane, Bennett, Richards, & Solaimani, 2001).

Once the problem is clear, it is often helpful to end the first paragraph with an intriguing question (or set of questions) suggested by your opening examples. These paragraph-ending questions accomplish three related goals. First, these questions outline the basic plot line of your story. Second, these questions invite your reader to join you in your effort toward solving an interesting puzzle. Finally, these questions serve as an effective transition into the second paragraph (and effective transitions are, as we have already discussed, paramount, if you ever hope to keep your readers' attention).

Having posed a number of intriguing questions, the second paragraph briefly summarizes how past research has addressed those questions and then, on the basis of that review, clearly articulates one to three meaningful gaps in the literature. This review of the literature does not need to be exhaustive, but it should communicate to reviewers that you have a good grasp of the key (and most recent and relevant) literature in the field.

An abbreviated (yet authoritative) review of the literature may seem like a paradox, but it is possible and can be highly effective. Reviewers are writers too, and they understand that you will soon follow up on your brief introduction with a more exhaustive review of the relevant literature. Nevertheless, many authors (especially young ones) are uncomfortable offering up an abbreviated summary of the literature because they believe that their main goal in the Introduction is to prove how smart they are by citing every single study ever conducted on the topic. Although it is important to establish yourself as an authority, it is always good to remember that "less is more." A shorter and more focused Introduction accomplishes a great deal more than a long and rambling survey of the literature that seems to be going nowhere. In sum, keep the second paragraph short, highlight one or two significant gaps in the literature, and quickly move on to the third paragraph where you promise to "solve the riddle."

As just noted, the third paragraph promises to address key gaps in the literature. If the second paragraph ends with the gaps, the third paragraph often starts with the straightforward sentence: *The present studies aimed to address these gaps by . . . [fill in the blank]*. If the second paragraph ends with one or two questions, the third paragraph can begin: *To address these questions, we . . . [fill in the blank]*. Regardless of how you frame it, the goal of the first sentence in the third paragraph should be to promise a solution.

The remainder of the third paragraph should outline the basic theoretical (or methodological) perspective you will use to find the solution, what you expect to find, and often your key findings. Authors, of course, differ as to whether they like sharing their key results up-front. On the one hand, sharing your hypotheses and key results up-front can help prime reviewers so they are not surprised when they subsequently get to these parts of the manuscript (thus potentially enhancing the fluency of the manuscript). On the other hand, some authors prefer to "hold their cards closer to the vest" and systematically build up to their hypotheses and key results. Either approach can work. Moreover, the same author may use different approaches for different papers and/or journals. As a matter of personal preference, we like to use the third paragraph to briefly introduce the theory, hypotheses, and often the key results.[1]

As an example of the three-paragraph approach, consider the following three-paragraph opening to Balliet, Li, and Joireman's (2011) paper exploring how two personality factors combine to predict forgiveness in social dilemmas (described in detail in Chapter 7):

> Forgiveness is a linchpin in successful relationships (Karremans & Van Lange, 2008; McCullough, Rachal, Sandage, Worthington, Brown, & Hight, 1998; McCullough, Worthington, & Rachal, 1997; Tsang, McCullough, & Fincham, 2006; Worthington, Van Oyen Wetviliet, Pietrinit, & Miller, 2007) and an important determinant of psychological well-being (Bono, McCullough, & Root, 2008; Karremans, Van Lange, Ouwerkerk, & Kluwer, 2003; Lawler et al., 2003). One factor that influences willingness to forgive is an individual's personality.
>
> Prior research linking personality with forgiveness has implicated a variety of traits. The majority of this work suggests that the forgivers of the world are basically "nice" people—high in agreeableness (e.g., Leach & Lark, 2004; McCullough & Hoyt, 2002) or empathy (McCullough et al., 1997, 1998, 2001; for a recent review, see Fehr, Gelfand, & Nag, 2010). More recent work suggests that the world's forgivers may also be "smart" people—high in trait self-control (Finkel & Campbell, 2001) or executive functioning (Pronk, Karremans, Overbeek, Vermulst, & Wigboldus, 2010). Integrating these two lines of research, the present work poses the following questions: Can a high level of trait self-control predict higher levels of forgiveness even among people with a proself orientation? Can a prosocial orientation positively relate to forgiveness even among those with a low level of trait self-control? Or does forgiveness require both a prosocial orientation and high trait self-control?
>
> To address these questions, we advance a trait × trait interactionist perspective on forgiveness, which gives rise to two competing theoretical models. Though both models are grounded

---

[1]Increasingly, editors and reviewers are asking authors to explicitly describe their paper's key contributions. Often, this happens following the third paragraph described here. For an example, see Joireman Grégoire, Devezer, and Tripp (2013; described in detail in Chapter 7).

in work on forgiveness and social interdependence theory, the models offer a notably different pattern of predictions. The compensatory model predicts that forgiveness requires a prosocial orientation or high self-control, and the synergistic model assumes that forgiveness requires both. We test these competing models across three primary studies exploring willingness to forgive an interaction partner who behaves noncooperatively in a social dilemma. (Balliet et al., 2011, p. 1090)

As this three-paragraph opener illustrates, the opening paragraphs (a) directly demonstrate that the behavior in question is an important one (forgiveness is a linchpin in successful relationships and an important determinant of psychological well-being); (b) quickly summarize research on key personality variables that predict forgiveness; (c) note that recent research suggests that the forgivers of the world are not only "nice" (as one would expect), but also (more intriguingly) "smart" (which raises the possibility that forgiveness may, at times, be selfishly motivated); (d) pose several interesting questions emanating from this observation (can self-control compensate for a proself orientation?); (e) inform readers that we will address these questions with a trait × trait interactionist perspective that gives rise to two competing models; (f) succinctly express those competing models; (g) help readers to understand how the competing models address the questions raised; and finally (h) inform readers broadly that we will test the models across three experiments exploring willingness to forgive a partner who behaves noncooperatively in a social dilemma.

In sum, over the course of three short paragraphs, and in a little over 300 words, Balliet and colleagues oriented readers to the problem, convinced them of its importance, reviewed what was known about the problem, raised intriguing questions about the problem on the basis of that review, and informed readers how they would address those questions. Interestingly, the opening paragraphs don't directly explicate gaps in the literature, per se, but rather imply those gaps with the questions raised. Later in the Introduction, the authors do explain why research testing the competing models is valuable. That said, we suspect reviewers' interest in the paper was piqued well before that justification was offered, as they recognized the theoretical value in testing the competing trait × trait compensatory versus synergistic models.

Two-Paragraph Opener

In the preceding section, we spent a fair amount of time outlining the logic and benefits of the three-paragraph opener because we believe it can be an extremely useful way to approach the opening paragraphs. At times, however, it is desirable or necessary to use some modification of that approach. One alternative is the two-paragraph opener. In this approach, two of the three elements (often the problem statement and key questions) are combined into a single paragraph.

Several years ago, Joireman and colleagues used this approach in a paper on sensation seeking, aggression, and the consideration of future consequences (Joireman, Anderson, & Strathman, 2003). To set up the questions in a compelling manner, we prefaced the first paragraph with two quotes, one from stalwarts in the field of aggression, the other from (Sir) Elton John. As it turned out, Huesmann and Eron raised an important question (Why do people engage in aggression when it often carries negative consequences?), and Elton John offered an intriguing answer that played perfectly into our focus on sensation seeking and aggression (because fighting can sometimes be fun). And so was born the "aggression paradox" (i.e., the notion that although aggression may provide immediate rewards, it can also carry long-term negative consequences).

As the reader will note, although we slightly rearranged the order of the introductory elements, the first two paragraphs managed to introduce the problem, raise intriguing questions, briefly review the existing literature, point out its gaps, provide a roadmap for where the paper was going, and articulate how it would address those gaps:

> One of the puzzling aspects of habitual aggressive behavior is why it persists in the face of so many apparently negative consequences.
> —Huesmann and Eron (1989, p. 102)

> Saturday night's all right for fighting. Get a little action in.
> —Elton John

> Of the many forms of self-control that must be mastered as one matures, perhaps none is more important than the control of aggressive behavior. Indeed, whether at work, home, school, or play, aggression often carries significant personal and social costs. That said, it is, as Huesmann and Eron (1989) note, "puzzling" that certain individuals habitually engage in aggressive acts, despite the apparently negative consequences. What accounts for this finding? Do aggressive individuals fail to consider the possible consequences of their actions, or might they perceive some benefit in behaving in an aggressive fashion? Perhaps the answer is both.

> In the present paper, we argue that individual differences in aggression are related, in part, to individual differences in sensation seeking (Zuckerman, 1979, 1994), impulsivity, and the consideration of future consequences (CFC) (Strathman, Gleicher, Boninger, & Edwards, 1994). At one level, our focus on these variables is not entirely new. Many studies, for example, have linked aggression with individual differences in impulsivity (e.g., Hynan & Grush, 1986; Buss & Perry, 1992; Zuckerman, Kuhlman, Joireman, Teta, & Kraft, 1993; Luengo, Carrillo-de-la-Pena, Otero, & Romero, 1994), and several studies have linked sensation seeking with broad indexes of aggression (Zuckerman,

1979, 1994). Few studies, however, have examined in detail how various dimensions of sensation seeking relate to different forms of aggression, and even fewer studies have explored how aggression may be influenced by individual differences in CFC (cf. Zimbardo & Boyd, 1999). In an attempt to better understand how aggression may be shaped by sensation seeking, impulsivity, and CFC, we integrate past work in these domains within a recent theory of aggression (Anderson & Bushman, 2002), and report a series of studies testing various aspects of the integrated model. (Joireman et al., 2003, p. 1287)

One-Paragraph Opener

If space is at a premium, and you need to get to the point as quickly as possible, you can accomplish all of the goals outlined previously in a single introductory paragraph. In one recent paper, for example, Joireman and colleagues were interested in whether a 2-week course of simple physical and cognitive exercises could reduce consumers' impulsive buying tendencies (Sultan, Joireman, & Sprott, 2012). Given the goals of the journal (rapid dissemination of novel findings), we needed to quickly "cut to the chase," which meant a compact Introduction. With work, we were able to accomplish all of our goals with the following paragraph, which was immediately followed up with a more comprehensive review of relevant theory and past research:

> Impulsive buying has been estimated to account for over $4 billion in retail store sales (Mogelonsky, 1998). Given its pervasiveness, researchers have been keen to identify the underlying causes of impulsive buying. One model that has recently been used to understand impulsive buying is the strength model of self-control (Baumeister & Heatherton, 1996; Vohs & Faber, 2007). Applied to impulsive buying, the strength model assumes that a consumer's ability to control urges to engage in impulsive buying can (a) become temporarily depleted as a result of prior self-control efforts (a depletion effect) and (b) built up over time through repeated self-control exercises (an exercise effect). The present research focuses on the latter by exploring whether simple physical and cognitive exercises, practiced over the course of two weeks, can reduce consumers' urges and intentions to engage in impulsive buying. (Sultan et al., 2012, p. 61)

THEORETICAL DEVELOPMENT

As we stressed in Chapter 2, one of the most important parts of any paper is the theoretical development section. It is particularly important at this stage to recall what theory is and what theory is not. To briefly reiterate our earlier points, assumptions are not theory; logic is not (necessarily) theory; and a review of the literature is not theory. *Theory* is a statement about the interconnection of relevant constructs and how those constructs combine to predict a given behavior of interest. Theory is a story about how reality, with respect to a given outcome, unfolds. Readers interested in a more detailed discussion of theory development and testing are encouraged to refer back to our earlier chapter, in which the ideals of truth, abstraction, progress, and applicability are discussed (cf. Van Lange, Kruglanski, & Higgins, 2012). With that being said, theory is often backed up with appropriate references to the extant literature.

LITERATURE REVIEW

When reviewing the literature, we recommend seven basic principles. First, use literature to back up your theoretical argument, rather than as the sole basis for your predictions. One of the most common mistakes new (and even long-time) scholars make in their introductions is that they tend to advance hypotheses on the basis (solely) of a review of the literature. If you find yourself saying something like, "Jones (2001) found X, Smith (2009) found Y. Hence, we hypothesize Z," it is time to go back to the drawing board and think harder about your theory. Obviously, making the transition from reviewing the literature to advancing theory and hypotheses on the basis of that theory is a difficult and time-consuming process. Nevertheless, to become a top-tier author, you must move beyond simply reviewing the literature.

Second, stay focused. Include only literature that is relevant to your study. Your goal in reviewing the literature is not (primarily) to impress your reader with your ability to cite each and every paper written since the dawn of time (i.e., the work of William James). Your job is to use your understanding of the literature to develop theoretical propositions and hypotheses.

Third, and on a related note, although classic research can be helpful in framing the broader goals of the paper, the bulk of the literature you review should be recent research in highly regarded journals. This sends the message that you understand the literature, which in turn can go a long way toward convincing your reviewers that you actually know where the gaps are.

Fourth, only discuss in detail the handful of previous papers that are most directly relevant to your study. It is not necessary to go into excruciating detail about the methods and results of every article you cite. In fact, this can be counterproductive, as it unnecessarily lengthens the manuscript (reducing the contribution-to-length ratio), and it dilutes your focus on the most important ideas behind your study.

Fifth, when you cite an article, be sure you know what it says. It pains us to recall how many times we have reviewed manuscripts by authors who have completely misinterpreted a study. At times, it is as if the author had never even read the paper (which in some cases may be a fair criticism). Needless to say, this sends a very bad message to reviewers (especially if you incorrectly interpret a study by your anonymous reviewer!). On the other hand, if you show reviewers that you are aware of not only the big picture behind certain papers but also the nuanced points made in those papers, you will have gone a long way toward establishing your credibility as an author.

Sixth, make sure to include relevant references from the journal to which you plan to submit. There has, justifiably, been some debate about the tendency for editors and reviewers to request such "self-citations." On the one hand, abuse of this technique can lead to an artificially inflated impact factor for the journal in question. On the other hand, taking the time to review your target journal's relevant research helps you to understand whether in fact your work fills a meaningful gap in the literature and will be of interest to readers of that journal. Carefully reviewing your target journal's related work also helps you understand how to position your manuscript. For example, perhaps a review of the journal's articles reveals that 80% of them have a section on "managerial implications." If so, it would be wise for you to include such a section as well.

Finally, don't let the tail wag the dog. What we mean here is that you should always be in charge of the literature, and you should not let the literature be in charge of you. Your Introduction should not simply read like an annotated bibliography of all previous studies. Rather, you should use the literature to make a point.

METHOD

The Method section is typically the easiest to write. The two major goals of the Method section are to allow readers to replicate your study and evaluate its validity. Keeping these goals in mind will help you determine what to include and not include. In short, include anything that is critical to the design or execution of the study, and eliminate unnecessary detail (e.g., participants used a No. 2 pencil).

In terms of organization, it is important to think carefully about the order in which you will discuss the various tasks—sometimes it might be good to discuss the task or measure that is most relevant to the hypotheses up-front, even if it was administered later in the experimental session. A good Method section should also be well structured in terms of appropriate headings. Thoughtful use of italics to highlight key constructs and conditions can also enhance readability. Indeed, the judicious use of italics helps readers quickly locate essential information. This is important because, although many readers may read through the method fully, others are likely to approach the Method section more like an encyclopedia, where the goal is to quickly locate specific details about a method or measure, without reading every word.

As you work through the Method section, take care to clearly explain all relevant characteristics of the sample, method of obtaining the sample, procedure, and measures. In addition, if the scales and methods you use have been well established, you can use a shorter description, referring readers to the original papers where the measures were developed. On the other hand, if you have designed a new measure or are using a new or intricate method, it is worthwhile spending some time carefully explaining them in the method section. And it is often wise to spell out the novel aspects of a new measure, because, as we will see in Chapter 10, methodological innovation is an effective way to make a contribution.

RESULTS

Like Method sections, Results sections are fairly straightforward, assuming you know your statistics. At the same time, you should be very careful to walk your readers systematically through your analyses, building from simpler results to more complicated results. In an experimental context, this means starting with any key manipulation checks and basic descriptive statistics (e.g., a correlation matrix) and working your way up through more complicated results (main effects, then interactions, then simple effects following an interaction).

Once the basic effects are established, it is appropriate to turn to process measures or underlying mechanisms to understand why you are getting the results you are getting. In an applied/correlational context, it is appropriate to begin with simple correlations and then build (where appropriate) to interactions and/or tests of overall theoretical structural equation models. Within the marketing domain especially, another important component of the Results section (or sometimes the Method section) is a detailed analysis of measurement properties, including construct validity and reliability. It is also important to note that you should not present the Results section as simply a summary of the statistical output. Rather, it is important to guide the reader through the results by highlighting the findings (e.g., F-tests) that are relevant to the hypotheses that you set out to test. Findings that are not relevant to the hypotheses should receive a less central position in the Results section, and sometimes might be even discussed briefly in a footnote (e.g., findings that are very complex and not directly relevant to the hypotheses). At the same time, authors should check and recheck whether they have reported all findings, so that readers always can tell which effects were significant and which were not. We also recommend taking time to prepare visually pleasing (and not overwhelming) tables and figures, as poorly constructed tables and figures can annoy reviewers and potentially lead to rejection, whereas carefully prepared figures can significantly enhance the impact of the paper; for creative examples, see the articles by Bateson, Nettle, and Roberts (2006) and Herrmann, Thöni, and Gächter (2008), discussed in Chapters 11 and 12, respectively.

DISCUSSION

The Discussion section offers authors an opportunity to recap their findings and explain how their work contributes to relevant literatures. The Discussion also often contains some speculation on the practical implications of one's findings, and careful reflection on the study's strengths and limitations, as well as future research directions.

Challenges and Goals of the Discussion

The Discussion is often the hardest section to write. By this point, authors may feel they have already said what they need to say and may consequently struggle to figure out what to say next without sounding redundant. It is also possible that the results did not completely support the hypotheses, in which case authors may feel a little defensive as they search for a plausible explanation for the unexpected results. Moreover, even if the results do support the hypotheses, authors must often find ways to rule out alternative explanations for the findings (frequently raised by reviewers!). Finally, authors may feel uncomfortable generalizing beyond the data as they try to highlight the theoretical and practical implications of the findings. In sum, the Discussion poses numerous challenges and can be difficult to write. Nevertheless, these challenges must be successfully navigated if the paper is to succeed. Assuming your theoretical rationale is strong, your method is sound, and the results are compelling, the Discussion is your opportunity to "seal the deal" with your readers. Next, we suggest an approach to the Discussion that can help you do just that.

Discussion sections will, of course, vary on the basis of the author's style, the journal's requirements, and the suggestions of reviewers. Generally speaking, however, it seems safe to say that you should accomplish at least four basic goals in the Discussion. Namely, you should briefly recap your paper's central goals and hypotheses, and discuss whether your results support (or do not support) your hypotheses; you should outline the theoretical implications of your findings; you should illustrate the practical implications of your findings (though journals differ on whether this is required); and you should outline the strengths and limitations of your study and outline directions for future research.

Opening the Discussion: Recapping Goals, Hypotheses, and Key Findings

The very first paragraph of the Discussion should succinctly remind readers of the paper's central goals, hypotheses, and key findings and should end by providing a brief overview of the remainder of the Discussion. One helpful technique for writing this first paragraph is to assume your reader skipped everything else in the paper and went immediately to the Discussion. If you imagine this possibility, it can put you in the right mind-set for writing the first paragraph because you must assume that your reader knows very little about the paper. With this in mind, a very logical first sentence would state: "The purpose of this study was . . . [fill in the blank]." Admittedly, this is not the most creative approach, but it gets the job done. With experience, you may choose to precede this boilerplate opening with a brief sentence reminding readers of the practical implications or real-world problem you are addressing.

Once you have stated the purpose of the study, the next few sentences should summarize the hypotheses and how the results either support or do not support those hypotheses. It is often helpful to have the first paragraph end with a transition sentence that provides an overview of the remainder of the discussion. When space is tight, reviewers and editors may recommend dropping such mini-overviews, but we recommend erring on the side of more rather than fewer transitions (as we have already articulated, you must lead the reader by the hand).

Theoretical Implications/Contributions

Once you have reminded your readers of your paper's goals, hypotheses, and results, it is time to convince them of its value and contributions to the literature. This section can be intimidating, but it is essential to the paper's success. It is here that you clearly explain why your paper is important (theoretically) and how it "makes a contribution." By the end of this section, readers should be convinced that your work fills a *meaningful gap* in the field and that the field now knows something important that it did not know before your work. This requires you to convincingly remind readers of that gap (which you explained in detail in your Introduction) and to clearly explain how your work fills that gap. If you hope to publish in top-tier journals, it is important that you do not fool yourself into thinking that a minor, incremental contribution is a groundbreaking theoretical advance. Incremental contributions are fine; they just shouldn't be confused with major contributions.

As you attempt to articulate your contribution, it is also important that you be familiar with (and cite) the recent literature relevant to your paper. A thorough understanding of the current literature helps to convince reviewers that you are in a good position to identify gaps in the literature and helps you know how to frame those gaps and explain how you address them.

As you outline the theoretical implications of your findings, it is usually necessary to offer an interpretation for your findings. Your preferred interpretation, most often, will be expressed in terms of your initial theorizing and hypotheses. However, even if your results support your hypotheses, it is usually possible that an alternative explanation can be offered (by reviewers). Through good experimental design (e.g., random assignment, avoiding confounds), relevant measures (e.g., mood checks), or analytic techniques (e.g., common method bias estimation), you may be able to rule out some of the more problematic alternative explanations. At times, however, you will need to rule out those alternative explanations logically. For example, if alternative explanation X is correct, then we would expect to observe Y, and we did not observe Y; therefore, alternative explanation X loses credibility.

Practical Implications/Contributions

Often, readers will be interested in the practical implications of your findings, though this can vary substantially according to the journal. As scientists, we tend to be reluctant to draw sweeping practical implications from our findings, yet some thought should go into this section. The practical implications should follow logically from your findings and should be offered with appropriate caveats.

Strengths, Limitations, and Future Directions

Having outlined the theoretical and practical implications of your work, it's time to brag a bit, show some humility, and give readers a vision for the future. We typically prefer to outline the limitations first, followed by the strengths (e.g., "despite these limitations, the present study has several strengths"), and end with the future directions, though future directions can be weaved in as a way to address the limitations.

The paragraph on limitations should convey to your reader that you have put serious thought into the true limitations of your project. Authors differ in terms of whether they like to express limitations; some prefer to let reviewers point them out. We feel, however, that it is an appropriate and good strategy to point out two or three limitations of your project. You don't want to overwhelm your reader with limitations; after all, you're trying to sell your paper. On the other hand, you don't want to be blindsided by reviewers who think you are not aware of the limitations of your study. As you consider whether to include limitations, remember that one of your goals is to establish your credibility to the reader. An author who is up-front about the key limitations of the study is also probably trustworthy when he or she claims to have made a certain contribution. That said, it is helpful, after you have outlined a limitation, to try to explain (if possible) why the limitation may not be a fatal flaw or to frame the limitation as a springboard for future research.

Once you have outlined two or three limitations, you can say, "Despite these limitations, the present study has several strengths," and then proceed to outline those strengths. Maybe you used multiple studies, interesting behavioral measures, or peer reports. Maybe you developed a novel method, conducted a longitudinal study, or collected data across numerous countries. Or maybe you used a sophisticated analytic technique. Don't be afraid to take some credit for the good things you have done. By this point, readers may have forgotten or may not be aware of those strengths. Remember: Lead your reader by the hand.

Finally, if you haven't outlined a large number of future directions in connection with your stated limitations, now is the time to suggest several directions for future research. Your job is not only to report what you have found but also to provide guidance for future researchers to build on your foundation. Leaving readers with some open questions can heighten their general enthusiasm for your work.

Concluding Comments

If you have room, you may want to wrap everything up with a Conclusion section. The Conclusion section, like the abstract, helps readers appreciate what you did, how you did it, what you found, and why it's important. Ending with a catchy sentence that ties back to your Introduction can also be a nice way to "tie a bow around" the paper.

MULTIPLE STUDY PAPERS

Before closing this section on the initial submission, we consider some of the issues involved in writing up multiple study papers. Multiple study papers, of course, have become the norm in the majority of top-tier journals in psychology and marketing. Thus, unless you have an impeccable study with impeccable results, it is likely that you too will be writing a multiple study paper for a top-tier journal. Multiple study papers offer several benefits, as we explain next, and require a few additional elements when it comes to writing.

Benefits

Multiple study papers have several benefits. To begin, if well assembled, the various studies tend to compensate for each other's weaknesses. For example, because correlation does not prove causation, it is helpful to replicate correlational results using an experimental method. Similarly, because experimental designs can suffer from low external validity, it is helpful to complement them with correlational data that uncovers similar relationships in the real world.

Second, multiple study papers allow an author to replicate and extend an interesting finding. The ability to replicate tends to be undervalued, but it is important. However, selling a pure replication is typically difficult. Thus, a good strategy in a multiple study paper is to start simple, for example, with proof of the basic concept, and then to replicate the basic finding and extend it by including a moderator or measuring a mediator. As we discuss in detail in Chapter 9, the moderator approach allows the author to identify boundary conditions, or factors that magnify a given effect, whereas the mediator approach allows the author to gain insight into the underlying process that accounts for the basic finding.

Finally, multiple study papers allow an author to establish generalizability across different methods, samples, or measures. This, in turn, gives readers more confidence that the findings are reliable and have broader applicability.

Overview of Studies

When writing a multiple study paper, two additional elements are typically included. First, usually at the end of the Introduction, it is a good idea to give readers an idea of the flow of the studies. This helps readers process and understand the flow of the studies. The overview can also help establish perceptual fluency for the reader. Depending on your style and space limitations, the overview may or may not summarize the key results.

Transitions Between Studies

Any time you write a multiple study paper, transitions between the studies are also critical. The approach we tend to favor is a quick transition between studies. In such a transition, you state the purpose of the previous study, review what you found, and highlight a (fixable) limitation. The limitation you note serves as the transition to the next study, which then addresses that limitation. It is not always necessary to frame the transition in terms of a limitation. For example, you could simply argue that you conducted a subsequent study to "enhance the generalizability" of the findings across cultures, or dependent measures, etc. However, pointing out a limitation and then addressing it tends to work well as a strategy.

CONCLUSION ON WRITING
THE INITIAL SUBMISSION

Good writing can go a long way toward eventually getting your contribution published. In this chapter, we have provided some recommendations for the more challenging parts of a manuscript. Beyond these recommendations, we encourage you to read top-tier journal articles carefully for ideas on what works well in each section of the manuscript. Modeling your writing on these publications should help you strengthen your writing and improve the likelihood that you too will publish in such journals.

Preparing a Successful Revision

As many readers are all too painfully aware, writing a strong first draft is only the beginning of the long and often arduous journey toward publication. If you are fortunate enough to receive a revise-and-resubmit decision (or even a reject-and-resubmit decision), the next obvious step is revision. This may involve reconceptualizing the theory, providing more support for the methods, conducting additional analyses, and/or collecting more data. In this chapter, we provide tips on navigating the review process. We begin by considering an intangible and often overlooked factor that is nonetheless extremely important: your attitude toward the review and revision process.

ADOPT THE CORRECT ATTITUDE

Let's face it: The review process is not usually pleasant. You worked hard on your project and firmly believe you did a great job on the initial draft, only to find out that, for instance, three anonymous reviewers (especially Reviewer 3 for some reason) raised "serious concerns" about your conceptualization, method, data analysis, or conclusions. The fact that you must undertake a significant revision of what you thought was a strong first draft can be irritating. Add to that the fact that reviewers sometimes seem ill-informed, hostile, or both, and the situation can be downright infuriating.

In light of these emotions, it is often tempting to respond to reviewers impulsively, emotionally, and with disrespect. However, this approach carries significant risks. Indeed, it is almost always advisable to override your immediate, gut-level desire to adopt a hostile posture and tell reviewers the myriad ways in which they are wrong. As rewarding as that approach may seem in the short run, in the long run, a more reflective, rational, and respectful approach (the

3R approach) will greatly increase the odds of your eventually getting published.

The 3R approach is rooted in two fundamental assumptions. First, though some may have a theoretical or political axe to grind, reviewers generally are interested in providing honest feedback that identifies important problems in a manuscript and offering suggestions for how to improve the manuscript. Second, despite its imperfections, the review process tends to identify the highest quality work and produce better revisions than the initial submissions. If you adopt these two assumptions, you will find it much easier to follow the 3R approach.

Admittedly, the 3R approach may not come automatically at first (or ever). It may take some time to cool off after you first receive the reviews, but that is time well taken. Indeed, it is often a good idea to put the reviews away for a week or so. As the reviews work their way down your inbox and your emotions begin to cool, remind yourself of the two key assumptions noted previously, perhaps by asking yourself: What are my goals and motives as an author? We suspect you will conclude that your goals and motives are consistent with the assumptions we just outlined, namely, that reviewers are often motivated to help improve your manuscript, and the review process generally improves manuscripts. Finally, when you are ready to adopt a 3R approach, return to the reviews and ask yourself: How can these reviews provide an opportunity for me to significantly enhance the quality of my manuscript and its eventual impact on the field? As you read the reviews, it may be necessary to repeat these steps, but over time, you may become more automatically inclined to adopt a 3R approach.

The 3R approach offers at least three benefits. First, it communicates to reviewers (and editors) that you have heard them and you understand their concerns, suggestions, and so forth. Second, as a result, it shows that you respect your reviewers. Third, it helps you better understand how to effectively respond to reviewer concerns and suggestions. When combined, hearing your reviewers, showing them respect, and responding to them effectively will go a long way toward helping you push through a successful revision. In the following sections, we provide additional suggestions that can help you prepare a successful revision.

DON'T FOOL YOURSELF AND DON'T TRY TO PULL THE WOOL OVER REVIEWERS' EYES

Our first piece of advice: Never cut corners as you prepare the revision. As a reviewer, it is very clear when an author is simply paying lip service to one of your comments. As an example, a reviewer might suggest that an author conduct a more thorough review of the relevant literature and provide two suggestions (as starting points). When an author comes back with the same two additional references, and no more, and incorrectly cites half of the new references, it is clear that he did not put in the time necessary to do a good job. This half-hearted job may allow the author to fool himself into thinking he has met the minimum requirement for a revision, but it will often not please the reviewer (especially at a top-tier journal). Given this, it is important to be complete and forthright in your revision.

RESPOND TO EACH (AND EVERY) COMMENT

Being complete and forthright requires that you respond conscientiously to each and every comment raised in the review process. You should incorporate as many of the reviewer comments as you can realistically manage (and live with), and you should approach the task seriously. At times, you will be forced to take a stand and argue against a reviewer for theoretical reasons, to clarify a misunderstanding, or to point out that the reviewer is (objectively) wrong (e.g., on a statistical technique). This is okay, if you feel it is absolutely essential, but we recommend using this approach sparingly, and respectfully. Either way, one thing you should always avoid is simply dismissing or failing to respond to a given comment, hoping perhaps that if you respond to the majority of the comments, reviewers and editors will let you slide on a few of the more minor ones.

OVERDELIVER

Responding to each and every comment is the minimum required. To be truly successful, we advise going one step beyond. Your goal should not be to provide only what reviewers want, but to go "above and beyond the call of duty" and overdeliver (within reason). If a reviewer hints that an additional study might be valuable, but does not ask for it directly, consider collecting the follow-up data and pleasantly surprising the reviewer. When you can read between the lines and correctly interpret what a reviewer is saying and then overdeliver as a result, it communicates a high degree of respect, intelligence, and motivation on your part, all of which should work in your favor.

WRITE A CLEAR, DETAILED, AND RESPECTFUL RESPONSE LETTER TO THE REVIEWERS

In the previous discussion on writing the initial draft, we stressed the importance of "leading the reader by the hand." The same principle applies to the revision and response letter, which should be clear and detailed (and written in a respectful tone). Though more general response letters may work (or even be requested by editors), in our experience as authors and reviewers, we find that a more detailed response letter works best. The response letter replicates each reviewer comment and follows with a detailed response to the comment (often in bold, a different font, or indented). When text is revised, it is important to let reviewers know on which page or pages they can find the revisions. And when not overwhelming, it is often useful to embed the relevant sections of revised text in the response letter. Although this can lengthen the response letter, it can also save reviewers from having to hunt through the manuscript, and it can bring into clear focus how you addressed the comment in question.

In addition to being clear and detailed, you should make an effort to be respectful. It may seem hard, or unnecessary, but thanking reviewers for raising an excellent point or suggesting a useful set of studies or analyses can go a long way toward establishing a positive response to your revision. The approach can be overdone, of course, and different authors will feel more or less comfortable with this approach (with some perhaps feeling it is too deferential). Our advice is to do what is comfortable and (if you can live with it) to err on the side of being overly polite.

INCLUDE A GENERAL LETTER TO THE EDITOR

In addition to writing a detailed response letter to the reviewers, it is important that you write some kind of letter to the editor. At a minimum, in this letter you should thank the editor for offering you an opportunity to revise and resubmit, acknowledge that the reviews helped you prepare a stronger manuscript (which, in general, should be the case), and offer to make any additional changes that the editor might believe could further strengthen the manuscript. Depending on the editor's letter, you may be asked to highlight the major changes you made to the manuscript (without going into as much detail as you did in your response to the reviewers).

REMEMBER, YOU ARE THE AUTHOR

As one of our reviewers noted, although the review process can often improve a manuscript, blindly following each and every reviewer comment can potentially make a paper worse. At the end of the day, it is important to recall that you are the author of the paper, and the paper should make sense as a whole product, and not simply reflect a patchwork of changes designed to satisfy reviewers. Furthermore, even if an author makes each and every change suggested by the review team, it is possible that the revision will be sent to at least one new reviewer to see if the revision makes sense to a fresh set of eyes. This reinforces the point that after all of the modifications have been made, the paper still must make sense as a whole. Thus, an author must balance respect for the review team with a respect for one's own position and provide a revision that offers the best chance of satisfying all parties involved.

DEALING WITH REJECTION

Unfortunately, despite our best efforts, manuscripts do get rejected, sometimes after as many as three or four rounds of reviews. At this point, a researcher must decide how to deal with the decision. Although challenging the decision can occasionally work, especially when the case for rejection was very weak, we do not advise challenging the editor's decision as a general strategy. Thus, an author with a rejected manuscript must decide where else to submit the manuscript—or even whether to shelve the project. If the reviewers raised clear and fatal flaws with the design or findings, our recommendation is to redesign the study and collect new data before resubmitting to a different journal. If, on the other hand, you still believe in the manuscript and think that reviewers "just didn't get it," new or additional data may not be necessary for submitting to a different journal. However, even in this case, it is generally advisable to look over the original reviews for any major issues that could be addressed before submitting to a different journal. It is possible that some of the original reviewers will review the manuscript for the next journal you select, and reviewers do not like to see that their suggestions have been plainly ignored. This does not mean that you need to do a painful, point-by-point change to the manuscript before submitting, but you should pay some attention to the major issues. Even if the same reviewer(s) do not review the manuscript, the changes may help increase your odds at the next journal. Whatever the case may be, our advice is to use the advice of the reviewers as you best see fit in an effort to strengthen the manuscript and its odds of being accepted at a different journal.

We would be remiss to end this section on revising and resubmitting without acknowledging that, at times, a manuscript may be rejected at a series of outlets. Although we generally recommend strong persistence, especially if you believe in the manuscript, there may be circumstances when placing the manuscript in the "file drawer" is the best option. This could occur if the manuscript was not an especially high priority to begin with, if the costs of completing the manuscript (e.g., time, money) outweigh its benefits (e.g., a low-tier journal), or when other high-priority manuscripts appear to offer a better chance of success. Early on in one's career, every manuscript seems vital to survival, but as one develops a bigger pipeline of projects, one is frequently faced with trade-offs between manuscripts offering different probabilities of success and impact. At that point, a researcher must carefully consider the costs and benefits of pursuing various courses of action. At the end of the day, whatever course you choose, our hope is that the recommendations provided in this chapter help you achieve your goal of publishing high-quality research in your field's top outlets.

Appendix 4.1:
A Checklist for Evaluating
the Quality of a Publication

The following checklist[1] can help you determine the quality of your own or another author's paper and whether that paper is likely to "make a contribution."

1. A High-Quality Publication Makes a Contribution. This can be done in a variety of ways. For example, the paper can
   - Integrate insights from multiple disciplines
   - Synthesize a large body of existing research via meta-analysis
   - Challenge long-standing assumptions
   - Test competing theories
   - Advance and test a new theory
   - Explain earlier contradictory findings via an integrated theory
   - Refine an existing theory by:
     - Showing the role of new causal variables
     - Demonstrating the influence of moderators
       - Moderators "change" the effect of X on Y (making it stronger or weaker, or changing its direction)
       - These moderators may (or may not) set "boundaries" on an effect
     - Identifying mediating mechanisms
       - Explaining why $X \rightarrow Z$, by demonstrating $X \rightarrow Y \rightarrow Z$
   - Introduce a novel individual difference construct and scale to assess it
   - Develop an innovative methodology that can advance an understanding of a domain
   - Illustrate the application of theory and prior research to a real-world problem or in a real-world setting
   - Examine the generalizability of past findings to a new population or culture
2. A High-Quality Publication Often Involves Multiple Studies (and Methods)
   - Does the paper have multiple studies?
   - Do the studies build on one another?
   - Do multiple methods complement each other (e.g., correlational and experimental designs)?
   - Do the studies tell an integrated story?

[1]Readers can download this checklist at http://www.cbe.wsu.edu/~jjoireman

3. A High-Quality Publication is Well Written. This means the paper
   - Has an hourglass organization (start broad, narrow, and end on a broad note)
   - "Leads the reader by the hand." To accomplish this, make sure to:
     - Think carefully about the organization of your paper
     - Provide overviews
     - Use clear headings and subheadings
     - Use effective transitions
     - Use straightforward language
     - Make sure that each sentence adds value
     - Use (some) redundancy
   - Has a compelling set of introductory paragraphs. The three-paragraph introduction, for example, is set up as follows:
     - Paragraph 1: What's the topic? Why should I care? And what's the puzzle?
       - A quote can help; they appear to be increasing in popularity
       - An interesting hook at the outset to capture reader's attention
       - A story (real life or hypothetical but realistic)
       - Real-world statistics (e.g., how many people were killed by guns last year)
       - This paragraph ends with a general question that can serve as a transition to the next paragraph (the "puzzle")
     - Paragraph 2: Filling in (part) of the puzzle, and highlighting the missing pieces
       - This paragraph (briefly) summarizes key findings (or a key finding) in the area and then proceeds to point out a limitation
       - This limitation serves as the transition to the next paragraph
     - Paragraph 3: Purpose of this article, or which pieces of puzzle we'll look at
       - Once they're interested and understand the limitation, readers need to know what you will do to solve the problem (fill in the pieces)
       - This paragraph clearly states the purpose of the study (first sentence, "the purpose of this paper/these studies is to . . .")
       - This paragraph may offer a general hypothesis (yes, it's OK; readers will understand that you will provide arguments for this hypothesis later on)
       - This paragraph should also highlight how the studies you propose will extend past research

- The remainder of article is characterized by clarity of expression:
  - Appropriate headings and subheadings
  - Occasional overviews of what's to come
  - In a multistudy paper, an overview of the studies (and how they fit together, and complement one another)
  - Clear statements, especially at the start of each paragraph
  - Transitions from one paragraph to another
  - Clear hypotheses
  - Results are clearly linked with hypotheses
  - Good transitions from one study to the next. For example,
    - Summarize findings of Study 1
    - Point out limitations of Study 1
    - Explain how Study 2 (etc.) will help address limitations of Study 1
- A discussion that
  - Summarizes most important findings
  - Recaps how findings relate to the hypotheses
  - Considers alternative explanations
  - Demonstrates relevance of findings for theory
  - Highlights possible applications
  - Accurately assesses strengths and limitations of the studies
  - Outlines avenues for future research

Appendix 4.2:
Revision Checklist

1. Adopt the "3R approach" (be reflective, rational, and respectful).
   - Carefully consider each comment, even if you may not initially agree.
   - Put emotion aside, and try to approach the reviews objectively.
   - Assume reviewers and editors are trying to help improve your paper.
2. Don't attempt to fool yourself or reviewers.
   - Do not "cut corners" or simply pay "lip service" to a reviewer's comment.
3. Respond to each and every comment (completely).
   - Show, through your careful and complete response, that you understand and have taken seriously each comment.
   - Showing a reviewer that you "got it" conveys respect and builds your credibility.

4. Overdeliver and leave reviewers pleasantly surprised.
   - This may include collecting additional data or a relevant analysis, even when it was only suggested, or simply alluded to in passing.
5. Include a clear, detailed, and polite response letter.
   - Provide each reviewer comment, followed by your response.
   - Thank reviewers for especially insightful suggestions, without going overboard.
6. Include a general letter to the editor.
   - Highlight the major changes (leaving the details for the response letter).
   - Thank the editor and reviewers and help them understand how their suggestions (and your changes) improved the manuscript.

PARADIGMS FOR PUBLISHING HIGH-QUALITY RESEARCH | **II**

Bridge Disciplines 5

In this chapter, we introduce the first of eight paradigms for publishing high-quality research: namely, bridging disciplines. Given our backgrounds and the nature of this book, the examples we provide focus largely on bridging the disciplines of social psychology and consumer behavior. However, because the fields of social psychology and consumer behavior have meaningful connections to many other fields of study (e.g., mental health, economics), the illustrations we provide are meant to underscore the broader value in building bridges between social psychology, consumer behavior, and a variety of other important fields of study. Before discussing the articles that illustrate the "bridging paradigm," we consider what bridging involves, as well as some of the costs and benefits associated with bridging.

http://dx.doi.org/10.1037/14525-006
How to Publish High-Quality Research, by J. Joireman and P. A. M. Van Lange

Background

WHAT IS BRIDGING?

Bridging can mean many different things to many different people (for a comprehensive review, see Van Lange, 2006). Bridging may mean forming collaborative relationships with colleagues from other disciplines, it may mean drawing on theory developed in a different discipline to shed light on a problem within one's own discipline, or it may mean borrowing novel methods or measures from other disciplines to broaden the scope of one's own research. In sum, bridging can be defined as an intentional effort to draw on the human, theoretical, methodological, and/or empirical resources of a related discipline to shed new light on one's own discipline, contribute new insights to a related discipline, and consequently advance progress in both disciplines. As we explain in more detail next, bridging consequently allows scientists to make significant progress in understanding broad theoretical questions as well as important societal issues.

BENEFITS OF BRIDGING

Bridging offers many benefits (cf. Van Lange, 2006). First, from a theoretical perspective, bridging allows researchers to address major scientific problems of a fundamental nature, such as whether people have free will, whether the person or the situation is the primary determinant of behavior, and whether people are good or bad by nature. Second, from a societal perspective, many issues are quite complex and multifaceted and therefore require expertise from various disciplines. For example, the problem of how to reduce environmental pollution often requires expertise from disciplines such as environmental science, economics, and psychology to fully understand the causes of pollution and how to reduce pollution. The same holds for other major societal issues, such as promoting public health, reducing international conflict, and promoting safety in communities. Third, and relevant to theory and society, bridging can also promote the development of broader theories that are applicable to those major theoretical and/or practical problems. Fourth, bridging often strengthens the quality of research in the domains of interest through the diffusion of alternative and sophisticated methods and data analytic techniques. Fifth, to many scientists, bridging is a stimulating exercise that can broaden the scope of one's research; revive, maintain, or strengthen one's enthusiasm for scientific inquiry; and build synergistic collaborations that pay big dividends in both productivity and career satisfaction. Sixth, bridging can also increase the likelihood that you will secure an extramural grant, given that most major granting agencies are now requiring an explicitly multidisciplinary approach. Finally, bridging disciplines can increase the impact of your research. Indeed, papers that bridge disciplines are often the most heavily cited papers, no doubt because they typically address big problems and appeal to such a wide audience (e.g., Markus & Kitayama, 1991, bridging social psychology and culture; Van Lange, Otten, De Bruin, & Joireman, 1997, bridging social, personality, and developmental psychology).

COSTS OF BRIDGING

Although there are many benefits of bridging, we should note that it is not always easy. Indeed, bridging involves several costs. For example, bridging requires keeping up with the literature in multiple disciplines; overcoming differences in terminology, assumptions, methods, and culture; and sometimes resisting institutional pressures to maintain a narrow identity, publish only in certain journals within one's field, and attend conferences only within one's narrowly defined field. Another challenge is that reviewers who are comfortable with their own "theoretical/disciplinary paradigm" may have trouble accepting or understanding how or why two seemingly disparate disciplines can (and should) be merged. On a related note, one of the biggest challenges is communication issues, because the disciplines often have different traditions, views, and (conceptual and operational) definitions. For example, psychologists are often inclined to define *altruism* in terms of motivation and goals, whereas economists may be more inclined to use behavioral definitions of altruism. As another example, psychologists tend to define *trust* in terms of interpersonal trust, whereas political scientists, management scientists, and economists are likely to also examine trust within larger units, such as organizational trust, institutional trust, or societal trust. These different definitions and approaches make miscommunication somewhat probable. At the same time, quite often such differences should be welcomed in that they help a scientist get the bigger picture that is relevant for broad theorizing, for broad methodology, and for broad applications—issues to which we now turn.

SUGGESTIONS FOR BRIDGING

How does one engage in bridging? To start bridging, we recommend first exposing yourself to the major journals in related fields. As an example, social psychologists would no doubt find many interesting articles in journals such as *Journal of Consumer Research, Journal of Marketing Research, Journal of Consumer Psychology, Journal of Public Policy and Marketing, Journal of Consumer Affairs, Journal of Advertising*, and *Journal of Retailing*, to name but a few. Researchers interested in consumer behavior, on the other hand, would benefit from reading *Journal of Personality and Social*

Psychology, Personality and Social Psychology Bulletin and Review, Journal of Experimental Social Psychology, Journal of Applied Social Psychology, Psychological Review, and *Psychological Bulletin,* among others. Second, we recommend attending (if not presenting at) at least one major conference outside your home discipline. Third, we recommend initiating collaborative relationships with researchers outside your home discipline. Here, it is not so important that you immediately know exactly what you would plan to do, but rather that you express an interest in a similar topic (e.g., how people respond to persuasive appeals in advertisements). Finally, we suggest being on the lookout for opportunities to join interdisciplinary teams of scholars on a large grant project, an increasingly prevalent activity within the academic community.

When it comes to writing a bridging paper, we also recommend being very conversant in the various disciplines to be merged and aware of the appropriate terminology and methods used in each. Recognizing these, it is possible to alert potentially skeptical reviewers to the subtle similarities and differences to smooth out the reviewers' openness to the new ideas.

In an effort to highlight the ways scholars can bridge domains, in what follows we discuss in detail six recent papers that successfully bridged multiple disciplines. In doing so, we decided to focus on bridges between the two fields that stand out in this book, given our expertise (i.e., social psychology and consumer behavior). With this in mind, we want to add that bridging has, over the years, proven fruitful in many other ways. For example, the entire field of social cognition (Fiske & Taylor, 1984) emerged out of a bridge between social psychology and cognitive psychology. Similarly, the field of social neuroscience emerged out of a bridge between social psychology and neuroscience (for a recent review, see Cacioppo, Berntson, & Decety, 2011). Many additional illustrations could be listed to show the usefulness of linking social psychology or consumer behavior to the fields of neuroscience and biology. For example, there are several productive programs of research focusing on the neurobiology of empathy, mind reading, fairness, trust, cooperation, social rewards and punishment, intergroup processes, self-evaluation, social support, and social exclusion (e.g., De Dreu et al., 2010; Eisenegger, Naef, Snozzi, Heinrichs, & Fehr, 2010; Singer et al., 2006; Taylor et al., 2010). Similarly, scholars have begun to build bridges between marketing and neuroscience to understand a range of outcomes (for a review, see Hubert & Kenning, 2008), including responses to aesthetic package design (Reimann, Zaichkowsky, Neuhaus, Bender, & Weber, 2010), brand loyalty (Lin, Tuan, & Chiu, 2010), celebrity endorsement (Stallen et al., 2010), and the ability of salespersons to understand consumer needs and intentions (Dietvorst et al., 2009). In addition, as we illustrate in Chapter 10, researchers have also begun to link ovulation with consumer behavior (e.g., see Durante, Griskevicius, Hill, Perilloux, & Li, 2011). Thus, bridging social psychology/ consumer behavior with insights from biology and social neuroscience is essential for a comprehensive understanding of these fields, as several of the illustrations in this (and other) chapters demonstrate.

Illustrations

DO PEOPLE "GO GREEN" TO BE SEEN?

In 2010, Griskevicius, Tybur, and Van den Bergh set out to answer what appeared to be a straightforward marketing-related question: Why is the Toyota Prius so successful? As the authors noted, desire for the Prius does not seem to be based primarily on financial or environmental concerns. Rather, the primary reason people say they buy a Prius is to "make a statement about me." The authors suggested that, "At first blush, it may seem puzzling why individuals would pay a premium to forgo luxury or comfort for the sake of displaying that they care" (p. 392). Drawing on insights from evolutionary social psychology (e.g., costly signaling theory and competitive altruism), the authors attempted to resolve this puzzle by hypothesizing that consumers might use conspicuous consumption of environmentally friendly products to enhance their status and reputation. By couching a timely and applied marketing-related question within the context of fundamental (and increasingly popular) social psychological theory, the authors provided a nice illustration of the value of the bridging paradigm.

After briefly reviewing more standard explanations for environmentally friendly behavior (EFB), the authors argued that many EFBs are also strongly influenced by social/normative factors and that people can use prosocial behaviors such as EFBs to enhance their reputations. The authors then outlined the ideas of competitive altruism and costly signaling theory. Briefly put, throughout history, people across cultures have competed to be seen as the most altruistic member of a group, and people often use costly altruism as a signal that they possess sufficient resources to sacrifice for the group (which, in turn, enhances their perceived status). With these principles as a framework, the authors proceeded to test whether people might use costly green purchases to enhance their status (or, in the words of the authors, "go green to be seen").

In Experiment 1, half of the participants read a short story designed to prime status motives; the other half were assigned to a control condition. All participants made three binary choices between a more luxurious nongreen option and a less luxurious green option (in the categories of cars, household cleaners, and dishwasher), with both options being equally priced. Results in all three product categories showed that participants primed with status motives were significantly more likely to prefer the less luxurious (but green) product.

In Experiment 2, the authors showed that status motives only led to heightened desire for the green product when the purchase was made publically (i.e., in a store), but not when made privately (i.e., online), in line with costly signaling theory.

In Experiment 3, the authors showed that people preferred the green option to the nongreen option when the green option was more expensive, but not when it was less expensive, than the nongreen option, again supporting the idea that people prefer green options because they connote status.

By studying how status motives lead consumers to prefer green products, and couching that work within the frameworks of competitive altruism and costly signaling theory, the authors shed new light on the conditions and motives encouraging adoption of green products. The theoretical framework is novel and intriguing, and the implications are at the same time quite practical for marketers. In short, bringing together evolutionary social psychological theory with a practical marketing problem allowed the authors to build a meaningful and profitable bridge between social psychology and consumer behavior.

CAN CONSUMERS BE SUBLIMINALLY PRIMED TO PREFER CERTAIN BRANDS?

In 2006, Karremans, Stroebe, and Claus brought together work on social psychology and consumer behavior to revisit an old legend. As the story goes, back in 1957, a marketing researcher named James Vicary claimed that he could get moviegoers to buy popcorn and Coca Cola by subliminally exposing them to the phrases "Eat Popcorn" and "Drink Coca Cola." As the authors noted, however, history suggests that Vicary was not telling the truth and that his fantastic claims were likely a publicity stunt. In light of this revelation and the subsequent controversy over subliminally priming consumers, the authors saw promise in evaluating "Vicary's fantasies" using two carefully conducted experiments drawing on recent developments in priming.

Prior to reporting their experiments, the authors reviewed past research that suggested that despite the concerns raised over "subliminally manipulating consumers," it is not always easy to subliminally prime consumers' brand preferences, choices, or consumption. One problem is that for subliminal primes to be successful, they must be very short; for example, the prime should simply present the brand name ("Coca Cola") as opposed to a longer and more complex phrase

("Go to the lobby and buy Coca Cola"). Second, the authors pointed out that many prior priming studies failed to consider a "crucial condition" (p. 793) that enables a primed brand to affect consumers' preferences: namely, the coexistence of a corresponding motivation to desire the product. In other words, priming a *satiated* consumer to want *more* Coke is likely a challenge, whereas priming a *thirsty* person to want *some* Coke should theoretically be much easier. Combining these two lines of reasoning, the authors set out to test whether the effect of a subliminally presented brand name (Lipton Ice) on consumer preferences only emerges when consumers are appropriately motivated (thirsty).

In Experiment 1, the authors randomly assigned Dutch participants to one of two conditions. Participants in the subliminal prime condition were exposed 25 times to the brand name Lipton Ice for 23 milliseconds (well below conscious awareness), whereas participants in the neutral prime (control) condition were exposed to the same set of letters arranged in a random order (Npeic Tol). Confirming the subliminal nature of the prime, participants reported not being aware of the primes. Following the priming task, participants made a choice between Lipton Ice and a Dutch brand of mineral water (Spa Rood) and rated their intentions to drink Lipton Ice, Spa Rood, and Coca Cola. Finally, participants rated their level of thirst at that moment in time. Results revealed that participants primed with Lipton Ice were only more likely to drink Lipton Ice when they were thirsty.

In Experiment 2, the authors aimed to replicate the prime × thirst interaction and enhance generalizability and confidence in the results by experimentally manipulating thirst rather than measuring it. Drawing on a technique introduced by Aarts, Dijksterhuis, and DeVries (2001), Karremans and colleagues led half of their participants to experience thirst by giving them a popular salty licorice candy (dropje) with a letter on one side. Participants were instructed to keep the candy in their mouth for 1 minute as they attempted to determine the letter on the candy. As a cover story, participants were told this was a "tongue detection" task. Participants in the control condition received no candy. Following the thirst induction, participants completed the same priming task used in Experiment 1. Conceptually replicating Study 1, results showed that subliminally priming Lipton Ice only increased choice of and intention to drink Lipton Ice among participants who had first been made thirsty.

Bringing together priming techniques, popular within social psychology, and brand choice within the context of an intriguing and controversial historical marketing legend, Karremans and colleagues (2006) illustrated the value in bridging disciplines. Their study also resolves a more fundamental and long-standing puzzle (why don't subliminal brand primes work well?) by highlighting a critical precondition that makes priming effects possible (the existence of a corresponding motivational state, in this case thirst). Taken together, multiple features of this article help to explain why this paper has had an impact.

DO SOCIALLY EXCLUDED PEOPLE SPEND MONEY TO REESTABLISH CONNECTION?

In 2011, Mead, Baumeister, Stillman, Rawn, and Vohs framed motives for consumer behavior within a hot topic in social psychology: social exclusion. The authors noted that social exclusion leads to many negative outcomes and that, despite growing interest in the topic within social psychology, little research has considered the impact of social exclusion on consumer behavior. The authors sought to fill this gap by testing the hypothesis that "socially excluded people spend and consume strategically in the service of affiliation" (p. 903).

To motivate that hypothesis, the authors first established that social exclusion increases people's desire to affiliate with others and showed that consumers use purchases and consumption to send others a message about the self. Two competing hypotheses were then advanced: socially excluded consumers will make purchases to differentiate themselves from others *or* they will make purchases to highlight their common identity with others (a prediction the authors favored). The authors also predicted that consumers' tendency to use consumption to facilitate affiliation is stronger among those high in the trait of self-monitoring (i.e., those who routinely adapt their behavior to please others) and only emerges when there is an opportunity to connect with others.

In Experiment 1, female college students were randomly assigned to an exclusion or control condition. Both groups believed they would exchange videotaped interviews with another student and then meet her in person. Participants first watched the confederate's videotape and were then told that after the confederate had watched the participant's videotape, she left before the actual interaction because she did not want to meet the participant (exclusion condition) or because she forgot an appointment (control condition). Participants were then told they could meet with a different student after they made choices in a mock store. Pretests indicated that one product in the mock store was likely to "send a message about who I am" (i.e., to help establish a connection with another fellow university student), whereas other products (pens, cookies) were not. As predicted, participants were more likely to pick the spirit bands when they had first been excluded.

In Experiment 2, participants received feedback on a personality questionnaire that ostensibly indicated that they would end up alone at the end of life (exclusion condition) or that they would end up with many friends (control condition). Participants then were told that they would have an opportunity to discuss with a partner who either valued "frugality" or "luxury" their evaluations of different types of products (a frugal product, a luxury product, and a neutral product). As expected, excluded participants evaluated more favorably products that matched the frugal/luxury orientation of their partner, and this effect only emerged among high self-monitors.

In Experiment 3, participants were excluded or not, using the Study 2 procedure. They were then given an opportunity to interact with a Chinese student who enjoyed eating chicken feet. Excluded participants evaluated chicken feet more favorably when they believed they would subsequently interact with the Chinese student and the student would be able to view the participant's food ratings.

In Experiment 4, participants recalled a time when they had been excluded, were ill (an aversive control condition), or had been accepted (a second control condition) and then indicated the likelihood that they would try an illegal drug (cocaine). Excluded participants stated stronger intentions to use illegal drugs, but only when drug use would occur in a public setting (i.e., a party), supporting the hypothesis that consumers might turn to risky behaviors to enhance connections with others.

Using a series of four creative experiments, the authors established that social exclusion leads people to spend money (strategically) on products that increase the likelihood of future affiliation. The range of exclusion manipulations and dependent variables (spirit bands, luxury watches, chicken feet, and cocaine) offers compelling evidence that the process is a generalizable one. The fact that this effect only emerges among those high in self-monitoring and when people have an opportunity to affiliate further strengthens the readers' confidence in the underlying claim: Consumer behavior can be motivated, in part, by a desire to reestablish connections following exclusion. Bridge built.

DOES MORTALITY SALIENCE MOTIVATE MATERIALISTIC PEOPLE TO CONNECT TO BRANDS?

In 2009, Rindfleisch, Burroughs, and Wong set out to "*bridge* [italics added] two important domains of consumer research (i.e., consumer values and brand connections) that are likely related but seldom intermingled" (p. 1). To do this, the authors argued that brands act as "security providers" and couched this idea within the framework of social psychological theory and research on terror management theory (TMT), allowing them to build further bridges between social psychology and consumer behavior.

Rindfleisch et al. (2009) began by highlighting a surprising gap in the literature: namely, that while much attention has been paid to materialism, little research has explored how materialism influences people's connection to brands. Defining *brand connection* as "the extent to which a consumer has incorporated a brand into his or her self-concept" (p. 1), the authors posited that materialistic people attempt to enhance brand connection as a way of dealing with existential uncertainty, or concern over one's own mortality. This prediction follows from TMT (cf. Burke, Martens, & Faucher, 2010; Hayes, Schimel, Arndt, & Faucher, 2010), which has received considerable attention within the field of social psychology but has, until recently, received relatively less attention in the consumer behavior domain. The authors argued that TMT is the "hinge" (p. 2) that links materialism to brand connection. They also established that brand connections often act as "security providers," helping consumers ward off uncertainty. As the authors noted, one important source of uncertainty is uncertainty or concern over our own mortality, and one way to deal with such existential uncertainty is to uphold valued cultural worldviews. Because materialism represents a value, it is hypothesized that highly materialistic people will show stronger brand connections when faced with existential uncertainty. To test this hypothesis, the authors conducted a field study and an experiment.

In their field study, the authors asked a representative sample of U.S. consumers to first think about the brand they most often use in the categories of cars, jeans, microwaves, or watches. Participants then indicated the extent to which they included that brand in their self-concept using established brand connection scales. Participants also completed scales assessing existential insecurity (i.e., the extent to which a person fears death) and materialism (i.e., the value they place on obtaining material objects). As predicted, results revealed that the positive relationship between materialism and brand connection was only significant among those high in existential insecurity.

To test the generalizability of their initial findings, in Study 2, the authors experimentally manipulated rather than measured existential insecurity, using standard procedures from the TMT literature. Specifically, half of the participants were asked to write down the thoughts and emotions that arose when thinking about death and dying (mortality salience condition); the other half wrote down thoughts and emotions that arose when listening to music (control condition). Participants then reported their brand connection to their favorite brand of sunglasses or MP3 players and completed the materialism scale. Confirming the authors' earlier findings, results showed that materialism was positively related to self-brand connections, but only in the mortality salience condition.

In sum, using survey and experimental methods, the authors provided clear support for the hypothesis that materialistic consumers turn to valued brands to ward off insecurity over their ultimate mortality. Moreover, by logically connecting work on materialism, self-brand connection, and TMT, the authors built bridges both within the field of consumer behavior (between materialism and self-brand connections) and between consumer behavior and social psychology (by using TMT/mortality salience as the critical "hinge" that connects materialism and self-brand connections).

DO PEOPLE STIGMATIZE MATERIALISTIC PEOPLE AND PURSUITS?

In 2010, Van Boven, Campbell, and Gilovich brought together work on social psychology and consumer behavior to address an interesting and important question: Namely, do people stigmatize materialistic people and pursuits and, if so, why? To motivate that question, the authors first cited a recent survey indicating that a large percentage of people believe Americans are too materialistic (88%) and reviewed studies suggesting that materialism has a number of negative consequences, including less fulfilling relationships. These findings, in turn, led the authors to wonder: "Why might materialistic behavior pose barriers to successful social relationships?" (p. 551). In response, the authors first reviewed research that links materialism to a number of unsavory personality traits, including low levels of empathy and high levels of Machiavellianism. The authors then considered a less obvious explanation that served as the basis for their investigation: Perhaps materialistic people have trouble in relationships because they are stigmatized due to the negative connotations associated with extrinsic (as opposed to intrinsic) pursuits. To test this hypothesis, the authors conducted a series of five studies.

The authors first reported a pilot study demonstrating that people do, in fact, like intrinsically motivated people better than extrinsically motivated people. Having established this basic premise, the authors set out to address the next important question: Why? More specifically, is preference for intrinsically motivated people based, in part, on negative stereotypes of materialistic people?

In Study 1, a first group of participants listed traits associated with one person they knew who was interested in materialistic pursuits and one person they knew who was interested in experiential pursuits. Results revealed that a second group of participants rated the traits stereotypically associated with materialistic people less favorably.

In Study 2, participants thought about people they knew who had made materialistic and experiential purchases and then rated the extent to which extrinsic and intrinsic motives influenced the purchase. As predicted, materialistic purchases were more strongly associated with extrinsic motives (than were experiential purchases), and experiential purchases were more strongly associated with intrinsic motives (than were materialistic purchases).

In Study 3, the authors evaluated whether people view consumers who make a stereotypically materialistic purchase (i.e., a new shirt) less favorably than consumers who make stereotypically experiential purchases (i.e., a ski pass). Results confirmed this prediction and also showed that participants rated the materialistic consumer less favorably because they viewed the consumer's purchase to be driven by extrinsic motives (i.e., perceived extrinsic motives partially mediated the impact of type of purchase on impressions of the purchaser).

In Study 4, the authors included a control condition to determine whether the perceptions uncovered in Study 3 were due to negative views of materialistic consumers, positive views of experiential consumers, or both. Results revealed that less favorable impressions of materialistic (vs. experiential) purchases is due to denigration of materialistic purchases (vs. the control), rather than admiration of experiential purchases.

In Study 5, pairs of participants were randomly assigned to discuss a recent materialistic or experiential purchase for up to 20 minutes. Participants then rated the conversation and their partner. Results showed that people rated their partners less favorably and enjoyed the conversation less when discussing materialistic purchases. Results also showed that the tendency to enjoy conversations about materialistic purchases less was mediated by less favorable impressions of the partner.

In sum, the authors built a bridge between social psychology and consumer behavior by systematically investigating the link between fundamental topics within social psychology (stereotypes) and consumer behavior (materialism). By demonstrating that materialistic people and purchases are perceived less favorably than experiential people and purchases, and underscoring the mediating role of perceived motives, results shed light on why materialistic people may have less fulfilling relationships.

DOES EGO DEPLETION LEAD TO IMPULSIVE BUYING?

In 2007, Vohs and Faber drew on the depletion or limited-resource model of self-regulation to shed light on how features of the situation could impact impulsive buying behavior. The depletion model assumes that an individual's self-regulatory resources are limited and thus susceptible to becoming depleted. More precisely, if an individual regulates his or her behavior in one domain, his or her ability to regulate their behavior in a subsequent domain should diminish.

Prior to Vohs and Faber's (2007) paper, the depletion model had been widely studied within the field of social psychology (for a review, see Hagger, Wood, Stiff, & Chatzisarantis, 2010). Consumer behavior researchers, however, had not used the theory. By drawing on the depletion model, which was centrally located within social psychology, to shed light on consumer behavior, Vohs and Faber provided an excellent illustration of the bridging paradigm.

In a series of three experiments, the authors used different manipulations of ego depletion and different dependent measures to establish the generalizability of their findings. In two of the three studies, the authors also tested for a theoretically and practically meaningful interaction between ego depletion and individual differences in trait impulsive buying tendencies, as measured by the Buying Impulsiveness Scale (BIS). The authors hypothesized that ego depletion would increase the likelihood of impulsive buying and that this effect would be especially pronounced among those high on the BIS.

In the first experiment, Vohs and Faber (2007) had those in the ego-depletion condition engage in an attention-regulation task (ignoring words at the bottom of a screen), previously used as an ego-depletion manipulation; control participants saw the same stimuli, but they did not have to ignore the words. As expected, results showed that those in the ego depletion condition said they would be willing to pay higher prices for a variety of consumer goods than those in the control condition.

Experiment 2 was designed to replicate and extend the initial results in two ways. First, to enhance the generalizability of the results, the authors used a different ego depletion manipulation (thought suppression) and a different dependent measure (actual purchase decisions). Second, the authors tested for the hypothesized ego depletion × trait BIS interaction. Results showed that those in the ego depletion condition were more likely than those in the control condition to spend the $10 they were allocated as part of the study on real products (e.g., candy) and that the effect of ego depletion was stronger among those high on the BIS.

Experiment 3 further tested the generalizability of the results using a third type of ego depletion (emotion suppression) and replicated the ego depletion × BIS interaction. Experiment 3 also evaluated whether the effect of ego depletion on impulsive buying was dependent on whether the product was affectively laden (e.g., chocolate cake) or cognitively laden (e.g., fruit salad; cf. Shiv & Fedorikhin, 1999). As expected, ego depletion led to an increase in impulsive buying, and this effect was again stronger among those high on the BIS. Results further showed that the effects did not depend on the type of product (affective vs. cognitive), suggesting that the ego-depletion model may operate differently than the Shiv and Fedorikhin model.

As the authors outlined, prior work on impulsive buying had largely focused on features of the product itself or features of the individual consumer. More recent work had begun to explore the impact of the situation on impulsive buying. Clearly, social psychologists have always been interested in the impact of the situation on thoughts, feelings, and behavior and have long been interested in the topic of self-control. Given that impulsive buying can be viewed as a form of self-control failure, Vohs and Faber (2007) saw an opportunity to capitalize on theory and research from social psychology (i.e., ego depletion) to shed light on the situational determinants of impulsive buying, providing an excellent illustration of the bridging paradigm.

Conclusion

In this chapter, we have illustrated the bridging paradigm by focusing largely on work bridging theories, methods, and topics within social psychology and consumer behavior. The six illustrations clearly show that social psychological theories and principles have made significant inroads into mainstream consumer behavior research, and consumer behavior represents a growing interest among social psychologists eager to apply social psychology to real-world behaviors. Although our focus has been on bridging social psychology and consumer behavior, our main goal was to encourage bridging more broadly. As we noted at the outset of the book, the illustrations described in the coming chapters apply to a wide range of additional disciplines (e.g., clinical, health, and organizational psychology), and many of those illustrations represent (secondary) examples of the value of bridging.

Author Interviews

Highlighted Author

What is your advice for publishing high-quality research that is likely to have impact?

What "bridging" paper would you recommend?

Vladas Griskevicius
Associate Professor of Psychology and Marketing, Carlson School of Management, University of Minnesota, Minneapolis

DON'T. Chasing "impact" is like chasing a dragon—you might end up frustrated for your entire life because you spent it chasing without a catch. Instead, my advice would be twofold: (a) Study what you're most passionate about and what you find intrinsically interesting. Enjoy the chase rather than focus on what you want to catch. (b) Try to study what you enjoy in a way that others can also value and enjoy. Making your work more valuable and interesting to others will help you get published in better journals. Although impact is nearly impossible to predict, publishing your work in better places will at least increase the chances that someone actually reads it.

My favorite bridging paper is by Ellis, Figueredo, Brumbach, and Schlomer (2009) published in *Human Nature* titled, "Fundamental Dimensions of Environmental Risk: The Impact of Harsh Versus Unpredictable Environments on the Evolution and Development of Life History Strategies." This paper bridges animal behavior, evolutionary biology, psychology, and economics. Although it is a long paper, it enables people to see the world through a very different perspective—and it contains about 100 testable hypotheses.

Johan Karremans
Associate Professor, Department of Social and Cultural Psychology, Radboud University Nijmegen, Nijmegen, the Netherlands

Sometimes curiosity and a fresh look at a topic that is outside of your core interest can lead to surprising new insights, but collaborate with experts in the field who can value the implications of your ideas. My own expertise is not on subliminal advertising or consumer behavior, but the other senior author on the paper, Wolfgang Stroebe, is an expert on attitude change and persuasion. My own work actually concentrates on a very different topic, forgiveness and revenge in interpersonal relationships. Sometimes a relative "outsider" (e.g., a master's student) raises an important issue that I had never thought of before, despite having worked on this topic for over 10 years. Collaborations that combine expertise and a certain level of naiveté are likely to be very fruitful.

I am a fan of recent work done by Kenrick, Griskevicius, Maner, and others. Taking a broad evolutionary perspective, their research bridges domains that otherwise would not have been connected easily. For example, several of their papers have examined the link between mating motives and consumer behavior, and mating motives and creativity. A nice example is Sundie et al.'s (2011) *Journal of Personality and Social Psychology* paper titled, "Peacocks, Porsches, and Thorstein Veblen: Conspicuous Consumption as a Sexual Signaling System."

Highlighted Author

What is your advice for publishing high-quality research that is likely to have impact?

What "bridging" paper would you recommend?

Nicole Mead
Assistant Professor of Marketing, Rotterdam School of Management, Erasmus University, Rotterdam, the Netherlands

Expose yourself to different disciplines and new ways of thinking each and every day. Be sure to interact with people from different disciplines and backgrounds. And perhaps most important of all, experience the world a new way, through traveling, art, music, or other forms of culture. All these things keep you in a learning mind-set and increase the chance that you will find connections you'd never find otherwise.

Every time I reread Hoch and Loewenstein's (1991) article in the *Journal of Consumer Research*, I learn something new. It is a fantastic example of scholarship that can inspire new ideas, ground old theories, and cut across theoretical boundaries in an effortless way.

Aric Rindfleisch
John M. Jones Professor of Marketing and Department Head, College of Business, University of Illinois, Champaign

Try to offer ideas that are newsworthy and make readers think new thoughts. This often is a challenge, as these types of papers require authors to go beyond the limits of an extant literature base. Thus, these types of papers usually require the development of new theory or a unique synthesis of two or more theories. This is what we tried to do in our 2009 article.

I am a big fan of "The Role of Customer Gratitude in Relationship Marketing" by Palmatier, Jarvis, Bechkoff, and Kardes (2009, *Journal of Marketing*). This article nicely bridges relationship marketing theory with gratitude theory from social psychology to identify a new driver of relationship marketing success. In addition to offering a fresh set of ideas to the relationship marketing domain, it also makes a nice empirical contribution by validating these ideas via both a field study as well as a laboratory experiment. It is a really nice paper. I wish I had written it.

Highlighted Author

What is your advice for publishing high-quality research that is likely to have impact?

What "bridging" paper would you recommend?

Leaf Van Boven
Associate Professor, Department of Psychology and Neuroscience, University of Colorado, Boulder

There are two related issues: How to do research that is high impact, and how to do research that is high impact beyond the confines of the academy. Social psychology is, in my view, the scientific study of what everyday life is like for the people who live it. That means our topic of study is how people experience the social world around them. Our science should therefore be relevant to people beyond the scientific laboratory. It is possible for one to conduct high-impact research by identifying unanswered questions by other psychological scientists. But this, it seems, misses the opportunity to explain common, everyday experiences. Studying the psychology of the common person is potentially of high scientific impact and of high broader impact.

Well, I've become really interested in the social psychology of politics and other social issues. One really interesting paper is on motivating voter turnout by Bryan, Walton, Rogers, and Dweck (2011). They show that admonitions that emphasize personal identity ("be a voter") influence behavior more than admonitions that emphasize behavior ("vote"). This is a really nice paper that bridges social psychology and political science.

Kathleen Vohs
Professor, Land O'Lakes Professor of Excellence in Marketing, Carlson School of Management, University of Minnesota, Minneapolis

Think big! Ask yourself how you could change the way that people think about the world with your idea. Read outside of your area; you will find not only fascinating ideas but methods too. Try to see the big picture.

There are so many. The Dunn, Aknin, and Norton (2008) work on the psychology of money is one of my favorite papers. It bridges relationship science to affective forecasting to happiness to economics. Brilliant work!

Conduct a Meta-Analysis | 6

The preceding chapter focused on bridging disciplines. In many ways, the present chapter emphasizes a similar theme by focusing on the integration of research findings, potentially across multiple disciplines, using meta-analysis. In what follows, we consider the history and growth in meta-analysis, provide an overview of the procedure, and discuss six high quality meta-analyses that illustrate its flexibility in contributing to a better understanding of theory, application, and research methods.

Background

HISTORICAL ROOTS

In 1977, Mary Smith and Gene Glass published a major review article on the effectiveness of psychotherapy in *American Psychologist*. Controversy had been swirling over the

http://dx.doi.org/10.1037/14525-007
How to Publish High-Quality Research, by J. Joireman and P. A. M. Van Lange

topic for many years, with some fervently arguing that psychotherapy was useless, and others just as fervently arguing that psychotherapy had real benefits. Rather than conducting a qualitative review, counting up the percentage of studies supporting psychotherapy, or averaging *p*-values for the difference between treatment and control, Smith and Glass used a technique originally introduced at the turn of the 20th century (by Karl Pearson), and which they greatly improved, commonly known as meta-analysis (or systematic research synthesis).[1] After a grueling process of locating relevant studies, coding, and analysis, Smith and Glass concluded that psychotherapy did lead to improvements in functioning (cf. Lipsey & Wilson, 1993).

As of this writing, Smith and Glass's (1977) meta-analysis has been cited over 2,000 times as this book goes to press. Although part of their impact is no doubt due to their introducing a systematic set of procedures for conducting meta-analysis, it is hard to ignore the more general, underlying conclusion: If you want to publish research capable of significant impact, consider conducting a meta-analysis.

GROWTH IN META-ANALYSIS

Following Smith and Glass's (1977) paper, the use of, and references to, meta-analysis have grown exponentially (cf. Carlson & Ji, 2011). Indeed, a large number of meta-analyses have been conducted. One of the most heavily cited meta-analyses is a paper by Barrick and Mount (1991)—cited over 5,400 times—which found that of the Big Five personality dimensions, Conscientiousness was the only one that reliably predicted three job performance criteria (job and training proficiency, and personnel data) among five occupational groups (professionals, managers, police, sales, skilled and semiskilled). Other dimensions such as Extraversion and Openness to Experience were only predictive for some criteria of job performance. In many ways, it should not be surprising that this meta-analysis has been exceptionally informative, because the Big Five were considered "the standard" set of personality traits, and it is theoretically and practically very important to know whom to select, and what to look for (above and beyond specific skills), when hiring personnel.

More recent examples include meta-analyses of the bystander effect (Fischer et al., 2011), the effect of violent video games on aggressive and prosocial behavior (Anderson & Bushman, 2001), terror management theory (TMT) predictions (Burke, Martens, & Faucher, 2010; J. Hayes, Schimel, Arndt, & Faucher, 2010), and why lie-catchers might

---

[1]For a fascinating behind-the-scenes look at several classic meta-analyses, see Hunt (1997).

fail (Hartwig & Bond, 2011). Several examples within consumer behavior include meta-analyses on the effect of music in retail settings (Garlin & Owen, 2006), the effect of humor in advertising (Eisend, 2011), the effectiveness of publicity versus advertising (Eisend & Küster, 2011), and the effectiveness of product warnings on safe behavior (Cox, Wogalter, Stokes, & Tipton Murff, 1997).

To help readers appreciate the breadth of meta-analysis, six additional meta-analyses are discussed in detail in this chapter. Prior to discussing those articles, we first define meta-analysis, consider its benefits, and briefly summarize key steps involved in conducting a meta-analysis.

WHAT IS META-ANALYSIS?

As most readers are probably aware, *meta-analysis* is a statistical technique for averaging effect sizes across studies and exploring how different study characteristics, such as the percentage of men and women in a sample, experimental methods, or outcome measures moderate (and/or mediate) the effect size. Given its ability to summarize a wide variety of data, meta-analysis is a very flexible tool. For example, in some cases, the meta-analysis focuses on a particular phenomenon, such as the bystander effect; in other cases, it addresses the robustness of a broad theoretical claim, as in the case of the TMT. Moreover, meta-analysis can be used to summarize differences between experimental conditions, correlations among constructs, or even statistical indexes such as Cronbach's alpha (e.g., Peterson, 1994) across a range of studies. Increasingly, meta-analysis is also being used to estimate the effect size *within* multistudy papers (e.g., Lee, Amir, & Ariely, 2009; Levav & Zhu, 2009).

BENEFITS OF META-ANALYSIS

Although highly time-consuming, there are many benefits to conducting and publishing a meta-analysis. To begin, meta-analysis can bring order to seemingly disparate and conflicting findings, allowing researchers to gain a better idea of the overall effect in a given area. This in turn can (though does not always) resolve long-standing controversies within the field. A good example is Smith and Glass's (1977) meta-analysis on psychotherapy. Although narrative and counting methods seemed to yield conflicting findings, Smith and Glass's analysis revealed a significant positive effect for psychotherapy (though, as Hunt, 1997, explained, it did not completely settle the long-standing debate).

Second, a meta-analysis can identify variables that had previously received little attention in the literature. For example, though they did not anticipate this finding, in their recent meta-analysis on the effects of reward and punishment on cooperation in social dilemmas, Balliet, Mulder, and Van Lange (2011) discovered that rewards and punishments were more effective when people were actually paid for their decisions (outcomes were material) than when they were not paid (outcomes were immaterial). As the authors noted, this unexpected finding could hold important practical and theoretical implications for future research.

Third, meta-analysis is able to identify how different study characteristics moderate the basic effect size. These moderators may give insight into how procedures affect the effect size or yield valuable theoretical insights into the phenomenon in question. As an example, in their meta-analysis of the terror management literature, Burke et al. (2010) examined the effects of mortality salience on worldview defense. That is, they focused on the question of whether reminders of one's mortality (e.g., through writing a paragraph about dying) would impact tendencies toward defending one's worldviews (e.g., beliefs about ethnic minorities, ideology, and political views). They found larger effects on worldview defense among Americans than among those from Europe, Israel, or Asia. From a methodological perspective, these findings could alert researchers using non-American samples that the effect of mortality salience may be weaker in their studies and thus require more participants to detect an effect. From a theoretical perspective, this difference in the effect of mortality salience on worldview defense may highlight intriguing cross-cultural differences worthy of future study.

Fourth, meta-analyses can uncover mediating mechanisms that help to explain why the primary predictor relates to the final outcomes measure (Shadish, 1996). As an example, in their meta-analysis of the attribution-emotion-helping literature, Rudolph, Roesch, Greitemeyer, and Weiner (2004) explored why people are less likely to help another when the potential help giver attributes the other's need for help to controllable causes. In short, they found that when people attribute another's need for help to controllable causes, they experience greater anger and less sympathy, which in turn reduces willingness; in other words, sympathy and anger mediated the relationship between attributions of controllability and helping.

Fifth, because of its ability to reduce a large and often technical literature down to a more manageable set of conclusions, meta-analysis can form the basis for more effective policy recommendations, as policymakers rarely have the time or resources to review a large body of research. Hunt (1997) provided several excellent illustrations of this policy benefit. For example, meta-analyses were able to inform policymakers that funding for schools enhances student performance (Hedges, Laine, & Greenwald, 1994) and doctors who prescribe antibiotic prophylaxis enhanced survival rates of patients undergoing colorectal surgery

(Baum et al., 1981). Relatedly, meta-analyses could serve as a strong basis for disseminating research findings to the media (and public in general); rather than experiencing confusion and a lack of confidence in the face of conflicting findings, media and the public may have more confidence in conclusions based on large scale meta-analyses.

Sixth, because of these favorable properties, meta-analyses are often the most heavily cited articles published. As an example, the six meta-analyses illustrated in detail in this chapter have been cited an average of 568 times.

Finally, conducting a meta-analysis can expose a researcher to a wide range of studies that further enhance his or her own research program. A researcher is likely to benefit by becoming exposed to different theories, methods, measures, and data analytic techniques. Moreover, the process of coding and analyzing the data can further refine the researcher's methodological and analytic skills.

COSTS OF META-ANALYSIS

Although meta-analysis is a valuable tool supporting high-quality research, it is important to recognize that meta-analyses can also pose some challenges. As we can both attest to firsthand, meta-analyses are very labor intensive. Gathering, coding, and analyzing the data takes substantial time and effort, and the researcher considering a meta-analysis should carefully count the costs before embarking on such a project. Second, certain schools may place relatively greater value on the dissemination of primary data collection than on meta-analyses. As such, researchers should clearly understand the value their department/university places on meta-analyses before undertaking one. Nevertheless, in our view and experience, meta-analyses make a very meaningful contribution to the advancement of a discipline and can thus represent a rewarding project for the motivated and incentivized researcher.

KEY STEPS IN META-ANALYSIS

Meta-analysis involves several key steps that, for the purposes of this chapter, we summarize very briefly in Exhibit 6.1. Readers interested in more technical treatments of these procedures can consult any number of excellent resources on the subject (e.g., Hedges & Olkin, 1985; B. T. Johnson & Eagly, 2000; Lipsey & Wilson, 2001; Rosenthal, 1991).

As can be seen in Exhibit 6.1, a researcher must first decide on the problem to be analyzed, as this will affect the studies selected and coded for the meta-analysis (e.g., do product warnings increase safe behavior, and what combination of factors leads to the most effective warning; Cox et al., 1997). Topics that are ripe for meta-analysis are those that

---

EXHIBIT 6.1

Basic Steps in Meta-Analysis

---

1. Decide on the problem (or question) to be analyzed.
2. Conduct a comprehensive search of the relevant published and unpublished literature, through multiple data bases, screening of relevant journals, use of reference lists of relevant papers (the ancestry method), citations to relevant papers (the descendancy approach), and direct solicitations to relevant scholars and research communities (the invisible college).
3. Determine whether a given study qualifies for inclusion in the meta-analysis on the basis of predetermined criteria (e.g., deals with a particular construct).
4. Have two researchers code relevant aspects of the studies (e.g., year of publication, sample size, sample characteristics, methods used) to be used as potential moderators.
5. Compute an effect size from each relevant unit (paper and/or study).
6. Compute a general effect size on the basis of all the data.
7. If sufficient variation (heterogeneity) in effect sizes exists (beyond what would be expected by chance), perform moderator analyses to determine how the study characteristics coded on Step 4 predict the effect size.
8. Report the findings in a meaningful and compelling manner, highlighting their practical and theoretical implications (cf. Rosenthal, 1995).

(a) have received significant attention in the literature but have not yet been quantitatively meta-analyzed; (b) have a common predictor (e.g., intelligence) or causal variable (e.g., effectiveness of a depression drug vs. a placebo drug) that would be suitable for comparing across studies; and (c) may have shown some mixed findings, suggesting the need for an overall quantitative synthesis of the literature and exploration of relevant moderators of the meta-analytic effect size.

Once the question has been defined, the researcher must conduct a comprehensive search of the published and unpublished literature, through multiple data bases, direct screening of relevant journals, use of reference lists of relevant papers (the ancestry method), citations to relevant papers (the descendancy approach), and direct solicitations to relevant scholars and research communities (the invisible college).

Third, the researcher must evaluate the gathered studies to determine whether a given study qualifies for inclusion in the meta-analysis (e.g., perhaps choosing to analyze only experiments or studies that involve random assignment to treatment and control conditions and deciding on whether to code for the quality of the study).

Once the relevant studies have been collected, a coding protocol must be developed to code relevant aspects of the studies (e.g., year of publication, sample size, sample characteristics, methods used), the papers should be coded by two researchers (to check on interrater reliability), and an effect size must be generated from each relevant unit (paper and/or study). Two common effect size statistics include d (the standardized mean difference) and r (correlation between predictor and outcomes), which can be computed on the basis of a combination of descriptive statistics (means, standard deviations, and sample sizes) or inferential statistics such as F and t.

With the studies coded, the researcher turns to data analysis and reporting. Here, a general effect size must be computed, and if sufficient variation (heterogeneity) in effect sizes exists (beyond what would be expected by chance), moderator analyses should be performed to determine how the coded study characteristics predict the effect size. Finally, results must be reported in a meaningful and compelling manner, highlighting their practical and theoretical implications (cf. Rosenthal, 1995).

Illustrations

DO THE THEORIES OF REASONED ACTION AND PLANNED BEHAVIOR PREDICT CONDOM USE?

In 2001, Albarracín, Johnson, Fishbein, and Muellerleile published a meta-analysis testing the ability of the theory of reasoned action (TRA) and the theory of planned behavior (TPB) to predict condom use. To motivate their paper, the authors first briefly summarized work that had failed to support the "perceived risk hypothesis," the idea that perceived vulnerability should lead to increased condom use. The authors then noted the large number of studies, and variable findings, applying the TRA and TPB to condom use, concluding that "a quantitative synthesis of this literature would prove valuable" (p. 142).

Although the TRA and TPB are probably well-known to most readers, a brief review may be helpful. According to both models, behavior is best predicted by intentions, and intentions are predicted by attitudes (a function of beliefs about consequences associated with a behavior × evaluation of those consequences) and subjective norms (a function of beliefs about what others think one should do × one's motivation to comply with those beliefs). According to the TPB, intentions and behavior are also predicted by perceived behavior control (one's belief that one has control over the behavior in question).

To test these models, the authors collected 96 data sets that had previously tested either theory as a predictor of condom use. The authors coded type of sex (e.g., anal, vaginal), type of partner (e.g., casual, regular), percentage of males and females, and risk level, among other moderators.

Across a range of conditions (e.g., different types of sex, partners, and risk levels), results provided excellent support for both the TRA and the TPB. At the level of individual parameters, attitudes emerged as the strongest predictor of intentions; subjective norms and perceived behavior control both showed roughly equal, but smaller, relations with intentions; and perceived behavior control was, with one exception, not significantly related to future behavior. Additional models incorporating past behavior also fit well, with past behavior emerging as a significant predictor of attitudes, subjective norms, perceived behavior control, intentions, and future behavior. A final model revealed an additional, direct relationship between attitudes and future behavior.

The authors concluded their paper with recommendations for practical interventions aimed at increasing condom use via messages designed to improve attitudes toward condom use, increase the perception that condom use is becoming more common, and enhance perceived behavior control. Noting that their meta-analysis showed much stronger effect for attitudes than subjective norms or perceived behavior control, the authors emphasized the greater potential of attitude change campaigns.

To date, their paper has been cited over 1,000 times on Google Scholar. How did their meta-analysis generate so much impact? Simply put, Albarracín and colleagues (2001) brought together insights from two of the most important social psychological theories linking attitudes to behavior and tested the application of those theories to one of the most important health behaviors of our time: condom use. In short, their meta-analysis is an excellent example of using sophisticated meta-analytic methods to integrate theory with application.

UNDERSTANDING WORKPLACE HARASSMENT FROM THE VICTIM'S PERSPECTIVE

In 2006, Bowling and Beehr advanced a comprehensive theoretical model of the antecedents and consequences of workplace harassment from the victim's perspective and used meta-analysis to test those parts of the model with sufficient data. The authors defined *workplace harassment* as "interpersonal behavior aimed at intentionally harming another employee in the workplace" (p. 998) and focused on forms of harassment that were not connected to the target's sex or race and did not represent aggression directed at the organization (e.g., theft).

Bowling and Beehr's (2006) model proposed that workplace harassment is a function of organizational climate, perpetrator and victim characteristics (which in turn are a function of human resource systems of selection, training, and rewards), and role stressors (e.g., role conflict, ambiguity). The model further assumed that the consequences of harassment would depend on the extent to which the harassment was attributed to the self, the perpetrator, or the organization; the three sets of relevant consequences included the victim's well-being, attitudes and behaviors toward the perpetrator, and work performance. Finally, the model assumed that role stress would have both direct and indirect effects on the relevant outcomes through workplace harassment. Framed another way, the model hypothesized that workplace harassment would predict the relevant outcomes above and beyond the "more traditional, better known stressors" (p. 1001; of role conflict and ambiguity).

Results identified several important antecedents of workplace harassment, including role conflict, ambiguity, and overload; work constraints; and victim's negative affectivity. In turn, workplace harassment was associated with a wide range of victim consequences, including higher strain, anxiety, depression, burnout, frustration, and negative emotions at work, and lower self-esteem, life and job satisfaction, organizational commitment, and positive emotions at work. Workplace harassment also had implications for organizational functioning, as it correlated with lower perceived organizational justice and higher counterproductive workplace behaviors, absenteeism, and turnover intentions.

Beyond these important findings, Bowling and Beehr (2006) conducted multiple regression analyses examining whether workplace harassment predicted the various consequences, over and above role conflict and ambiguity. They also tested the indirect effect of role conflict and ambiguity on the consequences through workplace harassment. In every case, workplace harassment added unique variance in predicting the 10 outcomes after controlling for role conflict and ambiguity, supporting the incremental validity of workplace harassment. With a few exceptions, results also revealed good support for the model's prediction that role conflict and ambiguity would have significant indirect effects on the outcomes via workplace harassment.

Bowling and Beehr's (2006) meta-analysis has already had a significant impact. As we write, the paper has been cited over 350 times on Google Scholar, and for good reason. To begin, the authors dealt with a problem that has important implications for the well-being of employees and organizations alike. Second, the authors framed their meta-analysis within the context of a comprehensive theoretical model. Finally, combining meta-analysis and multiple regression analysis, the authors showed that workplace harassment predicts key individual and organizational outcomes above and beyond more traditional role stressors, including role conflict and ambiguity, supporting the unique value of the construct.

DOES THE IMPLICIT ASSOCIATION TEST PREDICT BEHAVIOR?

In 2009, Greenwald, Poehlman, Uhlmann, and Banaji published a meta-analysis on the predictive validity of the Implicit Association Test (IAT). As many readers know, the IAT is a reaction time measure designed to assess implicit associations between attitude objects and descriptor terms. Respondents are shown pictures of the attitude objects and descriptors, and they must hit a key to categorize each image on the left or the right of the screen. A classic example is the race IAT. On some trials, objects and descriptors are grouped to reflect a favorable attitude toward Whites (e.g., white faces and good words on the left, black faces and bad words on the right). On other trials, objects and descriptors are grouped to reflect a favorable attitude toward Blacks (e.g., white faces and bad words on the left, black faces and good words on the right). Shorter reaction times reflect stronger implicit associations, and a difference in reaction times between the two types of trials is used to indicate the extent to which the respondent has more favorable associations with one race or the other.

The authors highlighted the need for a meta-analysis on the predictive validity of the IAT by noting the large number of IAT studies; the interest in using the IAT in applied settings, such as law; and the expressed need to evaluate the construct validity of the IAT. Given that the majority of IAT studies also measured self-reported attitudes, the authors were also able to use their meta-analysis to assess the relative strength of self-reports (vs. the IAT) as predictors of behavior (predictive validity estimates).

Overall, results revealed moderate-sized predictive validity estimates for the IAT ($r = .27$) and self-reports ($r = .36$), and a small (and highly variable) average positive relationship between implicit and explicit measures ($r = .21$). Drilling down, the authors next compared the predictive validity estimates within nine specific domains (e.g., race, intergroup, consumer behavior, political behavior). Results yielded several important findings: (a) Self-reports and the IAT tended to be most strongly related to behavior within the political realm; (b) compared with self-reports, the IAT was more strongly related to behavior within race and other intergroup settings; and (c) in all other domains, self-reports were more strongly related to behavior than was the IAT. Subsequent moderator analyses revealed that predictive validities tended to be larger in studies involving a larger number of effect sizes but did not depend on the order of the measures (relative to behavior). Results also indicated that the social sensitivity of the topic being studied (e.g., consumer behavior vs. racial attitudes) was more strongly related to the self-report predictive validities than the IAT predictive validities and that the IAT predictive validities were larger in studies involving "complementary" attitude objects (e.g., when judging Republicans vs. Democrats). Finally, partial correlation analyses indicated that self-reports and the IAT were significant predictors of behavior in the various domains, even after controlling for the effect of the other, supporting each measure's incremental validity.

Greenwald and colleagues' (2009) meta-analysis, which has now been cited over 900 times on Google Scholar, was a significant contribution to the literature for several reasons. To begin, prior to their meta-analysis, the IAT had become very widely used, and a large number of studies had tested the IAT's ability to predict behavior—in total, yielding 526 IAT effect sizes—and researchers were keen to understand the measure's predictive validity (both in isolation and relative to self-reports). Second, many were intrigued by the potential to use the IAT in applied settings; before widespread application, it was important to determine the degree to which the IAT had practical relevance. Finally, their meta-analysis helped illustrate the benefits of the IAT versus self-reports by showing that the strength of the IAT's predictive validities were not strongly affected by the domain's social sensitivity, whereas social sensitivity had a much larger impact on the self-reported predictive validities. In sum, Greenwald and colleagues' meta-analysis addressed key issues regarding measurement, construct validity, incremental validity, and practical utility of a very popular measure of attitudes, resulting in a review that will, like Wicker's (1969) classic review, be cited for many years to come.

DOES RESEARCH SUPPORT THE STRENGTH MODEL OF SELF-CONTROL?

In 2010, Hagger, Wood, Stiff, and Chatzisarantis published a large-scale meta-analysis on the strength model of self-control (Baumeister, Bratslavsky, Muraven, & Tice, 1998; Muraven, Tice, & Baumeister, 1998). The strength model assumes that self-control operates like a muscle. Building on the muscle metaphor, the strength model suggests that when people engage in an initial act of self-control, it can deplete their self-control resources and subsequently reduce their ability to engage in self-control in a second context (known as the *ego depletion effect*). On the other hand, just as a muscle can be built up over time, the strength model also assumes that the capacity for self-control can become strengthened over time with repeated use (the *training effect*). To help readers appreciate the importance of their meta-analysis, the authors highlighted the wide range of personally and socially relevant outcomes that are impacted by self-control, including academic performance, health behavior, violent behavior, and crime. The authors then noted the large number of studies testing the strength model's assumptions, the presence of several nonsignificant findings, and several unresolved questions (e.g., whether some tasks are more depleting than others) that together highlighted the need for a systematic, meta-analytic summary of this large literature.

In one of the more interesting features of this meta-analysis, the authors next outlined a range of alternative explanations for the depletion effect and considered whether those explanations are in conflict with, consistent with, or complement the depletion model's assumed mechanism (depleted self-control resources). The alternative explanations suggest that self-control represents a skill that is learned over time and that reduced self-regulatory performance is due to decreased motivation, reduced self-efficacy, increased fatigue, negative affect, and/or experimenter demand. By assessing the impact of an initial task requiring self-control on relevant dependent variables (e.g., self-efficacy, affect) and exploring relevant moderators (e.g., motivation), the authors creatively used their meta-analysis to provide an empirical test of these alternative explanations. In addition, the authors explored how several additional methodological variables may moderate the effect of an initial act of self-control on subsequent ability to engage in self-control (e.g., the nature or length of the depletion task). Finally, the authors explained several extensions of the strength model, which they also explored in their meta-analysis. These include the idea that people at times strategically conserve their self-control resources, people can improve their self-control capacity through training, opportunities for recovery can restore self-control capacity, and depleted glucose represents a physiological mechanism that explains depletion effects, suggesting that depletion effects are more than just a metaphor.

To address the issues just raised, the authors drew on a set of 198 independent tests of the ego depletion effect. At the broadest level, results revealed that participants required to engage in initial self-control task (vs. a control task) showed significantly lower self-control in subsequent tasks; significantly lower blood glucose; and significantly higher self-reported effort, task difficulty, and fatigue, with all effects characterized as medium to large in magnitude. Results revealed non-significant depletion effects on positive affect and self-efficacy and a small but significant effect on negative affect. With a few exceptions, moderator analyses subsequently revealed a high degree of similarity in the ego depletion effect across various methodological moderators (e.g., type of depletion task). Significant methodological moderators indicated that the ego depletion effect was weaker among studies with shorter depletion tasks, when no interim task was used between the initial depletion and subsequent self-control tasks, when the depletion task involved making volitional choices, and when the final self-control task was less complex.

Building on these results, the authors then reported results bearing on extensions of the strength model, which led to several interesting findings. First, the ego depletion effect was significantly stronger when participants anticipated a third self-control task (supporting the idea that people strategically conserve self-control resources). Second, the ego depletion effect was weakened when participants were given motivational incentives for continued high performance (supporting the moderating role of motivation). Third, training in self-control enhanced subsequent self-control (supporting the training effect). Finally, giving people glucose led to a significant reduction in the ego depletion effect (supporting the idea that ego depletion involves an actual, physiological mechanism).

Taken together, Hagger and colleagues' (2010) meta-analysis provided compelling support for the strength model of self-control and several of its extensions. Although a number of method factors affected the size of the ego depletion effect, the overwhelming conclusion is that the ego depletion effect is robust across a wide range of settings. Consistent with the strength model, results also showed that depletion tasks are viewed as difficult and effortful and lead to feelings of fatigue, and that depletion tasks affect an underlying physiological mechanism, most notably depleted glucose, indicating that depletion is more than a useful metaphor. Equally important, results failed to support a number of alternative explanations for the depletion effect, including reduced self-efficacy. However, results did reveal a small negative effect on negative affect, which the authors noted is not necessarily inconsistent with a depletion model (i.e., people may be expending additional effort trying to regulate the negative affect, which in turn further depletes self-control resources). Finally, results showed that people strategically conserve self-control resources and can recover those resources following a period of rest. The authors concluded their meta-analysis by suggesting several profitable directions for future research, such as identifying the exact resource (or mechanism) responsible for ego depletion effects and clarifying what precisely constitutes a self-control task.

To date, Hagger and colleagues' (2010) meta-analysis has already been cited nearly 400 times on Google Scholar, which is quite remarkable for a paper published in 2010. This high level of impact is no doubt due to the relevance of the topic at the center of their meta-analysis, the strength of their findings, and their ability to deal with alternative explanations and extensions of the basic theory. Researchers looking to use meta-analysis to test a theory would do well to read Hagger and colleagues' ego depletion meta-analysis carefully.

DOES EMOTIONAL INTELLIGENCE ENHANCE JOB PERFORMANCE?

In 2010, Joseph and Newman articulated a "cascading model" of emotional intelligence (EI) as a predictor of job performance and tested the model using meta-analysis. To grab readers' attention, the authors first noted the long-standing academic interest in emotional (social) intelligence, which they traced back to Dewey in 1909, and the large number of organizations now offering training in emotional intelligence. The authors then observed that despite the popularity of the EI construct, "critics remain dubious on the definition and measurement of EI and whether EI has incremental validity in organizational contexts beyond personality traits and cognitive ability" (p. 54).

To address these issues, the authors reviewed two different models previously used to define EI and outlined their cascading model of EI as a predictor of job performance. Prior to Joseph and Newman's paper, the two dominant models of EI included ability models (in which EI is more narrowly assumed to be a form of intelligence) and mixed models (in which EI is a combination of noncognitive abilities and wide variety of other traits, e.g., self-esteem). Noting several conceptual problems with the latter, the authors argued for an ability-based cascading model of EI.

The cascading model assumes that EI is composed of the ability to perceive, understand, and regulate emotion. These abilities are arranged sequentially, such that emotion perception precedes emotion understanding that precedes emotion regulation, which predicts job performance (*emotion perception → emotion understanding → emotion regulation → job performance*). Building on this core model, the authors further outlined how two traits (conscientiousness and emotional stability) and cognitive abilities can be integrated into a broader model. In addition to hypothesizing direct positive effects of these traits and abilities on job performance, the authors made a logical argument for three indirect effects, such that conscientiousness would predict higher emotion perception, cognitive ability would predict higher emotion understanding, and emotional stability would predict higher emotion regulation.

In addition to testing the cascading model, the authors addressed three other critical issues, including (a) the convergent and discriminant validity of different construct-measurement approaches to EI (i.e., as performance-based abilities, self-reported abilities, or self-reported mixtures of abilities and traits), (b) the incremental validity of EI in predicting performance over and above cognitive abilities and personality traits, and (c) differences in EI on the basis of sex and race.

To address these questions, the authors combined results from 21 prior meta-analyses with 66 of their own original meta-analyses. Results led to several important conclusions. First, performance-based EI measures overlapped very little with self-reported EI abilities and self-reported mixtures of abilities and traits, though the latter overlapped considerably, calling into question the convergent validity of the various EI measures. Second, using performance-based EI facets, structural equation modeling indicated that the cascading model fit the data well, with all but one of the hypothesized paths significant; subsequent analyses showed that the positive link between emotion regulation and job performance was only significant within jobs involving high emotional labor. Third, all construct-method approaches to EI predicted job performance, above and beyond the Big Five traits and cognitive ability, especially within jobs involving high emotional labor. Finally, women and Whites scored higher on performance-based EI, but sex and race differences were either nonexistent or inconsistent using self-reported EI.

Joseph and Newman's (2010) meta-analysis is noteworthy for several reasons. First, it shows how meta-analysis can be used, not only to test differences between groups or relationships between variables, but also to clarify the nature of relevant constructs. Second, it shows how a combination of past and original meta-analyses can be used to test an overarching theoretical model. Finally, it refines our understanding of a construct that has fascinated psychologists and practitioners for over 100 years. It is thus understandable why this paper has already been cited more than 260 times.

DO ORGANIZATIONAL CITIZENSHIP BEHAVIORS YIELD POSITIVE CONSEQUENCES?

In 2009, N. P. Podsakoff, Whiting, Podsakoff, and Blume published a meta-analysis assessing the consequences of organizational citizenship behaviors (OCBs). According to Organ's (1988) original definition, OCB is "behavior that is discretionary, not directly or explicitly recognized by the formal reward system, and that in the aggregate promotes the effective functioning of the organization" (p. 4). Put another way, OCBs are behaviors that go "above and beyond the call of duty" at work which (in theory) are not directly rewarded and facilitate the functioning of the organization. Examples include staying at work late to help a coworker who is struggling to complete a report, voicing one's opinions for constructive change, and not complaining in the face of difficult circumstances.

Prior to their meta-analysis, a large number of studies had focused on identifying predictors of OCBs, such as personality traits or leader–member exchange processes, and this literature was well established (e.g., P. M. Podsakoff, MacKenzie, Paine, & Bachrach, 2000). A key assumption underlying the search for predictors of OCBs was that OCBs facilitate organizational functioning. Another assumption, reflected in Organ's original definition, was that OCBs were discretionary and not formally rewarded. Both assumptions pointed to the practical and theoretical value in exploring the consequences of OCBs for employees and the organization, with two broad questions in mind: Are OCBs positively associated with performance ratings and rewards? And do OCBs predict superior organizational outcomes?

After articulating the value of their meta-analysis, N. P. Podsakoff and colleagues (2009) reviewed different classifications of OCBs and advanced several hypotheses concerning their individual and organizational consequences. At the individual level, the authors hypothesized that OCBs would be positively related to managerial ratings of employee performance and rewards given to employees, and negatively related to turnover and absenteeism. At the organizational level, they predicted that OCBs would be positively associated with unit productivity, efficiency, profitability, reduced costs, customer satisfaction, and reduced unit-level turnover. The authors also identified several potential moderators of these effects, including the source of the ratings, the target of the OCBs, and the study design (cross-sectional vs. lagged).

At the individual level, results revealed several interesting findings. First, OCBs and task performance showed roughly the same moderately strong positive correlation with performance ratings. Subsequent analyses revealed that OCBs also predicted reward recommendations and, to a lesser degree, actual rewards. As predicted, OCBs were also associated with lower turnover intentions, actual turnover, and absenteeism. Finally, the strength of these relationships did not vary substantially as a function of whether the OCBs were directed at other coworkers or the organization, but the OCB-performance relationships were stronger when the ratings came from the same source rather than different sources.

At the organizational level, results showed that a higher level of OCBs at the group or unit level was positively associated with performance ratings and customer satisfaction, and negatively with unit-level turnover. Also interesting, group-level OCBs were more strongly related to performance in time-lagged studies than in cross-sectional studies, suggesting that OCBs cause unit-level performance.

N. P. Podsakoff et al.'s (2009) meta-analysis made a significant contribution to the field by addressing two fundamental assumptions underlying OCBs. On the one hand, counter to the field's initial definitions, their meta-analysis clearly showed that OCBs were rewarded. On the other hand, in support of another long-standing assumption, their meta-analysis showed that OCBs do facilitate organizational functioning. Taken together, their findings helped clarify the nature of OCBs and highlight their practical relevance for employees and managers, a valuable balance that helps to explain why this article has already been cited over 400 times on Google Scholar.

Conclusion

In this chapter, we reviewed a statistical technique that allows researchers to publish papers that can have a significant impact. Although labor intensive, meta-analysis is very flexible, as the illustrations covered in this chapter highlight. Meta-analysis can be used to explore the consequences of an action, such as organizational citizenship behaviors (N. P. Podsakoff et al., 2009); the predictive validity of a measure, such as the IAT (Greenwald et al., 2009); and the underlying nature of a construct, such as EI (Joseph & Newman, 2010). Meta-analysis can also be used to test an overarching theory such as the theory of planned behavior (Albarracín et al., 2001), the strength model of self-control (Hagger et al., 2010), the cascading model of emotional intelligence (Joseph & Newman, 2010), or a theory of workplace harassment (from the victim's perspective; Bowling & Beehr, 2006). In sum, meta-analysis is a useful tool to add to one's professional arsenal. Although many meta-analyses have already been published, the explosion of research in general and the need to bring order to the rapidly expanding body of research suggests the future is bright for scholars wishing to publish research using meta-analysis.

Author Interviews

Highlighted Author

Nathan A. Bowling
Professor of Psychology and Industrial and Organizational Psychology and PhD Concentration Area Leader, Wright State University, Dayton, OH

What is your advice for publishing high-quality research that is likely to have impact?

I believe that the "best" research provides theoretically grounded insights into real-world problems. Thus, I would encourage basic researchers to consider the practical implications of their work, and I would encourage applied researchers to concentrate on theory-based solutions to practical problems.

What "meta-analytic" paper would you recommend and why?

One recent meta-analysis that I believe makes a significant scientific contribution is Meyer, Dalal, and Bonaccio's (2009) *Journal of Organizational Behavior* paper, "A Meta-Analytic Investigation Into the Moderating Effects of Situational Strength on the Conscientiousness–Performance Relationship." A distinguishing feature of this particular paper is that rather than simply aggregating the findings of previous studies as many meta-analyses do, Meyer et al. tested the theoretically (and practically) important hypothesis that situational strength moderates the relationship between personality and behavior. The significance of this paper is in the fact that despite limited empirical evidence, researchers have long assumed that situational strength moderates personality–behavior relationships. I would encourage researchers to follow Meyer et al. by identifying and then empirically testing the many "truisms" found among psychologists and among laypeople.

Highlighted Author

Anthony G. Greenwald
Professor, Department of Psychology, University of Washington, Seattle

What is your advice for publishing high-quality research that is likely to have impact?

Think seriously about working on improving research methods. Theory is important (and I've certainly made attempts in that domain), but my most-likely-to-endure contributions will likely be ones that produced and refined methods that others were persuaded to take up (and the Implicit Association Test [IAT] is certainly the best known of these).

What "meta-analytic" paper would you recommend and why?

I'm involved now in a sequel to the 2009 meta-analysis, made possible by the continued rapid accumulation of predictive validity research on the IAT. Fortunately (considering the work required of the lead researcher in a large meta-analysis), a colleague stepped forward to take the lead role in the new meta-analysis (and I hope she has the endurance to see it through). My involvement in the previous meta-analysis convinced me sufficiently of the value of meta-analytic methods to prompt me to use them on a smaller scale in combining results of smaller sets of studies to draw stronger conclusions than would otherwise have been possible.

Martin S. Hagger
Professor of Psychology, John Curtin Distinguished Professor, Health Psychology and Behavioural Medicine Research Group, School of Psychology and Speech Pathology, Curtin University, Perth, Australia

The key is always to be extremely familiar with trends in research through regularly reading scholarly psychology journals. The best researchers are extremely well read and know where the gaps in the research are. Meta-analyses and systematic reviews are also an excellent compendium of the zeitgeist of research in a particular field and usually overtly identify the gaps in the field that would make a major contribution to understanding. It is also important to understand the political landscape—what is relevant to governments, funding organizations, and the media is inevitably going to be impactful. Finally, many journals now list the articles that have been most frequently downloaded on their homepage—this gives an excellent indication of the immediacy of impact of particular research in that journal. Not surprisingly, articles on sexual behavior, racism, violent video games, fame and celebrity, and psychopathology and criminality usually appear at the top of those lists!

I think for technical excellence, precision, and attention to detail, I would thoroughly recommend Patall, Cooper, and Robinson's (2008) meta-analysis of choice on intrinsic motivation and related outcomes. The topic is of theoretical and practical importance given the value placed on choice in education and consumer contexts. The authors demonstrate a command of the important fundamental elements of meta-analysis, such as extraction and coding of data and identification of salient moderators, but also demonstrate some important additional components that further embellish the relationships they look at, including interactions among moderators, which is seldom examined in meta-analyses.

Highlighted Author

Dana L. Joseph
Assistant Professor,
Department of
Psychology, University
of Central Florida,
Orlando

What is your advice for publishing high-quality research that is likely to have impact?

I have always enjoyed reading and working on research that offers a new insight into a controversial topic (such as emotional intelligence) but does so in a way that is strong theoretically and methodologically. Offering a new theoretical model that integrates (rather than ignores or omits) past findings while using strong methods (e.g., large sample size, replicable findings/high statistical power, and a concern for psychometric construct validity) can allow one to "use data against dogma" and make a true high-impact contribution to the literature.

What "meta-analytic" paper would you recommend and why?

My academic inspiration for high-impact meta-analytic work is Harrison, Newman, and Roth's (2006) paper in *Academy of Management Journal* titled, "How Important Are Job Attitudes? Meta-Analytic Comparisons of Integrative Behavioral Outcomes and Time Sequences," which has also been heavily cited in organizational sciences, despite being a relatively recent publication. Similar to how my meta-analysis challenged popular opinion about emotional intelligence, this meta-analysis changed many scholars' minds by showing that job attitudes predict work behavior more strongly than previously thought (supporting the notion that "a happy worker is a productive worker"). Not surprisingly, this paper also proposed a new theoretical model (i.e., the attitude-engagement model) that integrated (rather than ignored) past findings, and used strong meta-analytic methods.

Highlighted Author

Nathan Podsakoff
Associate Professor,
Eller College of
Management, The
University of Arizona,
Tucson

What is your advice for publishing high-quality research that is likely to have impact?

This is a good question asked by doctoral students and senior scholars alike. Fortunately, the field is starting to accumulate some empirical data that provides answers to this question. Research by Judge, Cable, Colbert, and Rynes (2007) in the *Academy of Management Journal* indicated that articles published in a variety of applied psychology and management journals tend to receive more citations when (a) the purpose of the research is to explore new areas, rather than simply refine previous theory or findings; (b) the authors are affiliated with prestigious institutions (which may be a proxy for skill or ability, as well as resources); and (c) the presentation of the research is clear and readable. (Interestingly, these authors also reported that meta-analyses had higher citation rates than did non–meta-analyses.) In addition, consistent with the findings of several other studies, they reported that outlet quality significantly affected the citation impact of an article; so publishing in quality journals is another recommendation for high-impact research. Although the suggestions based on these findings are not exhaustive, they do provide a preliminary understanding of what factors may lead to high citation impact research. In addition, although it is important to recognize that citations are not the only way we define impact, many of my suggestions would be similar if I based them on more subjective measures of impact. However, I encourage scholars to continue the scientific exploration of these issues.

What "meta-analytic" paper would you recommend and why?

This is a tough question; frankly I could not narrow it down to one, or even a few. There are meta-analyses that make a significant contribution because they provide a summary of a very large literature on a specific relationship or set of relationships, because they test a theory or competing theories using previously reported research, and/or because they provide information on the validity of a measurement technique or research design. Because most of the low-hanging fruit from the psychology literature has already been picked, it would seem that the significant contributions from future meta-analysis will be more likely to come from reviews that test theory and/or estimate increasingly complex models.

Launch a Paradigm Shift 7
Challenge Existing Assumptions and Test Competing Theories

Background

The preceding paradigms both focus on finding similarities and structure across potentially disparate domains. Bridging, for example, looks for ways to integrate theories and methods across disciplines, and meta-analysis attempts to synthesize research findings into a coherent whole (while also recognizing meaningful variations based on moderator analyses). That is, both paradigms can bring about important shifts in ways of thinking (as we have seen) and can be explicitly used to bring about theoretical change. However, it is often not the primary goal of bridging or meta-analysis to challenge existing assumptions or to replace an establish theory with a new theory.[1]

---

[1]This is not to say that bridging and meta-analysis are unable to offer novel theoretical insights. In fact, often they do (e.g., LePine & King, 2010). Our point, rather, is that these two paradigms have more of a tendency to focus on convergence than the paradigm covered in this chapter, which has the explicit goal of pushing boundaries and challenging assumptions.

http://dx.doi.org/10.1037/14525-008
How to Publish High-Quality Research, by J. Joireman and P. A. M. Van Lange

As we outlined in Chapter 2, finding the truth, discovering abstract principles, and applying those principles across situations (i.e., convergence) are vital functions of theory development and scientific inquiry. Broad and integrative principles support the goal of parsimony, whereas true and applicable principles support the goal of accuracy. Thus, bridging and meta-analysis are powerful paradigms for scientific progress.

Complementing these paradigms, researchers often find it important to "push the boundaries" of existing theory and challenge existing assumptions. Although theories are useful road maps, few, if any, will remain unaltered in the face of empirical data. Inevitably, opposing theories will be proposed, boundary conditions will be identified, and additional mediators will be established that require a theory to undergo modification or be replaced altogether. Sometimes, the required changes represent more incremental alterations. Other times, the changes required are more dramatic, leading to a fundamental shift in the way a field views a phenomenon, commonly known as a *paradigm shift* (Kuhn, 1962).

This chapter focuses on how researchers can create paradigm shifts by testing competing theories and challenging existing assumptions. It is important to note that subsequent chapters echo and support this (boundary pushing) theme; for example, theories are advanced by identifying and understanding moderators and mediators (Chapter 8, this volume), developing a new individual difference construct (Chapter 9), introducing an innovative new method (Chapter 10), evaluating the real-world implications of a theory or finding (Chapter 11), and testing the cross-cultural generalizability of findings (Chapter 12), to name just a few.

In what follows, we consider some benefits and costs of pushing boundaries, discuss ways a researcher can challenge existing assumptions and test competing theories, and then describe a number of papers that nicely illustrate this paradigm.

BENEFITS OF PUSHING BOUNDARIES

We begin by considering some benefits of pushing boundaries. The idea of pushing boundaries is, by definition, an inherent part of scientific inquiry. Whether we are proposing a minor or a more major change in a field's understanding of a phenomenon, at some level, we are "rocking the boat" in an effort to extend what we know by stepping out into uncharted territory. In short, the TAPAS criteria discussed in Chapter 2 (truth, abstraction, progress, and application) require us to continually push boundaries.

Second, pushing boundaries makes for an interesting, if potentially controversial, journey. As researchers, reviewers, and readers, we are often more interested in the unexpected than the expected. We love wrestling with complicated puzzles and solving intriguing mysteries.

Thus, a paper that confirms a common-sense prediction, although possibly valuable, may generate less enthusiasm and impact than a more groundbreaking paper that challenges existing assumptions. Indeed, scholars and editors who have written about successful theory building and publication have long implored authors to "make it interesting" and "explicate the novel aspects" (e.g., Zaltman, LeMasters, & Heffring, 1982) and to be "forward thinking" in the sense of anticipating emerging issues that require theoretical advancements (e.g., Corley & Gioia, 2011).

Finally, pushing boundaries can increase your professional standing, in part because boundary-pushing papers often receive significant attention and because boundary pushing locates you at the beginning of a new movement. This may, of course, take time. Old ideas often die hard. But eventually, if the idea takes off and you publish the seminal paper responsible for launching the shift, your paper can become one of the "classic citations" future researchers find essential to include in the first paragraph of their introductions.

COSTS OF PUSHING BOUNDARIES

Scientific progress, intrigue, and enhanced standing are desirable outcomes associated with pushing boundaries, but it would be misleading to suggest that boundary pushing does not entail some costs, at least in the short run. To begin, boundary pushing is, by its very nature, controversial. Pushing boundaries means challenging what others before you have held up as truth or long assumed as truth, and the defenders of those truths can sometimes be resistant to change. At the end of the day, reviewers and editors are in fact human, and altering the way we think about a phenomenon takes work and can be threatening, even for these gatekeepers. This does not mean that the gatekeepers will inevitably defend flawed assumptions in the face of compelling evidence, but it does mean that one short-term cost associated with boundary pushing can be a difficult and lengthy review process.[2]

A second, and unfortunate, cost of pushing boundaries is the possibility of offending or alienating certain scholars. As we said, reviewers and scholars in general are sometimes heavily invested in their theories, methods, and preferred interpretations, and any challenge to "their system" may be seen as a threat. It would be easy to suggest that one could simply brush off the possibility of offending another scholar, guided by the idea that if they aren't open-minded enough to entertain

---

[2]Although the tone in this section may seem somewhat negative, in our experience (as authors, editors, and reviewers), editors and reviewers usually try to help authors improve their manuscripts, and long and difficult review processes almost always end with a much stronger manuscript, as we discussed in Chapter 4.

your new idea, then you may not wish to associate with them anyway. But, of course, this approach can be risky, especially if the offended scholar holds the "purse strings" to important benefits. Having said all of this, we do not advocate taking an extreme position in either direction (avoiding controversy altogether vs. adopting a dismissive attitude toward "competitors"). Rather, as we explained in detail in Chapter 4, we encourage scholars to approach their initial draft and the revision process in a respectful (if challenging) manner, with the primary goals of framing advances as interesting extensions and improvements on existing work, even when the improvement requires a substantial rethinking of a phenomenon. In the following sections, we outline two of the most common ways to push boundaries and pay attention to how to strategically frame those approaches to facilitate greater acceptance.

CHALLENGING EXISTING ASSUMPTIONS

When one thinks about pushing boundaries, a natural starting point is to evaluate strongly held assumptions. These assumptions may deal with the appropriateness of a certain method or measure; the dimensionality of a construct; the causal mechanism responsible for an effect; or the generalizability of an effect across time, people or situations. Because each method, measure, construct, mechanism, or effect has been established for a limited set of purposes and in a limited set of contexts, each is open to criticism. A method that has been used for years may contain a fundamental confound, a measure that has been used for years may be based on a flawed theory, a construct that has long been assumed to be unidimensional may have multiple dimensions, an existing mechanism may be an incomplete explanation for a causal chain, and an effect established in one domain may have limited application in another domain. As we show through this chapter's illustrations, challenging these assumptions has the potential to contribute not only to the practice of one's field (e.g., by developing a better method or measure), but also, and perhaps more significantly, to the field's theoretical understanding of a phenomenon.

Often, challenging assumptions involves questioning the nature of a construct or process, or the generalizability of a theory or finding to a new domain or phenomenon. The ability to successfully challenge assumptions, in turn, rests significantly on a researcher's comprehensive knowledge of past theory and research—not only in one's own area but also in related areas. This broad and interdisciplinary knowledge base can, in turn, help identify significant conceptual gaps and ensure that the researcher is not simply "reinventing the wheel." As we have said from the outset, the ability to publish high-quality research rests on the researcher's ability to fill a meaningful and novel gap, rather than filling in a hole that does not, in fact, exist. We also suspect that the ability to challenge assumptions requires a good deal of creativity, a willingness to "think outside the box," and careful attention to detail, nuance, and the gap between our sometimes artificially clean and simple methods (scenario experiments with college students) and the more complex real world. Although carefully controlled lab experiments have their place, they leave many practical, and more important, theoretical questions unanswered. Attention to the similarities and differences between the lab and real world can thus pay significant dividends for the researchers who take time to dip their feet in the real world.

A good example is Van Lange, Ouwerkerk, and Tazelaar's (2002) work on the use of strict tit-for-tat versus generous tit-for-tat strategies in social dilemmas involving noise, which we illustrate in this chapter. To briefly summarize, Van Lange and colleagues reasoned that when people interact in social dilemmas (involving a choice between more or less cooperative behavior), a strict tit-for-tat strategy may be appropriate in lab settings, because each person's choice in a social dilemma is clear. However, in the real world, choices in social dilemmas are affected by noise (e.g., one may come across as less cooperative than one intended because of uncontrollable factors), and in such situations, it may be better to "give the other person the benefit of the doubt" and be a little bit more generous to one's partner than the partner was to the self (e.g., returning six coins if the other gave you five coins). Van Lange et al.'s paper represented an important conceptual shift in the field, because it called into question the ubiquity of strict tit-for-tat, which had long been assumed to be the strategy that is most effective in promoting and sustaining cooperation in social dilemmas. The idea of generous tit-for-tat also opened up a number of interesting, theoretical questions for future research, as we explain next.

When challenging assumptions, Zaltman and colleagues (1982) argued that one should challenge firmly held beliefs, rather than weakly held beliefs or fanatically held beliefs. Challenging weak beliefs is unlikely to be viewed as a significant contribution, and challenging fanatically held beliefs is unlikely to be successful. Thus, the most interesting and pragmatic beliefs to challenge are those that many in the field might adhere to, but could (with compelling argumentation and empirical evidence) come to question.

Strategically, when challenging assumptions, it is advisable if at all possible to frame the challenge as an interesting open question, rather than as an outright attack. Open questions are invitations for your reviewers to join with you on a quest; attacks are likely to give rise to defensiveness and counterattack. The key is to make the question, rather than the scholar, the point of questioning (if at all possible) and to frame the previous theory and/or scholar as a valuable stepping stone that paved the way for your contribution.

TESTING COMPETING THEORIES

A second way one can push boundaries is to test competing theories. This can happen in one of two ways. The more ambitious approach, in our view, is to challenge a previous scholar's theory with your own theory. A somewhat less provocative, but still valuable, approach is to pit two competing theories against each other, where neither theory is one that you, personally, developed. A final approach is to suggest that different theories (or principles) are appropriate under different circumstances, which in many ways relates closely to the idea of identifying boundary conditions for an effect.

Challenging another's theory is difficult. To succeed, the existing theory must have significant conceptual gaps, and your competing theory must be better defined and reasoned. This requires attention to appropriate construct definition and a more compelling explanation for the causal process underlying a phenomenon. Taking on another's theory is not impossible, of course, but it can be a challenge, especially for the young scholar.

An alternative is to test competing theories. It is possible that the theories exist, as theories, or that competing theories are suggested by disparate hypotheses and findings. A good example of this approach can be found in Balliet, Li, and Joireman's (2011) illustration in this chapter. In their paper, Balliet and colleagues focused on how two traits (concern with others and self-control) combine to predict forgiveness. In reviewing the literature, the authors recognized that two competing models had been suggested to explain how these traits might combine, a compensatory model and a synergistic model. The authors articulated and labeled each model, illustrated their competing pattern of predicted results, and tested the theories across three primary studies.

Finally, competing theories can also be set up by suggesting that what we have long observed in one context may not be applicable in a different context—in other words, by identifying a boundary condition for an effect and explaining the relevance of the boundary condition (and different pattern of expected results) for theory. One way to identify a boundary condition is to note important conceptual differences between the lab and field, explain why results observed in the lab may not extend to the field, and use the expected differences to expand on existing theory. Here again, Van Lange et al.'s (2002) work on generous tit-for-tat strategies is a good example.

Illustrations

CAN HIGH TRAIT SELF-CONTROL PROMOTE FORGIVENESS WITHIN PROSELFS?

In 2011, Balliet, Li, and Joireman published a paper testing two competing models explaining how trait self-control and trait concern with others (trait forgiveness and social value orientation) interact to influence forgiveness in social dilemmas. According to the *compensatory model*, forgiveness requires either a prosocial disposition or high trait self-control (i.e., forgiveness is only low in proselfs with low trait self-control); according to the *synergistic model*, forgiveness requires both traits (i.e., forgiveness is only high in prosocials with high trait self-control). To illustrate the nature of the competing models, the authors visually depicted the contrasting nature of the interactions predicted by the two models (e.g., Figure 1, p. 1093) and explained, in detail, the pattern of simple slopes that would be expected on the basis of the competing models (for a discussion of different types of interactions, see Chapter 8, this volume).

Prior to their publication, both models had been indirectly suggested by past theory and research, but the models had never been labeled as compensatory or synergistic models, or put to a competitive test. As such, Balliet, Li, and Joireman's (2011) paper is a good example of how researchers can recognize the (implicit) existence of competing models, articulate and label them, and put them to a competitive test, rather than attacking a previous theoretical model with the author's preferred model. Indeed, early on in the introduction, Balliet and colleagues were careful to frame the test of competing models as an open question by asking, "Can a high level of trait self-control predict higher levels of forgiveness even among people with a proself orientation? Can a prosocial orientation positively relate to forgiveness even among those with a low level of trait self-control? Or does forgiveness require both a prosocial orientation and high trait self-control?" (p. 1090). Importantly, the authors followed up these questions with a detailed explanation of the logic behind the competing models.

To test the competing models, the authors conducted two preliminary and three primary studies. The first two studies were done to determine whether trait self-control was positively related to trait forgiveness (Study 1a) and whether priming state self-control would promote state forgiveness (Study 1b). The three primary studies explored how trait self-control and state concern with the well-being of others interacted to impact forgiveness in a variety of social dilemmas, including a two-person prisoner's dilemma, a two-person give-some dilemma, and a two-person maximizing difference game.

Each study provided evidence for the compensatory model: In sum, a high concern with the well-being of others (or high trait forgiveness) led to high levels of state forgiveness, even among those with low trait self-control, and high trait self-control led to high levels of state forgiveness, even among those with a low concern with the well-being of others. Thus, high levels of each trait "compensated" for low levels of the other trait.

Balliet, Li, and Joireman's (2011) paper helps to illustrate how to test competing models in a nonthreatening way. The authors were careful to frame the competing models test as an open question, rather than an attack on any one position. Moreover, the authors clearly articulated the theoretical reasoning behind the models and visually illustrated the nature of the results predicted by each model. In addition, the authors used a variety of methods to establish the generalizability of their findings, including different measures of concern with others (trait forgiveness and social value orientation), different types of social dilemmas, and different measures of forgiveness. Finally, the authors used the finding that self-interested people forgive if they have high self-control to raise an interesting question for future research: namely, whether forgiveness may sometimes be motivated by long-term self-interest.

CAN INSINCERE FLATTERY ACTUALLY WORK?

In 2010, E. Chan and Sengupta set out to demonstrate that insincere flattery actually works, in contrast to common wisdom, theory, and research. To set up their argument, the authors first defined *insincere* flattery as occurring "when the recipient knows that the flatterer is offering an insincere compliment, presumably driven by an ulterior motive" (p. 122). Whereas previous research has shown that *sincere* flattery "works" (e.g., leads to more favorable impressions of the flatterer), theory and research have suggested that recipients would likely discount (or correct for) insincere flattery because of a perception of ulterior motives, rendering it ineffective. Although E. Chan and Sengupta acknowledged this "characterization-correction view" (cf. Gilbert, Pelham, & Krull, 1988, p. 123), they also suggested that "despite such correction, a positive impact of flattery may still be observed" (p. 122).

To reconcile the seemingly opposing ideas that insincere flattery may be discounted, but it may also work, the authors drew on a dual attitudes distinction between explicit and implicit attitudes. Specifically, they argued that whereas insincere flattery may have little effect on (more conscious and deliberately formed) explicit attitudes, insincere flattery could significantly enhance (less conscious and association based) implicit attitudes, which should be less susceptible to deliberate correction processes.

E. Chan and Sengupta (2010) tested their reasoning using four experiments set within a consumer context. In each study, participants imagined receiving a flattering leaflet inviting them to shop at a hypothetical store known as PerfectStore. The leaflet informed participants that they were being contacted because PerfectStore knew they were fashionable and stylish and had exceptional taste and a classy and chic sense of dress. A pretest, involving different participants, indicated that the leaflet was recognized as insincere flattery (i.e., flattery with an ulterior motive, which was designed to persuade the recipient to visit the store).

In Studies 1a and 1b, the researchers aimed to demonstrate that implicit attitudes toward PerfectStore were more favorable than explicit attitudes and that implicit attitudes were more strongly related than explicit attitudes to (delayed) purchase intentions. In Study 1a, participants were assigned to either an implicit or an explicit attitudes condition. Those in the implicit condition were required to respond to each attitude rating within a limited amount of time (5 seconds), while those in the explicit condition were given unlimited time to provide their ratings, providing sufficient time for retrieval. Three days later, participants returned to the lab and indicated their willingness to shop at the PerfectStore. Consistent with E. Chan and Sengupta's (2010) reasoning, implicit attitudes were significantly more favorable than explicit attitudes, and implicit attitudes were more strongly related to (delayed) purchase intentions. In Study 1b, using a within-subject design, the authors again showed that following receipt of the insincere flattery leaflet, implicit attitudes toward the store were more favorable than explicit attitudes.

In Study 2, the authors assigned participants to either an implicit attitudes condition (with time-constrained ratings) or an explicit attitudes condition (with unlimited time to respond). The authors then administered a behavioral choice task either immediately or after a three-day delay. In this task, participants were asked to select a coupon worth approximately $6 that they could use at either PerfectStore or RovoStore (a similar store that would carry a variety of brands at different price points). Although the names of the stores were hypothetical, participants were informed that the stores were real and that their names had been changed to maintain their confidentiality. Consistent with Studies 1a and 1b, implicit attitudes were more favorable than explicit attitudes. In addition, and consistent with the authors' reasoning, explicit attitudes were a stronger predictor of immediate than delayed behavioral choice (of coupon), presumably because of the decay in explicit attitude accessibility over time, and delayed choices were more strongly related to implicit than to explicit attitudes, given the more automatically activated nature of implicit attitudes on exposure to the attitude object.

In Study 3, E. Chan and Sengupta (2010) were interested in evaluating whether the desire for self-affirmation was a likely explanation for why insincere flattery works and whether implicit attitudes were more resistant to attack than explicit attitudes. To test these hypotheses, the authors first led participants to experience high self-esteem (self-affirmation) or low self-esteem (self-threat) by writing about a positive aspect of their self or an aspect of their self they would like to change. The authors hypothesized that the tendency for implicit attitudes to be more favorable than explicit attitudes would be reduced when participants had first experienced self-affirmation. Next, participants read PerfectStore's flattering leaflet and then provided either implicit or explicit attitudes toward the store, as in the previous studies. After a brief distractor task, participants read an unfavorable review of the store, ostensibly from another shopper. Subsequently, participants once again provided implicit or explicit attitudes toward the store, using slightly different scale items. Results showed that implicit attitudes were more favorable than explicit attitudes in the self-threat condition, but not in the self-affirmation condition, and that following the negative store review, implicit attitudes did not change, whereas explicit attitudes became significantly less favorable, showing that implicit attitudes were less susceptible to attack.

In sum, E. Chan and Sengupta (2010) creatively drew on the dual attitudes distinction between implicit and explicit attitudes to show—counter to previous theory, research, and intuition—that insincere flattery actually works. Whereas recipients of insincere flattery appear to "correct" their explicit attitudes in light of the flatterer's ulterior motive, insincere flattery also appears able to "fly under the radar," leading to favorable implicit attitudes that are resistant to counterattack and serve as strong predictors of future behavioral intentions. E. Chan and Sengupta's final study, moreover, supports the hypothesis that insincere flattery's success is based, in part, on recipients' desire for self-enhancement. Taken as a whole, E. Chan and Sengupta's work provides a nice model for how a dual-process model can be used to challenge assumptions, identify boundary conditions, and bring additional nuance to our understanding of an intriguing phenomenon.

CAN SPENDING MONEY ON OTHERS PROMOTE HAPPINESS?

In 2008, Dunn, Aknin, and Norton set out to address an apparent paradox: Although much of modern media would have people believe that "money can buy happiness," studies correlating income with happiness often show a fairly weak, albeit positive, relationship between the two. With this in mind, the authors suggested that "an emerging challenge, then, is to identify whether and how disposable income can be used to increase happiness" (p. 1687). In their quest to answer this question, the authors subsequently noted, "ironically" (p. 1687), that thinking about money can lead people to focus less on others and avoid (prosocial) behaviors that have been linked with higher happiness.

To provide preliminary insight into the link between spending on the self, others, and happiness, the authors first conducted a survey using a panel of Americans. Respondents reported how much they normally spent, per month, on bills, gifts for themselves, gifts for others, and charitable donations. Prior to analysis, the first two categories were combined into an index of spending on the self, whereas the latter two were combined into an index of spending on others. Results revealed that spending on the self was unrelated to happiness, but spending on others was positively related to happiness—results that held, even after controlling for income.

Dunn and her colleagues (2008) next conducted a longitudinal study to complement their initial correlational findings. Employees who would soon receive a profit-sharing bonus were asked to rate their happiness before receiving the bonus. Six to eight weeks after receiving the bonus, the employees again indicated their happiness and their spending on the self (bills, rent/mortgage, and gifts for the self) and others (gifts for others and charitable donations). Results confirmed Dunn et al.'s earlier findings: Whereas spending on the self was unrelated to Time 2 happiness, spending on others was a significant predictor of Time 2 happiness, even after controlling for income and bonus amount.

To provide an even stronger demonstration, Dunn et al. (2008) conducted a final experiment in which they gave participants a windfall of $5 or $20 and instructed them to spend the money on themselves or others that day. Participants were then contacted at 5:00 p.m. the same day and asked to rate their happiness. Results revealed a main effect for the target of the spending: Those who spent money on others reported higher levels of happiness than those who spent money on themselves. Interestingly, results revealed no effect for the size of the windfall or the interaction between windfall size and target. On the basis of their findings, the authors concluded that "how people choose to spend their money is at least as important as how much money they make" (p. 1688).

In one of the paper's more interesting twists, the authors then observed that although spending on others promoted happiness, participants in their studies spent a very small fraction of their income on others. This raised an intriguing paradox: Although spending on others promotes happiness, people do not appear to be aware of that link. To test this hypothesis, the authors asked an additional sample to predict which of the conditions in their final study would lead them to experience the greatest happiness. As the authors noted, participants were "doubly wrong": Participants predicted they would be happier after spending money on the self (vs. others), and they would be happier after spending a windfall of $20 (vs. $5). In sum, participants seem unaware that prosocial spending can promote happiness.

Dunn and colleagues' (2008) paper provides a nice model of how researchers can translate a highly interesting and practical question into a testable series of studies that is able to resolve an apparent paradox. In so doing, Dunn and colleagues also provided an excellent example of how to challenge existing assumptions—in this case, that money can buy happiness. In contrast to much of modern media, Dunn et al. showed that money spent on the self does not buy as much happiness as money spent on others, a counterintuitive finding with valuable theoretical and practical implications.

DO CUSTOMERS ALWAYS WANT REVENGE FOLLOWING FAILED SERVICE RECOVERIES?

In 2013, Joireman, Grégoire, Devezer, and Tripp reported three studies examining how customers respond to failed service recoveries. Failed service recoveries occur when a service provider fails to provide satisfactory service and then fails to offer an acceptable recovery, as when a restaurant delivers suboptimal food and fails to correct after a customer complains.

Prior to their work, theory and research largely assumed that failed service recoveries would lead consumers to experience anger and a desire for revenge, which in turn would increase the likelihood of retaliatory behaviors (e.g., spreading negative word of mouth about the firm; *failed recovery → anger → desire for revenge → retaliatory behaviors*). Joireman and colleagues (2013) challenged the assumption that customers would always desire revenge, arguing that customers may prefer reconciliation to revenge, under some well-specified conditions.

To develop their argument, the authors first articulated an expanded process model of responses to failed recoveries. This new model added several new constructs to the basic model. First, Joireman et al. (2013) argued that many of the factors shown to increase customer anger (blaming the firm, severe failures, and unfair treatment) have their impact through inferred negative motives. In other words, customers become angry when they believe a firm's actions are guided by greed and a desire to take advantage of the customer. Second, Joireman and colleagues argued that firms could take actions to encourage the perception of positive motives through explanations, apologies, and compensation. Finally, Joireman et al. suggested that when customers infer positive motives, they would be more likely to want to reconcile with the firm than seek revenge against it. Restated, customers would offer firms a "second chance," as long as they inferred that the firm's motives for the failed recovery were positive.

To test their model, the authors conducted three studies. In the first study, the researchers surveyed airline passengers who had complained about a failed service recovery. Survey respondents indicated the severity of the failure, the extent to which they blamed the airline for the failure, and the extent to which they felt they had been treated fairly during the recovery process. Respondents also indicated their level of anger, their desire for revenge, and the extent to which they believed the firm had negative (or positive) motives for the failed recovery. Results showed that respondents were significantly more likely to believe the firm had negative motives when respondents rated the failure as severe, blamed the firm for the failure, and felt the firm had treated them unfairly. Customers who believed the firm had negative motives, in turn, had higher levels of anger and desire for revenge.

In the second study, participants imagined they ordered a video-game console and were told they could pick it up at the store. When they arrived, participants were told the console was not available. When they arrived 1 week later to get their console, participants were told they had to wait 30 minutes before being helped. Some participants were then led to believe the firm had negative motives for the failed recovery, some were told nothing about the firm's motives, and others were led to believe the firm had positive motives for the failed recovery. Results showed that participants were more likely to desire revenge than reconciliation when led to believe the firm had negative motives, and more likely to desire reconciliation than revenge when led to believe the firm had positive motives for the failed recovery.

In the third study, participants imagined the same failed recovery at the electronics store. Next, participants were led to believe the firm offered the customer compensation, an apology, both, or neither. Results showed that when the firm offered *neither* compensation nor an apology, desire for revenge was higher than desire for reconciliation; when the firm offered *either* compensation or an apology, desire for revenge and reconciliation were equal; and when the firm offered *both* compensation and an apology, desire for reconciliation was higher than desire for revenge. Additional analyses revealed that when the firm offered both compensation and an apology, participants believed the firm had a positive motive, which in turn, led participants to offer the firm a "second chance" (via reconciliation).

In sum, Joireman and colleagues' (2013) research revealed that firms can encourage reconciliation following failed recoveries if they directly explain their positive motives or communicate their positive motives indirectly by offering an apology paired with compensation. This research effectively challenged the widely shared assumption in consumer behavior (and other fields) that failed service recoveries, especially in business settings, are almost always interpreted in terms of negative intent and often lead to anger and revenge. This work shows the potential of prosocial communication—expressing clarity, apologizing, and willingness to compensate—that seems to weaken feelings of revenge and instead promote reconciliation. Many of these examples of prosocial communication are helpful, especially when things go wrong, to maintain good relationships. It is to be expected that future research will extend this line of reasoning, not only for theoretical reasons (because it does challenge the assumption of narrow self-interest) but also for practical reasons: For many businesses, it pays to explain errors, to apologize, and even to compensate. It may help to maintain trust, and this seems important to many contexts—from interpersonal contexts to the exchange contexts examined in this article.

CAN LOW-STATUS CONSUMERS EXERT SOCIAL INFLUENCE TOO?

In 2012, Shalev and Morwitz published a paper challenging the prevailing assumption that influence sources are always more effective when they have high as opposed to low status. The authors opened by inviting readers to imagine how they would react if they observed a low-status individual using a piece of technology that the reader herself was considering purchasing. Traditional models of social influence would predict a reduced interest in purchasing the product because of the low status of the person using the device. In contrast, the authors argued that under certain well-specified conditions, the reader may in fact become more likely to want to buy the device.

The authors outlined their reasoning by first distinguishing between two types of influence: *identification-based influence* (where sources high in status have more influence because of an observer's desire to identify with the source) and *comparison-based influence* (where sources low in status have more influence because of their ability to lead an observer to generate an unfavorable social comparison, suggesting that the observer's relative standing on a desired trait is lower than the observer thought). Building on social comparison theory, the authors then detailed the conditions under which consumers will be influenced by what they referred to as *comparison-driven self-evaluation and restoration* (CDSER). In short, CDSER occurs when an observer sees a lower status person using a product that the observer does not own; generates an unfavorable social comparison, which leads the observer to reason that his relative standing on the focal trait is lower than he thought; and is motivated to restore a positive sense of self by purchasing the product. On the basis of social comparison theory and research, the authors argued that CDSER should be more likely when the "focal trait" associated with a product is self-relevant, and the observer is not confident about his or her standing on the focal trait.

As an example, consider a consumer who feels creativity is an important part of his self-concept, but he is unsure of his standing on the trait of creativity. Now assume this consumer observes a homeless person using the latest photo-editing software, which the consumer does not own. In this case, the focal trait associated with the product (creativity) is self-relevant, the consumer is uncertain of his standing on the trait, and the consumer is likely to infer that his relative standing on creativity is lower than he thought. The consumer may think to himself: "If even a homeless person is using this software, then everyone has become more creative." This, in turn, should lead the consumer to take steps to restore a positive self-evaluation by purchasing the photo-editing software.

To test this reasoning, the authors conducted four studies. In Study 1, college students indicated the likelihood they would purchase a T-shirt after reading a positive review ostensibly written by a grocery packer or by a college student—the low- and high-status targets, respectively (based on pretests). The T-shirt was said to have been made by a company that manufactured well-designed clothes that appealed to a sophisticated group of consumers. Consistent with CDSER, purchase intentions were higher after reading the review by the grocery packer. In Study 2, a panel of consumers read a review for a new wireless charging device written by a security guard (pretested as low status) or an architect (pretested as high status) and then rated their self-affect and purchase intentions. Results revealed that the low-status review led people to feel worse about themselves and more likely to purchase the new product, but only among those who considered the focal trait (being innovative) an important part of their self-concept. In Study 3, female college students rated their wiliness to purchase a Wi-Fi detector after reading a review ostensibly written by a high or a low socioeconomic status user. Results revealed higher willingness to purchase in the low- versus high-status condition, but only when women had been led to feel uncertain about their standing on the focal trait. In Study 4, the authors showed that CDSER is more likely when the focal trait associated with a product is clear, whereas identification-based influence is more likely when the focal trait associated with a product is ambiguous.

Shalev and Morwitz's (2012) paper serves as an excellent illustration of how researchers can effectively challenge long-standing assumptions by carefully specifying the conditions under which the past assumptions do, and may not, hold; articulating a compelling theoretical explanation for their counterintuitive hypothesis; and systematically documenting, with multiple methods, support for their paradigm-shifting argument.

IS TIT-FOR-TAT ALWAYS THE BEST STRATEGY? NOT IN NOISY SITUATIONS

In 2002, Van Lange, Ouwerkerk, and Tazelaar published a paper questioning the long-standing assumption that a tit-for-tat (TFT) strategy is always the most effective reciprocal strategy in social dilemmas involving repeated interactions. The TFT (or eye-for-an-eye) strategy involves returning to one's partner the same level of cooperation that the partner demonstrated on the previous trial. Prior to Van Lange et al.'s (2002) publication, many studies, including an influential computer simulation tournament by Axelrod (1984), supported the effectiveness of the TFT strategy by showing that it elicits high levels of cooperation and leads to higher long-term outcomes for the self and others. As Axelrod noted, TFT is an effective strategy for four reasons: (a) it is nice (it always starts out making a cooperative choice); (b) it is forgiving (it never initiates a noncooperative choice before the partner defects, and it returns to cooperation once a previously noncooperative partner has chosen to cooperate); (c) it is retaliatory (it immediately matches the partner's noncooperative choice); and (d) it is clear (it is easy for the partner to learn the contingency between their choice and the TFT strategy's choice).

Although there was little doubt that TFT was an effective strategy in the social dilemma paradigms typically used by researchers (e.g., prisoner's dilemma, public goods dilemma), Van Lange and colleagues (2002) observed that TFT is "not without limitations." Most notably, the authors stressed that TFT can lead to a suboptimal pattern of negative reciprocity, or *echo effect* (Axelrod, 1984), which can, in part, be due to the presence of negative noise (i.e., factors beyond an actor's control that lead the actor's choice to be less cooperative than intended). As an example, a coauthor may be unable to return a manuscript in the agreed-on time frame because of an unexpected family emergency.

Van Lange and colleagues (2002) argued that instances of negative noise are quite prevalent in daily life, whereas the vast majority of social dilemma paradigms had never incorporated noise; rather, choices in previous paradigms were unaffected by noise and were communicated clearly between partners. If Person A decided to give Person B five coins, Person B would learn that Person A gave five coins. As readers will recall, clarity is one of the reasons the TFT strategy is so effective: When choices are unaffected by noise, the consequences of one's choices are clear.

After recognizing the prevalence and importance of noise, Van Lange et al. (2002) next argued that in situations of noise, TFT may not be the most effective strategy. In contrast, building on Axelrod's (1984) suggestions, Van Lange and colleagues suggested that when noise is present and echo effects are likely, it is arguably beneficial to show one's partner generosity (i.e., being a little bit more cooperative than the partner was on the preceding trial). Van Lange and colleagues also argued that the benefits of generosity in situations involving noise would likely be due to more favorable (benign) impressions of the generous partner.

To test these ideas, Van Lange and colleagues (2002) used a "coin game" representing a two-person give-some dilemma. On each trial of the game, each player was given 10 coins and had to decide how many coins to keep or give to their partner. Coins were worth one point to the self, and two points if given to the partner. Thus, from a collective perspective, the players were better off giving each other all of the coins, as each would end up with 20 points, for a collective outcome of 40 points. However, it was in each person's own self-interest to keep all of the coins, regardless of what one's partner did. For example, a partner who kept the 10 allotted coins and received 10 coins from the partner would end up with 30 points. Consequently, if both partners followed this individually rational strategy and gave each other no coins, they would each end up with only 10 points, for a collective outcome of 20 points. As a result, the give-some coin game was a social dilemma in which individual and collective interests were at odds.

Although Van Lange and colleagues (2002) noted that positive noise was (theoretically) possible, in this study they chose to focus on the more problematic form of negative noise. To manipulate negative noise, the researchers arranged for some of the players' choices to be negatively impacted by noise. Specifically, for those assigned to the noise conditions, on roughly 15% of the 53 trials, the computer subtracted two coins from the participant's intended contribution to the partner. Participants were led to believe that noise would affect the participant's choices only, the partner's choices only, or both. A fourth (control) condition involved no noise.

Van Lange et al. (2002) also manipulated the strategy of the preprogrammed partner. For half of the participants, the partner (in reality, a preprogrammed strategy) followed a strict TFT strategy, always giving the participant what he or she gave on the preceding trial. By contrast, for the other half of the participants, the partner followed a more generous TFT+1 strategy, giving the participant what he or she gave on the previous trial plus one coin.

Results revealed a very clear pattern: Relative to the (no noise) control condition, noise reduced cooperation, but only when the partner followed a strict TFT strategy. When the partner used a more generous TFT+1 strategy, noise had no effect on cooperation rates. Moreover, when noise was present, TFT+1 led to higher levels of cooperation than TFT. As predicted, favorable impressions of the partner followed an identical pattern, and favorable impressions mediated the interaction between noise and partner strategy on cooperation.

Van Lange and colleagues' (2002) paper illustrates how a conclusion that has been accepted for some time (TFT is the best reciprocal strategy) can be challenged by identifying key practical and theoretical boundary conditions. By noting that many real-world interactions involve noise, the authors were able to question the benefits of a strict TFT strategy and outline the benefits of a more generous strategy. The study's methodology also provides a nice illustration of how to model real-world phenomena in a lab under carefully controlled conditions.

Conclusion

Researchers often seek to launch paradigm shifts by challenging the status quo of existing theory and assumptions. This chapter illustrated several ways researchers have used the paradigm-shifting paradigm to test competing theories concerning predictors of forgiveness (Balliet, Li, & Joireman, 2011); challenge the assumption that insincere flattery does not work (E. Chan & Sengupta, 2010); and demonstrate, counter to many lay theories, that spending money on others leads to greater happiness than spending money on the self (Dunn et al., 2008). This paradigm was also helpful in showing that customers do not always seek revenge following failed service recoveries (Joireman et al., 2013); that low-status consumers can, counter to the prevailing assumption, sometimes significantly influence the consumption patterns of other consumers (Shalev & Morwitz, 2012); and that a strict tit-for-tat is not always the most effective way to promote cooperation in social dilemmas, especially when they are characterized by negative noise (Van Lange et al., 2002). Researchers who see an opportunity to challenge assumptions, or fundamentally shift the way a field views a phenomenon are likely to find many valuable lessons in these articles and the additional readings our highlighted authors recommend.

Author Interviews

Highlighted Author

Daniel Balliet
Associate Professor,
Department of Social
and Organizational
Psychology, VU
University, Amsterdam,
the Netherlands

What is your advice for publishing high-quality research that is likely to have impact?

As this book indicates, there are several ways to make a scientific contribution. Two that I enjoy involve (a) setting up experiments to test competing theoretical perspectives on a specific phenomenon and (b) using meta-analysis to resolve long-standing inconsistencies in prior literature, while simultaneously using the meta-analysis to test theory of the phenomenon under investigation.

What "testing competing theories" paper would you recommend and why?

I would recommend reading Cosmides, Barrett, and Tooby's (2010) work testing competing theories about human reasoning abilities, published in the *Proceedings of the National Academy of Sciences, USA*. In this paper the authors pit several general human intelligence theories of reasoning abilities against an evolutionary account of domain specificity in reasoning. The results across four studies consistently support an evolutionary theory of domain specificity for our ability to detect cheaters during social exchange. Such a contribution has broad implications across both the biological and social sciences for understanding human intelligence and reasoning abilities. A long-standing assumption is that humans possess a general reasoning ability that is applied to all forms of decisions. The current research challenges these claims and opens several new directions of research about how humans reason to solve many different social and ecological problems.

Highlighted Author

What is your advice for publishing high-quality research that is likely to have impact?

What "paradigm-shifting" paper would you recommend and why?

Elaine Chan
Assistant Professor of Marketing, Tilburg School of Economics and Management, Tilburg University, Tilburg, the Netherlands

I would encourage researchers to think more about how their research questions are related to real-world problems. Sometimes when I read a paper, I think about how it translates to a real-life situation, because it helps me to go beyond the existing literature and think from a broader perspective. Besides considering the impact of one's research, I believe that it is also very important for the researchers to conduct research in an area that they themselves are passionate about.

There are a lot of papers that I would like to recommend. I very much like the research by Wilson, Lindsey, and Schooler (2000) on dual attitudes. Similar to other researchers, they also provided a new perspective on attitudes by recognizing the important role of implicit attitudes. They further offered a broad perspective on how implicit attitudes could differ in awareness and the motivation to be overridden. Their framework suggests a number of interesting questions that still remain to be answered.

Elizabeth Dunn
Associate Professor, Department of Psychology, University of British Columbia, Vancouver, British Columbia, Canada

Let your curiosity about the world lead you, rather than doing "research on research." Sometimes I'll start by reading the literature on a topic and then formulate hypotheses, but I get more interesting results when I start by looking at the world around me first. My best projects have always been driven by my curiosity about something I noticed in the world, rather than in the scientific literature.

When I was in graduate school, I did almost all of my research with undergrads at the University of Virginia. I realized that, sure, they weren't perfectly representative of all of humanity, but Henrich, Heine, and Norenzayan's (2010) paper convinced me that these sorts of samples are actually some of the weirdest people in the world. Their paper made me truly appreciate the importance of pushing the cultural boundaries of my own work, leading my original collaborators and me to team up with economists at the University of British Columbia and researchers in Africa to test whether spending money on others promotes happiness around the world.

Highlighted Author

Jeff Joireman
Associate Professor,
Department of
Marketing, Washington
State University,
Pullman

What is your advice for publishing high-quality research that is likely to have impact?

Pick a topic you are passionate about and that can hold your attention for a sustained amount of time. Ground your work in existing theory, or advance a new or improved theory or model. Work with a team of competent, reliable, and agreeable coauthors with complementary skills. Put together a collection of studies, drawing on a combination of field and experimental methods. Use and communicate statistics appropriately. Learn how to write, and strive for perfection. Don't overcomplicate the message; find the "nugget" and sell it. And last, approach the revision process with care: Take the reviewers' comments to heart, figure out how to improve your manuscript with their input, address everything, and overdeliver.

What "challenging assumptions" paper would you recommend and why?

I really like Paul's 2002 noise paper (Van Lange, Ouwerkerk, & Tazelaar, 2002). I pushed hard to include it in this chapter, and Paul finally agreed. In my mind, this paper represents a huge shift in the way researchers will eventually think about reciprocal strategies in social dilemmas. There is no doubt that a strict tit-for-tat strategy is effective at increasing cooperation (for most people), but the strict tit-for-tat strategy is simply not flexible enough, or "forgiving," in less controlled, and noisy, real-world settings. Paul's work shows that in noisy situations, adding a little generosity (tit-for-tat + 1) goes a long way toward ensuring mutually beneficial outcomes. As such, Paul's paper challenged existing assumptions by noting a key difference between the lab and the real world, and highlighted why a more generous strategy would be beneficial in more realistic settings, contributing important theoretical and practical insights into a topic that has interested social dilemma scholars for decades.

Highlighted Author

Edith Shalev
Assistant Professor,
William Davidson
Faculty of Industrial
Engineering and
Management Technion,
Israel Institute of
Technology, Technion
City, Haifa, Israel

What is your advice for publishing high-quality research that is likely to have impact?

Be sensibly counterintuitive. Don't try to shock people with an enigmatic effect. The counterintuitive part of the research may highlight an overlooked angle or an innovative application of an old theory. One does not need to challenge the entire theory. People like to understand phenomena in behavioral science, and thus a totally inexplicable effect may leave them doubtful and perplexed.

What "paradigm-shifting" paper would you recommend and why?

There are quite a few paradigm-shifting papers out there, making it difficult for me to choose one. Furthermore, it is not always easy to identify precisely how the paradigm-shifting idea evolved. A paradigm shifter is often thought of as a massively cited, seminal paper. However, we should note that big papers often build on a series of smaller, less-cited papers. In our paper, for example, we cite a largely unknown 1942 paper by Festinger, where he reports a surprising finding that did not fit with his subsequent social comparison theory. Seventy years later, that finding becomes relevant to our paper and theoretical framework. To me, such smaller papers, although not necessarily framed as such, are also paradigm shifting.

Highlighted Author

Paul Van Lange
Professor of
Psychology and Chair,
Department of Social
and Organizational
Psychology, VU
University, Amsterdam,
the Netherlands

What is your advice for publishing high-quality research that is likely to have impact?

My experience as editor tells me that it is not fully predictable which papers will make an impact. Sometimes, excellent papers do not receive much attention. But the bottom line is that the paper should be well written. Beyond that, it is a combination of scientific excellence, broad interest (including relevance), and novelty, and I think that often two of these three criteria must be met to have impact. For example, sometimes a well-written paper that addresses a novel issue that captures a broad interest (or is relevant from some perspective, such as measurement tool) may be sufficient to generating considerable impact, even if the quality of the research is good but not excellent. Also, sometimes research that is not especially novel, but provides excellent research tools that are of broad interest, may be very influential. There are several roads to Rome.

What "challenging assumptions" paper would you recommend and why?

Social psychology has many good theories. One theory that I found particularly challenging at the time is the theory of "tend-and-befriend" by Shelley Taylor and colleagues (2000). Fight and flight were seen as the dominant responses to stress, but they noted that tending-and-befriending could also be an adaptive response to stress. Tending involves the nurturing behaviors toward the self and offspring to promote safety and reduce stress, and befriending is the creation and maintenance of social networks that may aid in this process. The paper was also seminal because it offers a theoretical integration of the biological system and interpersonal system, providing social behavioral and neuroendocrine evidence for their theory, as well as outlining some important social and political implications of their theory. I think the theory scores well on truth (which is also up to future research), but it certainly is a theory that scores highly on abstraction, progress, and applicability.

Combine Mediators and Moderators
Mediated Moderation and Moderated Mediation

8

Background

Throughout this book, we have emphasized that publishing high-quality research involves pushing the boundaries of established theories and findings. We have also argued that one of the main goals of theory is to explain why a phenomenon occurs and identify the conditions under which a phenomenon is more or less likely to occur. This chapter discusses two powerful methodological techniques that allow researchers to accomplish both goals simultaneously, namely, testing for mediated moderation and testing for moderated mediation.

In our experience, the terms *mediation, moderation, mediated moderation,* and *moderated mediation* are often confused and sometimes difficult to distinguish. Given this, we begin this chapter with a brief review of these four terms before discussing the procedures in greater detail.

http://dx.doi.org/10.1037/14525-009
How to Publish High-Quality Research, by J. Joireman and P. A. M. Van Lange

MEDIATION VERSUS MODERATION

Mediation

Mediation addresses the question "Why does X (the primary predictor) lead or relate to Y (the primary criterion)?" Restated, mediation analyses are designed to provide insight into the "causal process" linking X to Y by testing whether the X–Y relationship "runs through" a mediator (Me). As an example, consider the "art infusion effect" (Hagtvedt & Patrick, 2008), the finding that placing artwork on the front of a product, or using artwork in a product's advertisement, enhances product evaluations. Across three studies, Hagtvedt and Patrick (2008) showed that the art infusion effect occurs because art increases perceptions of a product's luxury, and perceptions of luxury, in turn, lead to enhanced product evaluations (i.e., the impact of art on product evaluations is mediated by perceptions of luxury).

As many readers know, mediation has long been established using the four conditions outlined by Baron and Kenny (1986): (a) X should be related to Y; (b) X should be related to the mediator (Me); and when X and Me are used together to predict Y (Y is regressed on X and Me), (c) Me is a significant predictor of Y; and (d) the relationship between X and Y is no longer significant (full mediation) or is reduced but still significant (partial mediation). Typically, researchers using the Baron and Kenny approach have also reported the Sobel (1982) test that evaluates the significance of the reduction in the X–Y relationship when Me is entered as a predictor.

More recently, scholars have begun complementing or replacing the Baron and Kenny (1986) approach with bootstrapped tests of the indirect effect of X on Y through Me, using the bootstrapping procedures outlined by Preacher and Hayes (2008; see also Zhao, Lynch, & Chen, 2010) and often testing the fit of the full structural model (X → Me → Y) using path analysis or structural equation modeling (when model variables include latent constructs).

Moderation

Where mediation deals directly with the question of "why," *moderation* deals with the question "When, or under what conditions, is X more or less likely to lead to Y?" Simply put, a moderator (Mo) changes the nature of the relationship between X and Y. As an example, consider a paper the current authors, along with Mark Van Vugt, published titled, "Who Cares about the Environmental Impact of Cars? Those With an Eye Toward the Future" (Joireman, Van Lange, & Van Vugt, 2004). In that study, we assessed the extent to which people believed cars harmed the environment (the primary predictor, X), respondents' preferences for public transportation (the criterion, Y), and individual differences in concern with future consequences (the moderator, Mo; Strathman, Gleicher, Boninger, & Edwards, 1994; see also Chapter 9, this volume). As expected, results revealed a positive relationship between perceived environmental harm caused by cars and preference for public transportation. More important, that relationship was *moderated* by individual differences in the consideration of future consequences (CFC), such that the relationship between perceived environmental harm and preference for public transportation was only significant among those who scored high on CFC (i.e., were highly concerned with the future consequences of their actions).

DEMONSTRATING MEDIATION WITH MODERATION

In the preceding section, we highlighted the classic distinction between mediation (used for testing mechanisms and addressing questions of why X leads to Y) and moderation (used for testing boundary conditions and addressing questions of when or under what conditions does X lead to Y). We should also briefly note that others have made a strong case that moderation, when used appropriately, can be used to gain insight into underlying processes (for an excellent discussion, see Spencer, Zanna, & Fong, 2005). As an example, if a researcher suspects a mechanism may be responsible for an effect, experimentally manipulating the mechanism and "turning it off" can also provide evidence for the mechanism's role in connecting X and Y.

MEDIATED MODERATION VERSUS MODERATED MEDIATION

With the terms *mediation* and *moderation* defined, we can now define mediated moderation and moderated mediation. Simply put, *mediated moderation* is a technique used to understand why an interaction occurs (i.e., what mediates the interaction between X1 and X2 in predicting Y), whereas *moderated mediation* is a technique used to determine whether a certain mediating process (X → Me → Y) is moderated by a fourth variable (i.e., whether the mediating process, or indirect effect, is different at different levels of a fourth variable). As we will show, mediated moderation is commonly used when a researcher has identified an interesting interaction and wants to understand why the interaction is occurring. By contrast, moderated mediation is used when a researcher has identified a mediation model (or indirect effect) and wants to determine whether that mediation model (or indirect effect) is different under different conditions (e.g., exists within women but not men).

That said, a number of scholars have pointed out that mediated moderation and moderated mediation are closely related (Edwards &

Lambert, 2007; Muller, Judd, & Yzerbyt, 2005; Preacher, Rucker, & Hayes, 2007). Researchers differ, however, on how to deal with this overlap and the confusion that sometimes arises over their distinction. Some suggest that it is acceptable to distinguish between mediated moderation and moderated mediation, depending on the theoretical perspective driving the study (e.g., whether understanding why an interaction occurs is the primary focus or not; e.g., Muller et al., 2005), whereas others have argued that mediated moderation and moderated mediation models are both, fundamentally, moderated mediation models and can be parsimoniously organized within the broader concept of "moderated path analyses" (Edwards & Lambert, 2007) or "conditional indirect effects" (Preacher et al., 2007). From our perspective, there is value in distinguishing between the two approaches conceptually, as researchers often start by focusing either on moderation (and then trying to explain it) or mediation (and then identifying conditions under which it is more or less likely). As such, we provide illustrations of both concepts and are careful to explain why the two labels are particularly relevant in each case. At the same time, we recognize that the two techniques are likely to continue to undergo additional refinements as conceptual and analytic tools are developed and discussed in the literature. In the final analysis, our suggestion is to thoughtfully consider the illustrations of mediated moderation and moderated mediation contained in the chapter, while continually following the discussion over these increasingly popular techniques.

INTERACTION EFFECTS

This chapter focuses on mediated moderation and moderated mediation. To clearly understand both techniques, it is essential to understand the related terms of *interactions* and *moderation*. Interaction effects occur when the effect of one independent variable (X1) on the dependent variable (Y) depends on the level of another independent variable (X2). When this occurs, researchers often say that the second independent variable "moderates" the effect of the first independent variable on the dependent variable (depending on the researcher's model, it is equally plausible to suggest that X1 moderates the impact of X2 on Y). In the following sections, we consider some major goals of using an interactionist framework, highlight different types of interactions, and discuss different ways to "break down" an interaction.

GOALS OF INTERACTIONS

Interactions serve a number of important goals. First, interactions can help identify meaningful boundary conditions for an effect. This may suggest, for example, that an intervention is more or less successful under certain circumstances or within certain populations. Existence of a boundary condition may also suggest the need to refine existing theory (e.g., Van Lange, Ouwerkerk, & Tazelaar, 2002; see also Chapter 7, this volume). Second, in a related vein, interactions are useful for identifying conditions that may help facilitate the effect of a primary variable or are even required for the primary variable to have its effect (e.g., Joireman et al., 2004, described earlier in this chapter). Third, interactions are useful for testing the validity of a construct. Often, this approach is used when validating a new individual difference scale— for example, by showing that a certain personality trait moderates the effect of a relevant situation manipulation or that the impact of the trait varies on the basis of the situation in a theoretically meaningful manner (e.g., Paharia, Keinan, Avery, & Schor, 2011). Finally, interactions are, at the broadest level, more consistent with the complex (interactive) nature of behavior, which is routinely a function of the interaction between features of the person (P) and the situation (S) (i.e., $P \times P$; $S \times S$; or $P \times S$).

TYPES OF INTERACTIONS

To better appreciate how researchers can capitalize on interactions (and moderators), it is helpful to consider some of their basic forms. In particular, most interactions take on one of four prototypes on the basis of how the moderator impacts the nature of the relationship between X and Y. To be precise, moderators can (a) amplify/enhance/magnify the relationship between X and Y, (b) reduce/mitigate/buffer the relationship between X and Y, (c) make people susceptible to the adverse impact of a variable on an undesirable outcome, or (d) reverse the relationship between X and Y.

Amplification

Figure 8.1, Panel A, depicts an amplification interaction. Here, the relationship between X1 and Y is stronger at "high" levels of X2 than at low levels of X2, but the relationship is significant at both high and low levels of X2. In other words, high levels of X2 amplify the impact of X1 on Y. Similarly, if X1 is treated as the moderator, high levels of X1 amplify the effect of X2 on Y. A good example of this amplification interaction is Bessenoff's (2006) article showing that social comparison processes (in response to exposure to thin ideals in the media) lead to higher levels of negative outcomes (e.g., depression), most notably among women with a high discrepancy between their actual and ideal body image.

A special type of amplification, which we refer to as the *catalytic* or *synergistic interaction* (e.g., Balliet, Li, & Joireman, 2011; see also Chapter 7, this volume), is shown in Figure 8.1, Panel B. Here, the

FIGURE 8.1

Panel A

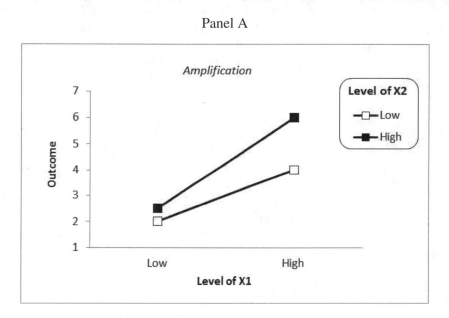

Panel B

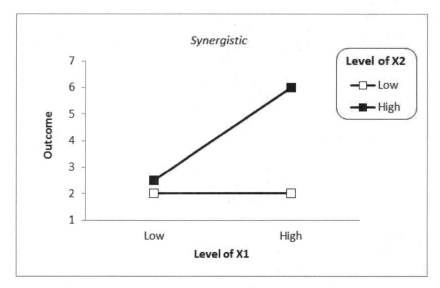

Amplification and synergistic interactions.

relationship between X1 and Y is only significant at high levels of X2; in other words, high levels of X2 are necessary to catalyze the effect of X1 on Y; or to state it differently, high levels of Y only occur when high levels of X1 and X2 work in synergy. Several of the illustrations in this chapter depict this form of interaction, including Paharia et al.'s (2011) work on the underdog effect.

It should also be noted that, technically, an amplification/catalytic/synergistic interaction could also occur if the relationship between X1 and Y is stronger at low levels of X2 (assuming X2 is negatively related to Y). For example, workers may be more likely to volunteer for extra-role tasks if they are treated fairly by their supervisor (X1 is high) and they have low family stress (X2 is low). Here, volunteering for extra-role tasks requires both fair supervisor treatment and low family stress, or low stress facilitates (or permits) the positive effect of fair treatment on extra-role tasks. The broader point here is that researchers who are considering framing their interaction in this way should think carefully about the nature (and interpretation) of their variables and the way the variables combine.

Buffering

As noted, another form of interaction is the *buffering interaction*. To understand the buffering interaction, it is important to note that buffering almost always implies protection against the effect of a vulnerability factor on an outcome. Like amplification interactions, buffering interactions can come in one of two broad forms. As shown in Figure 8.2, Panel A, *partial buffering* (or *mitigation*) may occur when high levels of X2 reduce (but do not completely eliminate) the negative impact of X1 (a vulnerability factor) on Y (a positive outcome). By comparison, as shown in Figure 8.2, Panel B, *full buffering* occurs when high levels of X2 completely eliminate the negative impact of X1 on Y. A good example of full buffering is Little, McNulty, and Russell's (2010) work, illustrated in this chapter, which explored whether frequent and satisfying sex (the moderator) could "buffer" (or protect against) the negative effects of attachment insecurity (the primary predictor) on relationship satisfaction (the criterion).

Susceptibility

Another type of interaction is the *susceptibility* (or *vulnerability*) *interaction*. Here, a feature of the person or situation may make a person more susceptible to adverse impacts of a primary variable on an outcome variable. People may vary in their degree of susceptibility (Figure 8.3, Panel A), or only certain types of people may be susceptible (Figure 8.3, Panel B). As can be seen, the pattern of the susceptibility interaction

FIGURE 8.2

Panel A

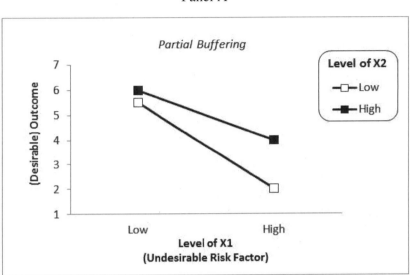

Panel B

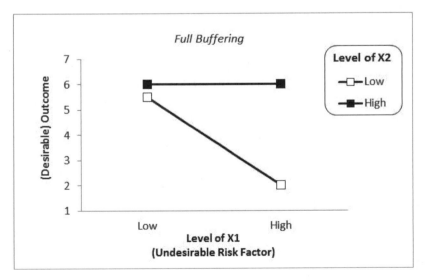

Partial buffering and full buffering interactions.

FIGURE 8.3

Panel A

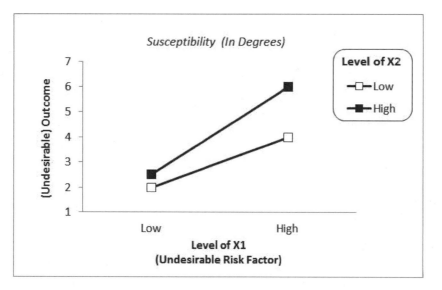

Panel B

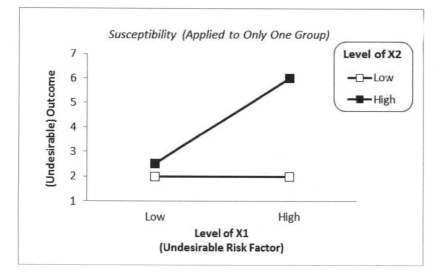

Susceptibility interactions.

is the same as the pattern of the amplification interaction (Figure 8.1). The distinction is that the label *susceptibility* is especially relevant when the primary predictor is a variable that can lead to a negative outcome. As an example, consider a recent study on predictors of credit card debt (Joireman, Kees, & Sprott, 2010). In that study, college students reported their compulsive buying tendencies, concern with future (and immediate) consequences, and credit card debt. As expected, results revealed a positive relationship between compulsive buying tendencies and credit card debt. More important, this relationship was much stronger among those high in concern with immediate consequences. Restated, a high concern with immediate consequences made people (relatively) more susceptible or vulnerable to the adverse impact of compulsive buying tendencies on credit card debt.

Reversal

A final type of interaction is the *reversal interaction*. In the reversal interaction, the direction of the effect of one or both predictor variables on the criterion variable is different at different levels of the other variable. In the less extreme case, the direction of the effect of X1 on Y is different at different levels of X2, but the direction of the effect of X2 on Y is (in actuality, or practically) the same at different levels of X1 (Figure 8.4, Panel A). In the most extreme case, the direction of the effect of X1 on Y is different at low and high levels of X2, and the direction of the effect of X2 on Y is different at low and high levels of X2 (Figure 8.4, Panel B). As an example of full reversal or cross-over interaction, consider Okimoto and Brescoll's (2010) work on backlash against power-seeking female politicians, illustrated in this chapter. Among their findings, Okimoto and colleagues reported that when male politicians expressed power-seeking intentions, it led to increases in perceived competence, whereas when female politicians expressed similar power-seeking intentions, it led to decreases in perceived competence. Moreover, male politicians were seen as more competent when they did (as opposed to did not) express power-seeking intentions, whereas female politicians were seen as more competent when they did not (as opposed to did) express power-seeking intentions.

BREAKING DOWN INTERACTIONS

As we have noted, interactions indicate that the relationship between one predictor (X1, primary predictor) and the criterion (Y) varies as a function of the other variable (X2, moderator). To better understand the "nature" of the interaction, researchers routinely follow up an

Panel A

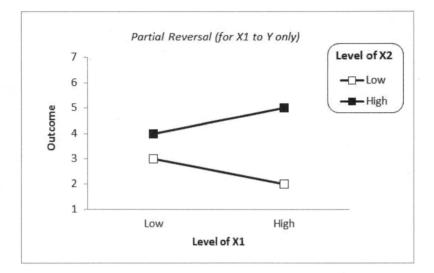

Panel B

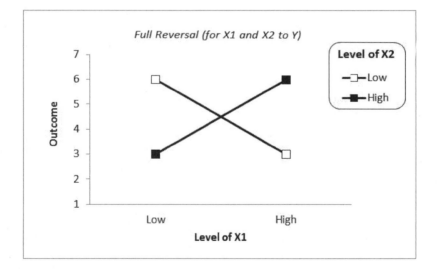

Partial and full reversal interactions.

interaction by conducting simple slope analyses (if the predictor is a continuous variable) or simple effect tests (if the primary "predictor" is an experimentally manipulated variable). In theory, it is possible to conduct two types of follow-ups: One can either test the effect of X1 on Y at different levels of X2, or the effect of X2 on Y at different levels of X1. Alternatively, it is not uncommon that a researcher will conduct both sets of follow-up analyses. Ultimately, the nature of the follow-ups one chooses is importantly determined by one's theory and, relatedly, the form of the interaction one expects, a point we will underscore in our discussion of the illustrations in this chapter.

TESTING FOR MEDIATED MODERATION

With a detailed discussion of moderation in place, we now briefly consider how to test for mediated moderation. To recall, mediated moderation is a technique used to understand why an interaction occurs (i.e., what mediates the interaction between X1 and X2 in predicting Y). Restated, mediated moderation is most likely to be of interest when a researcher has first identified an interaction of interest (theoretically or empirically) and is consequently interested in understanding why that interaction occurs. As an example, consider the theoretical models at the heart of our three mediated moderation illustrations, depicted in Figure 8.5.

In our first illustration, Little, McNulty, and Russell (2010) sought to answer two key questions. First, can frequent sex buffer the negative impact of an insecure attachment on relationship satisfaction? And second, might perceptions of partner availability explain that interaction? These questions implied a mediated moderation model in which (a) frequency of sex moderated the relationship between insecure attachment and relationship satisfaction (the primary interaction); (b) frequency of sex moderated the relationship between insecure attachment and perceptions of partner availability; and (c) once controlled, perceptions of partner availability explained the primary interaction of interest.

In our second illustration, Okimoto and Brescoll (2010) were interested in whether power-seeking intentions were harmful for female (but not male) politicians (i.e., led to reduced intentions to vote for the candidate) and whether the interaction between power-seeking intentions and candidate gender was mediated by a collection of cognitive and affective mediators (i.e., perceived communality, agency, and competence as well as moral outrage against the candidate).

In the final illustration, Paharia, Keinan, Avery, and Schor (2011) aimed to determine whether the tendency for consumers to be more likely to purchase brands that express an "underdog biography" was

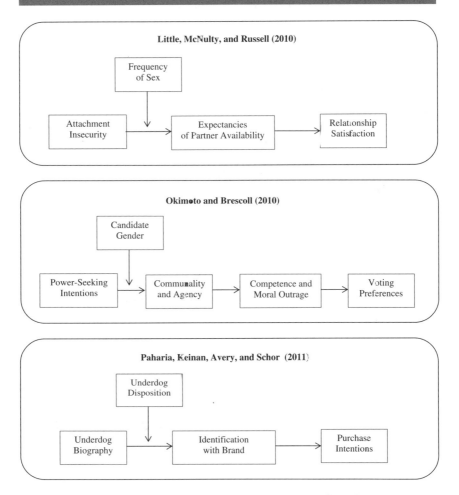

FIGURE 8.5

Theoretical models underlying illustrations of mediated moderation.

stronger among consumers scoring high on an "underdog disposition" and whether this Underdog Brand × Underdog Disposition interaction could be explained by heightened feelings of identification with the brand.

As can be seen, one common feature of the mediated moderation models shown in Figure 8.5 is that the moderator affects the strength of the relationship between the primary predictor and the mediating variable. This implies that there is an interaction between the primary predictor and the moderator on both the mediator and the final outcome, and once the mediator is controlled statistically, the significance of the primary interaction is reduced or eliminated.

An examination of the literature reveals several approaches to testing for mediated moderation. One approach involves estimating a series of three regressions (Muller et al., 2005). Regression 1 tests for the primary hypothesized interaction between X1 and X2 in predicting Y. Regression 2 tests for the hypothesized interaction between X1 and X2 in predicting the mediator. Regression 3 explores how the primary interaction established in Regression 1 is reduced or eliminated when the mediator and the interaction between the mediator and moderator are entered into the equation. According to Muller et al. (2005), in Regression 3, the primary interaction should become non-significant or "less significant," and one or both of the two new terms (mediator, mediator x moderator) should be significant. An example of this approach can be found in Paharia et al.'s (2011) illustration in this chapter.

A second approach involves multiplying the coefficients from two regressions to arrive at an estimate of the indirect effect of the interaction on the primary outcome via the mediator (MacKinnon, Fritz, Williams, & Lockwood, 2007). Regression 1 involves estimating the interaction between X1 and X2 in predicting the mediator, whereas Regression 2 involves estimating the relationship between the mediator and the final outcome variable. An example of this approach can be found in Little et al.'s (2010) illustration in this chapter.

A final approach involves using bootstrapping procedures to estimate the strength of the indirect effect from the hypothesized interaction to the final outcome measure via the proposed mediator (or mediators; e.g., Shrout & Bolger, 2002). An example of this approach can be found in Okimoto and Brescoll's (2010) paper on backlash against female politicians in this chapter.

TESTING FOR MODERATED MEDIATION

Moderated mediation is the focus when the researcher has first identified (empirically or theoretically) a mediational model of interest and is subsequently interested in determining whether the fit of the mediation model (or strength of the indirect effect) varies as a function of a moderator. More formally stated, the essential argument in moderated mediation is that the hypothesized mediation effect (X → Me → Y) varies as a function of a moderator variable (Mo). Often, the moderator is a fourth variable, but it is also possible for the primary predictor (X) to serve as a moderator of the Me → Y relationship, as the article by Wiedemann, Shüz, Sniehotta, Scholz, and Schwarzer (2009) illustrates in this chapter. Moreover, because the indirect effect conceptually represents the *product* of the two proximal paths (X → Me and Me → Y), it is

FIGURE 8.6

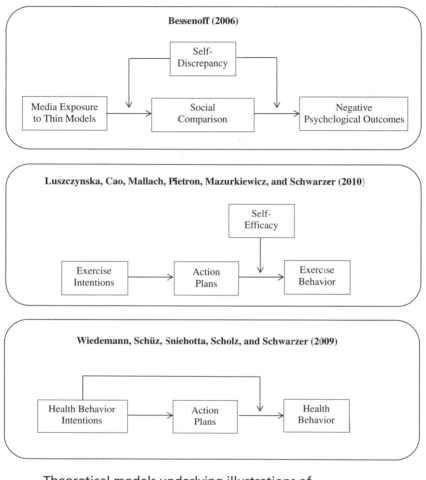

Theoretical models underlying illustrations of
moderated mediation.

important to note that moderation (of the indirect effect) may occur at
Stage 1 (X → Me) or Stage 2 (Me → Y), or both. As shown in Figure 8.6,
the articles we selected as illustrations of moderated mediation reflect
these three different approaches.

Bessenoff (2006), for example, was interested in how social comparison processes mediate the impact of exposure to thin models on
negative psychological outcomes (e.g., depression). Prior to her work,
research had provided mixed support for the mediating role of social
comparison processes. Bessenoff argued that conflicting support for the

mediation model may be due to the presence of a theoretically relevant moderator (ideal vs. actual self-discrepancy). Specifically, as we explain in more detail next, Bessenoff proposed a moderated mediation model that suggested the negative impact of exposure to thin models on social comparison and the impact of social comparison on negative psychological outcomes would be stronger when a woman's level of self-discrepancy was high (i.e., self-discrepancy moderated both paths in the mediation model).

As can be seen in the second panel of Figure 8.6, Luszczynska et al. (2010) focused on how action plans mediate the relationship between exercise intentions and physical activity. Luszczynska et al. also proposed that action plans are most likely to lead to actual exercise when perceptions of self-efficacy are high. Thus, in this case, moderated mediation involved a moderator (self-efficacy) acting on the strength of Stage 2 in the mediation model.

Finally, as can be seen in the final panel of Figure 8.6, Wiedemann et al. (2009) began by focusing on a core mediation model that suggested that health behavior intentions (for physical activity and interdental hygiene) lead to action plans, which in turn lead to engagement in the health behaviors of interest. More important for our purposes here, Wiedemann and colleagues suggested that actions plans were most likely to lead to actual health behaviors when intentions were high. In other words, in this case, moderated mediation involved the primary predictor (X) moderating the Stage 2 relationship of the mediation model.

As was the case with mediated moderation, researchers have used a number of techniques to test for moderated mediation (for reviews, see Edwards & Lambert, 2007; Preacher et al., 2007). One common approach is the moderated causal steps approach (Edwards & Lambert, 2007). This approach involves a series of regressions, for example, to determine whether the moderator impacts the strength of the relevant paths (or stages) within the moderated mediation model. Examples of this approach can be found in the chapter's illustrations by Bessenoff (2006) and Luszczynska et al. (2010). Another approach is based on Preacher et al.'s (2007) suggestion that moderated mediation models be treated as "conditional indirect effects." Treated as such, researchers can perform a bootstrapping analysis to estimate the distribution of the indirect effect, derive confidence intervals for the indirect effect, and determine ranges of the moderator variable for which the indirect is significant. Complementing this approach, researchers can then graphically depict the "confidence bands" around the indirect effect as a function of the moderator, an adaptation of the P. O. Johnson and Neyman (1936) technique. An example of this approach is provided by Wiedemann et al. (2009).

Illustrations: Mediated Moderation

SEX, ATTACHMENT INSECURITY, PERCEIVED PARTNER AVAILABILITY, AND RELATIONSHIP SATISFACTION

In 2010, Little, McNulty, and Russell published a paper exploring whether frequency of sex and sexual satisfaction could buffer the negative relationship between insecure attachment and relationship satisfaction. The authors also identified and tested one theoretically relevant mechanism that could explain (or mediate) the Sex × Attachment Insecurity interaction, namely, expectancies of partner availability.

The authors rooted their work in theory and research on secure versus anxious versus avoidant attachment styles and sex. The authors began by reviewing Mikulincer and Shaver's (2003) model of attachment activation, which suggests the reason insecurely attached people experience less satisfaction in relationships is that they respond ineffectively when their attachment systems become activated (e.g., during a separation or fight). Whereas securely attached partners may still feel confident in their partner's ability and ultimately seek closeness, anxiously attached people may fear being abandoned and thus continually search for signs of potential abandonment, and avoidant partners may simply withdraw, with both strategies leading to lower relationship satisfaction. With this logic in place, the authors then posed the (buffering, moderation) question: What might happen if the attachment systems of anxious and avoidant types could be reduced, and what might reduce the likelihood of such attachment system activation? To answer these questions, they turned to research on the benefits of sex (i.e., enhanced feelings of closeness). Combining these lines of research led to their primary mediated moderation hypothesis, namely that frequent and satisfying sex buffers the negative impact of insecure attachment on relationship satisfaction because frequent and satisfying sex leads to heightened perceptions of partner availability (and thus, reduced activation of the attachment system). Restated, the authors argued that positive expectancies of partner availability mediate the hypothesized interaction between frequency of sex and attachment insecurity.

To test their mediated moderation hypothesis, the authors recruited two groups of newlyweds for a 7-day diary study. During Phase 1, participants completed an attachment scale yielding scores on attachment styles' two major underlying dimensions (anxiety and avoidance; Brennan, Clark, & Shaver, 1998), reported the frequency with which they had sex over the previous 30 days and rated their marital satisfaction and expectations of their partner's availability. On every day of the subsequent week, each partner rated his or her sexual satisfaction, relationship satisfaction, and expectation of partner availability on the next day.

Because of the nonindependent nature of the data (repeated measurements from husbands and wives), the authors used multilevel modeling to test their interaction hypothesis. In line with their reasoning, results revealed two "buffering" interactions. First, frequency of sex buffered the negative relationship between attachment anxiety and relationship satisfaction, such that the relationship between attachment anxiety and relationship satisfaction was eliminated when sex was frequent. Similarly, more satisfying sex buffered the negative relationship between attachment avoidance and relationship satisfaction, such that the relationship between attachment avoidance and relationship satisfaction was eliminated when sex was more satisfying. Additional analyses, using procedures outlined by MacKinnon, Fritz, Williams, and Lockwood (2007), established that the interactions just described between insecure attachment dimensions and sex on relationship satisfaction were mediated by perceptions of partner availability, supporting the mediated moderation hypothesis.

Little et al.'s (2010) paper provides an effective illustration of how researchers can use strong theory and methods to build and evaluate a mediated moderation model in a practically meaningful context. The authors highlighted the importance of attachment insecurity and used attachment activation theory to reason that factors that enhance partner availability might prevent activation of the attachment system, with corresponding benefits for insecurely attached partners. The use of a diary study further strengthened the findings by allowing the authors to test the hypothesized mediated moderation model using two conceptually related sets of model variables (static and ongoing relationship satisfaction and expectations of partner availability, and two dimensions of sex, frequency and quality).

POWER SEEKING AND BACKLASH AGAINST FEMALE POLITICIANS

In 2010, Okimoto and Brescoll published a paper aiming to gain insight into why women are underrepresented in positions of political power. The authors immediately capture readers' attention with a quote from a *Los Angeles Times* article suggesting that Hillary Clinton may face obstacles in her bid for the presidency because "many voters see [her] as coldly ambitious" (p. 923). Using data from 2009, the authors subsequently cited the large discrepancy between men and women in the House (15% women) and Senate (17% women), and then posed their key question: What might explain this imbalance?

The authors hypothesized that one of the reasons women may face obstacles in getting elected is that voters apply different standards to the power-seeking intentions of male and female candidates. More specifically, although voters may approve of a male politician who expresses power-seeking intentions, they may show backlash against female politicians who are perceived to have, or directly express, power-seeking intentions. The authors built support for their hypothesis by reviewing the literature on gender stereotypes, which suggests that men are expected to (and "ought to") act in an agentic manner, whereas women are expected to (and "ought to") act in a communal manner, and citing literature indicating that women often experience negative consequences when they act in a manner inconsistent with these stereotypes. The authors then noted the lack of research exploring whether women will experience similar backlash when they simply express power-seeking intentions (rather than actually engage in power-seeking behavior) and the absence of research exploring these issues within the political domain. Ultimately, the authors advance a theoretical model suggesting that gender of the political candidate will interact with (perceived or expressed) power-seeking intentions such that female candidates who seek power will be judged to have a "communal deficit," which in turn will lead to moral outrage (contempt and disgust) and reduced willingness to vote for the candidate; by contrast, power-seeking male candidates will not experience these negative consequences.

To test their hypotheses, the authors conducted two studies. In the first study, participants read experimenter-generated webpage biographies of two state senators (one male, one female). The biographies did not include political affiliation or pictures, and the descriptions were counterbalanced (i.e., Descriptions A and B were based on a female politician half the time, and vice versa). After viewing the biographies, participants indicated whom they would vote for, the extent to which they believed each candidate expressed a desire for power, and their own political orientation. Results revealed the anticipated interaction between sex of politician and perceived power-seeking intentions: Perceived power seeking was negatively related to likelihood of voting for the female (but not the male) candidate.

In Study 2, the authors extended their original study by manipulating (vs. measuring) power-seeking intentions and measuring the variables (perceived communality, agency, competence, and moral outrage) hypothesized to mediate the primary (candidate sex × power-seeking intentions) interaction on voting intentions. Results revealed the anticipated interaction on voting intentions: Participants were less likely to vote for a female candidate when she did (vs. did not) express power-seeking intentions, whereas the opposite was true for male candidates. In addition, when female candidates expressed power-seeking intentions, they were seen as less communal and participants expressed more moral outrage, whereas stated power-seeking intentions had no effects within male candidates. Finally, a series of multiple regression analyses revealed that when perceived communality and agency were entered into the model, the primary interaction between sex of candidate and expressed power-seeking intentions became nonsignificant, and a path analysis showed good fit for the mediated moderation model (interaction → communality and agency → moral outrage and competence → voting intentions).

Okimoto and Brescoll's (2010) paper provides a very nice illustration of the value of the mediated moderation paradigm and high-quality research in general. The authors immediately help readers appreciate the practical and theoretical importance of their studies; provide a concise and logical review of the literature to motivate their model; point out specific gaps in the literature and how their work fills those gaps; use multiple methods; and provide clear support for their prediction that the interaction between candidate sex and power-seeking intentions (or backlash against female politicians) is due to the judging of power-seeking female candidates as less communal, which evokes moral outrage and a reduced willingness to vote for the candidate.

IDENTIFYING WITH AND SUPPORTING THE UNDERDOG

In 2011, Paharia, Keinan, Avery, and Schor highlighted the prevalence of "underdog biographies" in the marketplace and set out to understand how (and why) underdog biographies impact consumers. Broadly defined, *brand biographies* reflect "an unfolding story that chronicles the brand's origins, life experiences, and evolution over time in a selectively constructed story" (p. 776) whereas *underdog biographies* "tell stories about entrepreneurs of humble origins who struggle against the odds to build their brands and businesses through sheer will and determination, despite lacking the resources of their well-endowed competitors" (pp. 776–777). As the authors illustrated, underdog biographies can be found in fiction (e.g., Rocky Balboa, a struggling boxer aiming to make it big) and nonfiction (e.g., Nantucket Nectars, the juice company said to have been started "with only a blender and a dream") and are often used strategically to attract and retain customers. Equally important, the authors argued, is that although people enjoy being associated with winners, they also love underdogs. The key question is, why?

The authors addressed this question by advancing an identification-based explanation. They first reviewed research indicating that consumers are more likely to form stronger connections with a brand if they can identify with the brand and then showed that consumers from the United States are, in general, more likely to view themselves (as opposed to others) as underdogs. Accordingly, the authors argued that consumers respond favorably to underdog brands because they strongly identify with them. They also assumed that people differ in the tendency to view themselves as underdogs on the basis of an underdog disposition and culture, with U.S. consumers more likely than East Asian consumers to favor the underdog.

The authors tested their reasoning using a series of studies, three of which use mediated moderation. They began by introducing their 18-item underdog scale, based on two underlying dimensions: (a) external disadvantage (e.g., "I've had to struggle more than others to get where I am in my life") and (b) passion and determination (e.g., "I always stay determined even when I lose"). Crossing the two dimensions, the authors identified and validated four prototypes: the victim (high disadvantage, low passion; homeless person), the underdog (high disadvantage, high passion; Rocky), the top dog (low disadvantage, low passion; Donald Trump), and the privileged achiever (low disadvantage, high passion; Paris Hilton).

The authors next tested the hypothesis that underdog biographies impact consumers favorably via heightened identification with the brand. In Study 1, participants read a top dog or an underdog brand biography, rated their identification with the company and purchase intentions, and completed the underdog scale. Results revealed the predicted interaction between brand biography and underdog disposition, such that the underdog disposition was positively related to purchase intentions and identification in the underdog condition but not the top dog condition. Mediated moderation analyses further showed that the interaction on purchase intentions was mediated via identification with the brand. In Study 2, participants read brand biographies corresponding to one of the four prototypes (victim, underdog, top dog, privileged achiever) and rated their purchase intentions and identification with the brand. Results revealed stronger identification with and purchase intentions for the underdog brand and showed the interaction on purchase intentions was mediated via identification. In Study 3, participants from the United States and Singapore read an underdog or top dog brand biography and rated identification with and purchase intentions toward the brand. As predicted, U.S. consumers showed stronger identification and purchase intentions for the underdog than the top dog brand, whereas no differences emerged in participants from Singapore. Mediated moderation analyses further supported the prediction that the Biography × Culture interaction on purchase intentions was mediated via identification. In Study 4, the authors showed that people (from the United States) are more likely to actually select a product from a company with an underdog (vs. top dog) biography.

Paharia et al.'s (2011) article is an excellent illustration of mediated moderation and many of the other elements described in this book that support a high-quality paper. The historical underdog illustrations immediately pique the reader's interest. The theoretical reasoning underlying the mediated moderation model is well articulated. The introduction of individual differences and cultural differences helps expand the theoretical and practical value of the paper. And the use of multiple methods, including an actual choice task, provides confidence in the reliability and generalizability of the results.

Illustrations: Moderated Mediation

SELF-DISCREPANCY MAGNIFIES THE IMPACT OF EXPOSURE TO THIN MODELS

In 2006, Bessenoff proposed a moderated mediation model to explain how exposure to thin models impacts a host of negative psychological outcomes, including weight concerns, depression, and low self-esteem within women. Bessenoff began by suggesting that exposure to thin models activates social comparison processes (Path 1) which in turn predicts the negative outcomes just noted (Path 2). Restated, Bessenoff's core model was a mediation model (exposure to thin models → social comparison processes → negative psychological outcomes). As Bessenoff noted, although some previous research had supported the basic mediation model, other studies had failed to find support for at least one of the paths in the model. This variability in findings suggested that the strength of the two key paths in the mediation model may be affected by theoretically relevant moderators. In particular, Bessenoff argued that the two key paths would likely be stronger among women who reported a high discrepancy between their actual and ideal body self-images.

To test this moderated mediation model, Bessenoff (2006) conducted an experiment using female psychology students. Several weeks prior to the study, participants completed a scale assessing the extent to which they were high or low on actual-ideal body self-image. In the primary study, participants were randomly assigned to one of two thin-ideal media conditions. Participants in the thin-ideal condition were exposed to eight clothing advertisements featuring thin female models, and those in the control condition were exposed to eight ads for nonclothing products that did not feature thin models. Participants evaluated the products featured in the ads; completed scales assessing mood, depression, and state self-esteem; and listed the thoughts they had after being exposed to the ads, including thoughts about social comparison and weight-regulatory activities (e.g., exercising, dieting).

Results from a series of analyses provided good support for Bessenoff's (2006) moderated mediation model. To begin, exposure to the thin-ideal ads led to a larger decrease in self-esteem and increase in weight-related thoughts, weight-regulatory thoughts, and negative mood among those high in actual-ideal self-discrepancy, a pattern consistent with the overall moderated mediation model. Bessenoff next tested the basic mediation model for each of the key dependent variables. In sum, Bessenoff found that social comparison processes either fully mediated, or partially mediated, the effect of exposure to the thin-ideal ads on self-esteem, depression, weight-related thoughts, and weight-regulation thoughts. With these findings in place, Bessenoff conducted a series of regression analyses to test for moderated mediation. Consistent with the first part of Bessenoff's model, results showed that the impact of exposure to thin-ideal ads on social comparison processes was stronger among women high in self-discrepancy. Confirming the second part of her model, social comparison processes, in turn, were more strongly related to weight-regulatory thoughts, depression, and reduced self-esteem among women high in self-discrepancy.

In sum, Bessenoff's (2006) work illustrated moderated mediation by showing that exposure to thin media ideals is much more likely to lead to social comparison processes among women who perceive a high discrepancy between their actual and ideal body image (moderation of Path 1) and that thoughts of social comparison are more strongly related to a host of negative outcomes within this same group (moderation of Path 2). In so doing, Bessenoff's article serves as a useful example of how researchers can use moderated mediation to test theoretically and practically important questions.

GOOD INTENTIONS PREDICT PLANS TO EXERCISE, BUT PLANS ONLY LEAD TO BEHAVIOR WHEN SELF-EFFICACY IS HIGH

In 2010, Luszczynska, Cao, Mallach, Pietron, Mazurkiewicz, and Schwarzer set out to test a moderated mediation model designed to explain the physical activity levels of Chinese and Polish adolescents. To motivate their article, the authors first reviewed the short- and long-term benefits of exercise alongside the troubling recent decline in adolescents' physical activity levels. As the authors noted, to follow recommended guidelines for exercise, it is helpful to form intentions. Yet, as the authors also observed, intentions do not always translate into action. To understand why, the authors articulated a moderated mediation model stressing the key role of planning and self-efficacy beliefs.

To begin, according to Luszczynska and her colleagues (2010), it is important to recognize that intentions have an indirect, rather than a direct effect, on physical activity. More specifically, intentions lead to plans and plans lead to behavior. With that said, the authors were quick to point out that plans do not always translate into action, and previous studies yielded some inconsistent findings regarding whether plans mediate the intention–behavior relationship. The authors also pointed out that the *intention-planning-action* mediation sometimes holds in one population, but not in another, suggesting that the indirect (mediated) path is likely to be altered by theoretically relevant moderators.

In this article, the authors focused on how self-efficacy beliefs would moderate the link between planning and behavior because "people harboring self-doubts might fail to act upon their plans" (Luszczynska et al., 2010, p. 268). This reasoning positioned self-efficacy as a moderator of the second path in the mediation model (planning to behavior), setting up a logical series of regression analyses, described next.

To test their model, the authors conducted two longitudinal studies. In Study 1, a sample of Chinese adolescents completed measures assessing intention to exercise and actual exercise (at Time 1), and then, 1 month later, scales assessing coping planning (planning to exercise despite obstacles such as bad weather), recovery self-efficacy (the belief that one can restart an exercise program if circumstances make a person stop, temporarily), and self-reported exercise behavior over the past month. To analyze the data, the authors used a program developed by Preacher et al. (2007): MODMEDC (Version 1; Model 3). Results from a series of multiple regression analyses revealed strong support for the authors' moderated mediation model: (a) Intentions predicted planning and correlated with Time 2 activity; (b) Time 1 activity, and Time 2 self-efficacy, planning, and their interaction predicted Time 2 activity (with planning showing a stronger relationship with activity as self-efficacy levels rose); and (c) when the predictors just noted (on Step 2) were entered into the model, intentions no longer predicted Time 2 activity. Restated, the indirect (intentions-planning-action) effect was only significant when self-efficacy reached an appropriately high level.

In an effort to extend the cross-cultural generalizability of their findings, the authors conducted a second longitudinal study drawing on a sample of Polish adolescents and using a different set of measures to tap related constructs (e.g., action planning as opposed to coping planning and maintenance self-efficacy as opposed to recovery self-efficacy). Consistent with their initial findings, the indirect (intentions-planning-action) effect was only significant at high levels of self-efficacy.

In sum, Luszczynska and her colleagues (2010) tested a clear and theoretically meaningful moderated mediation model predicting physical activity levels of adolescents that showed that the indirect effect of intentions on actions (via planning) is moderated by self-efficacy. Readers interested in setting up and testing moderated mediation models will find this article an extremely helpful guide. The article contains a clear logic, an easy to understand conceptual diagram, and a systematic approach to the analytic procedures, all couched within an important theoretical and practical domain.

STRONG EXERCISE AND INTERDENTAL HYGIENE INTENTIONS "CATALYZE" ACTION PLANS INTO ACTION

In 2009, Wiedemann, Schüz, Sniehotta, Scholz, and Schwarzer proposed and tested a moderated mediation model to predict physical activity and interdental hygiene. Wiedemann and her colleagues argued that to understand why intentions do not always translate into behavior, researchers must consider "individual differences in post-intentional processes of goal pursuit and action planning" (p. 67). In particular, the authors proposed the need to develop a parsimonious moderated mediation model in which the second path in the core mediation model (*intentions → action planning → behavior*) is moderated by the strength of the initial intentions (i.e., more significant when intentions are strong).

Wiedemann and her colleagues (2009) advanced two lines of reasoning for why intentions should moderate (i.e., catalyze) the relationship between action planning and behavior. First, high intentions lead to a deeper encoding of the situational cue related to the action plan, as well as the connection between the cue and the desired response. This, in turn, leads a person's "if–then" contingency plans to become more efficacious. Second, high intentions lead if–then plans to be more specific, which in turn, leads them to be more effective. To test their model, the researchers conducted two longitudinal studies using samples of German adults.

Study 1 focused on physical activity levels within the context of cardiac rehabilitation. At Time 1, participants completed scales assessing intentions to engage in physical activity and relevant action plans (e.g., "I have developed a specific plan on where to exercise"). Four months later, participants completed a self-reported physical activity scale.

To provide evidence for moderated mediation, the researchers first established that intentions predicted action planning and action planning partially mediated the effect of intentions on physical activity. Next, the authors conducted a series of analyses to test for moderated mediation. To begin, they estimated a regression model including intentions, action planning, and the interaction between intentions and action planning. Consistent with their moderated mediation model, this analysis revealed a significant interaction between intentions and action planning. Next, the authors estimated the significance of bootstrapped indirect effects estimates at low (−1SD), medium (mean), and high (+1SD) levels of intentions. Results revealed that the indirect effect (intentions → action planning → activity) was only significant at medium and high levels of intentions, providing additional insight into the nature of the moderated mediation model. Finally, to illustrate the significance of the indirect effect as a function of intentions, the authors graphed the confidence interval around the mean indirect effect as a function of intentions (see Wiedemann et al., 2009, Figure 3, p. 73).

To cross-validate their model, the authors subsequently conducted a second study applying the model to interdental hygiene (flossing). At Time 1, participants completed scales assessing intention to engage in interdental hygiene and action planning and were given appropriate tools and instructions on how to engage in the target behavior. Three months later, participants self-reported how often they engaged in the target behavior.

Similar to Study 1, Wiedemann et al. (2009) first established that intentions predicted action planning, and action planning partially mediated the effect of intentions on behavior. Second, using regression analysis, the authors showed that intentions and action planning interacted to predict interdental hygiene behavior. Finally, they estimated the significance of the bootstrapped indirect effect at low, medium, and high levels of intentions. Consistent with their model, results revealed that the strength of the (intention → planning → behavior) indirect effect became stronger as intentions increased, though in this study, the indirect effect was significant at all three levels of intentions. The authors once again graphed the confidence bands around their indirect effects as a function of intentions, facilitating an interpretation of the moderated mediation findings.

Wiedemann and colleagues' (2009) work provides a useful model for articulating and testing moderated mediation models. The authors clearly explained how the basic mediation model is likely to be moderated, and they provided a systematic four-step approach to the moderated mediation analysis by which they (a) established basic mediation, (b) established the interaction between the moderator and mediator, (c) showed that the bootstrapped indirect effect varies as a function of the moderator, and (d) displayed the confidence intervals around the indirect effect as a function of the moderator. Related to the final point, another feature of the paper that stands out is that rather than testing the indirect effect only at arbitrary levels of the moderator (−1SD, mean, +1SD), the authors used a continuous moderator approach, which made it possible to show (in the figures) the strength of the indirect effect at *all values* of the moderator in the dataset and to identify the threshold at which the indirect effect becomes significant.

Conclusion

An important goal of research is to understand when and why a phenomenon occurs. Answering these questions, in turn, rests on a firm understanding of moderation (which helps identify the conditions under which an effect is more or less likely to occur) and mediation (which deals with why certain effects occur). Increasingly, researchers are also combining moderation and mediation into the same design and testing more sophisticated models using mediated moderation and moderated mediation.

In this chapter, we illustrated mediated moderation with three examples, including research aimed at understanding why frequency of sex moderates the impact of attachment insecurity on relationship satisfaction (i.e., through expectations of partner availability; Little et al., 2010), why power-seeking intentions lead to backlash against female (but not male) politicians (i.e., through a perceived communal deficit; Okimoto & Brescoll, 2010), and why dispositional underdogs support brands with an underdog biography (i.e., via identification with the underdog brand; Paharia et al., 2011). This chapter also illustrated moderated mediation. These illustrations showed that self-discrepancy magnifies the impact of exposure to thin models on social comparison and the impact of social comparison on negative psychological outcomes (Bessenoff, 2006); good intentions lead to plans to exercise, but plans to exercise only predict actual exercise when self-efficacy is high (Luszczynska et al., 2010); and strong exercise and dental hygiene intentions magnify the impact of action plans into action (Wiedemann et al., 2009). Researchers whose primary aim is to understand why an interaction occurs, or when a mediation model holds, can refer to these examples as a source for ideas on how to conceptualize and analyze models containing a mix of mediation and moderation.

Author Interviews

| Highlighted Author | What is your advice for publishing high-quality research that is likely to have impact? | What additional "moderated mediation" paper would you recommend and why? |

Gayle R. Bessenoff
Associate Professor, Department of Psychology, Southern Connecticut State University, New Haven

I don't think a researcher should go into a project with the intent to publish high-impact research. I strongly believe in researching what one is genuinely interested in learning about. That said, having high impact seems to depend mainly on citation rates—so one needs to take into account where the paper would have the widest relevant audience and also get as much PR as possible. One way to do this is to have one's home institution (e.g., university, research company) put out a press release.

I recommend Baron and Kenny (1986) and Muller, Judd, and Yzerbyt (2005) for excellent theoretical and statistical writings on mediators and moderators.

Aleksandra Luszczynska
Professor of Psychology, University of Social Sciences and Humanities, Wroclaw, Poland, and Associate Research Professor at Trauma, Health, and Hazards Center at University of Colorado at Colorado Springs

Think of burning issues that are in the "Pasteur quadrant": research that targets basic issues (or understanding of fundamental scientific problems) but, at the same time, seeks to be eventually beneficial to society. Luckily, the majority of scientific disciplines have some burning issues within their Pasteur quadrant.

I like the experimental study by Gholami and her coauthors, published in 2013 in *Appetite*. Applying the moderated mediation approach, Gholami et al. show that her behavior change intervention is effective. Further, she provides arguments why this health behavior change intervention works ("why" is explained by testing the underlying mediating processes) and for whom it works (testing age as a variable that moderates this mediation).

Highlighted Author

James McNulty
Associate Professor,
Department of
Psychology, Florida
State University,
Tallahassee

What is your advice for publishing high-quality research that is likely to have impact?

I think the most important thing to do is start with an important question. Let that question guide your research. For us, the question was "How can insecure people remain happy with their relationships?" Then, use existing theories to try to answer that question.

What additional "mediated moderation" paper would you recommend and why?

Readers interested in other papers on mediated moderation may enjoy McNulty and Russell (2010). This paper examines whether certain spouses, namely, those facing more frequent and severe problems, benefit from engaging in problem-solving behaviors typically assumed to be negative during interactions with their partners. The research demonstrates that the severity of the problems spouses tend to face in their relationship moderates the effects of their tendencies to blame, command, and reject their partners during discussions, such that these behaviors are associated with steeper declines in satisfaction among spouses facing relatively minor problems on average, but with more stable satisfaction among spouses facing more severe problems on average. Further, consistent with the idea that these behaviors can help spouses who face more severe problems by motivating their partner to change, this interactive effect was mediated by changes in the severity of the problems themselves.

Highlighted Author

Tyler Okimoto
Senior Lecturer, UQ
Business School,
The University of
Queensland, Brisbane,
Australia

What is your advice for publishing high-quality research that is likely to have impact?

Maintain your curiosity for understanding social behavior, and pursue the questions that you are passionate about. If you notice an interesting social phenomenon in your daily life, it is probably intriguing because it does not yet fit into your theoretical understanding of the world. And if the questions you pursue are also important to you and to society more broadly, your search for understanding (combined with good research design and statistics training) will lead to work with high potential for impact.

What additional "mediated moderation" paper would you recommend and why?

Mediated moderation techniques can make for more impactful work by revealing both psychological processes and important outcomes. Theoretically derived conditional effects (i.e., moderation) shown on key psychological variables is often the best way to evidence theoretical processes, but those processes only become important when also showing that those psychological variables have downstream behavioral consequences. An excellent paper that also uses mediated moderation techniques in this way is "Testing a Social-Cognitive Model of Moral Behavior" by Aquino, Freeman, Reed, Lim, and Felps (2009; *Journal of Personality and Social Psychology*). Their work shows that situational triggers interact with moral identity centrality to increase the accessibility of moral identity, which subsequently affects moral behavior. The use of mediated moderation has helped make this contribution impactful by offering theoretical precision, while also relating those processes to important moral outcomes such as social responsibility in business (Study 1) and lying in an employment negotiation (Study 2).

Highlighted Author

Neeru Paharia
Assistant Professor of
Marketing, McDonough
School of Business,
Georgetown University,
Washington, DC

What is your advice for publishing high-quality research that is likely to have impact?

I would say to find a real-world phenomenon and use that as a starting point. It is harder, and messier, but in the end you may find that you have come up with something that really resonates with people.

What additional "high-quality" paper would you recommend and why?

One additional high-impact paper I would recommend, an example of the innovative method paradigm covered in Chapter 11, is by Kronrod, Grinstein, and Wathieu (2012) in the *Journal of Marketing* titled, "Go Green! Should Environmental Messages Be So Assertive?" This paper uses Study 3 to see whether people are more or less likely to click on an assertive environmental message. I think that's very clever!

Highlighted Author

Amelie U. Wiedemann
Dr. phil. at the Division
of Health Psychology,
Department of
Education and
Psychology, Freie
Universität, Berlin,
Germany

What is your advice for publishing high-quality research that is likely to have impact?

If you introduce new methods, allow them enough space in your work and explain them step-by-step in easy language and with sufficient detail for replication. That helps convince both reviewers and readers. And take challenging coauthors on board that function as devil's advocate. Further, cross-validating novel findings in unrelated data sets, as we did in our study, provides confidence in findings.

What additional "moderated mediation" paper would you recommend and why?

The processes that guide human behavior are complex. If we restrict our thinking to simple mediation or moderation models, we are not doing justice to this complexity. Combining mediation and moderation assumptions and testing them in integrative models is a step toward a more fine-grained investigation of the processes that guide human behavior. In his book, *Introduction to Mediation, Moderation, and Conditional Process Modeling* (Hayes, 2013), and several accompanying papers, Andrew Hayes explains the concepts of moderation, mediation, moderated mediation, and mediated moderation and uses easy-to-follow examples to explain statistical approaches for their analyses. A must-read for researchers of all subdisciplines of psychology.

Develop a New Tool to Assess Individual Differences

9

Background

Researchers in many disciplines have long been interested in the role of individual differences—and for good reason, given that personality is an important source of variance and a meaningful moderator of the impact of the situation on thoughts, feelings, and behavior.[1] To date, researchers have developed scales to measure hundreds of individual difference constructs (for reviews, see Bearden, Netemeyer, & Haws, 2011; Haugtvedt, Liu, & Min, 2008; Leary & Hoyle, 2009; Robinson, Shaver, & Wrightsman, 1991). Despite this plethora of constructs, researchers continue to develop scales to measure new individual difference constructs or improve

[1]As one reviewer rightly noted, certain disciplines place less emphasis on individual differences and may even marginalize them. Accordingly, readers should recognize that the paradigm covered in this chapter is most relevant to and beneficial within those disciplines where individual differences are recognized as important sources of variance.

http://dx.doi.org/10.1037/14525-010
How to Publish High-Quality Research, by J. Joireman and P. A. M. Van Lange

existing scales. If you are able to identify and assess a truly novel individual difference construct, or significantly improve an existing scale, you stand a good chance of making a significant contribution in the field.

In this chapter, we discuss the most important issues involved in developing an individual difference scale and establishing its validity. Our emphasis is conceptual rather than mathematical, as our goal is to provide readers with a broad perspective on how a scale "makes a contribution." Much of our discussion therefore focuses on the relevance of the scale and evidence supporting its validity.

PERSONALITY TAXONOMIES

Before considering key steps for developing an individual difference scale, we set the context for the discussion by briefly reviewing some broader issues in the field of personality taxonomies. We do this because understanding where the field has been can help readers better understand where their new construct fits within the broader scope of personality variables and thus how their construct/scale can make a contribution to the field.

Obviously, personality variables can be viewed from a broadband perspective (e.g., extraversion) or a narrowband perspective (e.g., need for cognition). Today, two of the best-known broadband taxonomies include the Big Five (for a review, see John, Naumann, & Soto, 2008) and the Alternative Five (Zuckerman, Kuhlman, Joireman, Teta, & Kraft, 1993). The Big Five consists of Agreeableness, Extraversion, Emotional Stability, Conscientiousness, and Openness to Experience, whereas the Alternative Five consists of Aggression–Hostility, Sociability, Neuroticism, Impulsive Unsocialized Sensation Seeking, and Activity. More recently, there is evidence to suggest that personality might perhaps be more accurately described in terms of six rather than five factors. The additional sixth factor in this HEXACO model (Ashton et al., 2004) is called Honesty–Humility, a relatively independent dimension that represents the personality facets of sincerity, fairness, greed avoidance, and modesty.

Whereas the list of broadband taxonomies is relatively small, the range of narrowband personality variables is quite large (for reviews, see Bearden et al., 2011; Leary & Hoyle, 2009; Robinson et al., 1991). Indeed, as Zuckerman (1994) once noted, "Personality traits and tests tend to proliferate like rabbits and it is often difficult to trace their ancestry or relationships with other dimensions of personality" (p. 56). Given that so many narrowband personality scales have already been developed, researchers interested in making a novel contribution to the field should carefully consider how their construct fits within the broadband taxonomies noted and review previous scales to ensure that they are not unnecessarily proliferating the already large number of existing scales.

QUESTIONS USED WHEN EVALUATING TOOLS FOR ASSESSING INDIVIDUAL DIFFERENCES

Whether one is developing a new individual difference assessment tool or improving an earlier one, the elements of successful tool development are quite similar. In a nutshell, when reviewers are asked to evaluate whether a new tool makes a significant contribution to the field, they ask themselves several questions, as summarized in Exhibit 9.1.

To begin, reviewers ask whether the new tool is a meaningful contribution to the literature (vs. a slight adaptation of an existing measure) and whether the scale is theoretically grounded. Reviewers are also interested in whether the scale is internally reliable and stable over time. It is also important to ask whether the new tool shows good convergent validity (correlating with similar constructs) and appropriate discriminant validity (i.e., is not too closely related to similar assessments) and where, as a result, the new construct fits within a broader "nomological net" of existing constructs. With convergent, discriminant, and nomological validity established, reviewers ask whether the tool provides good predictive validity (i.e., whether the tool can predict novel, intriguing, and practically relevant outcomes). In this chapter, we discuss six papers in social psychology and consumer behavior that

---

EXHIBIT 9.1

Questions Used When Evaluating Tools for Assessing Individual Differences

1. Does the tool truly address a gap in the literature, or does it simply represent a slight revision of an existing tool with a new name?
2. Is the tool theoretically grounded, and does it have the potential to fundamentally advance our understanding of an important aspect of human behavior?
3. Is the tool reliable (internally and over time)?
4. Does the tool assess what it is intended to assess? That is, does it show good convergent validity, relating to other measures intended to assess similar constructs?
5. Is the tool distinct from previously published assessments? That is, does it show good discriminant validity with respect to other tools that measure similar constructs?
6. Where does the tool fit within the broader "nomological net" of existing constructs (the broader, overall pattern of existing constructs)?
7. Does the tool predict outcomes it should predict (including theoretically relevant interactions with features of the situation), and does it predict those outcomes above and beyond existing measures?
8. Are the validity data compelling and generalizable? In other words, have the authors made an effort to use different methods to explore whether the tool can predict novel, intriguing, and practically relevant outcomes?

Note. Typically, researchers assess individual differences using self-report scales. However, because individual differences can be assessed using other techniques (e.g., choice tasks; Van Lange, Otten, De Bruin, & Joireman, 1997), we have chosen to use the broader term *tool* in place of *scale*.

successfully address each of these questions. Our discussion centers on both classic and contemporary measures.

BENEFITS OF DEVELOPING INDIVIDUAL DIFFERENCE TOOLS

If scales truly are "proliferating like rabbits" (Zuckerman, 1994, p. 56), why continue to develop them? This is an important question, and one that should be answered before undertaking this (often lengthy) process. From our perspective, developing a tool to assess individual differences offers several benefits. One benefit is that in the process of thinking through how to measure a construct, the researcher can gain greater insight into the underlying construct. It may be, for example, that a researcher will discover that the construct he is trying to assess contains an additional dimension. As an example, researchers often adopted the view that personality is composed of five broad factors (i.e., the Big Five or Alternative Five reviewed earlier). As noted, however, recent research has identified a sixth major dimension of personality called Honesty–Humility, tapping the degree to which a person is sincere, fair, modest, and not greedy (Ashton et al., 2004). No doubt, this sixth dimension of personality will spur a new line of research that will advance our understanding of how personality impacts a person's thoughts, feelings, and actions.

A second benefit is that high-quality tools and scales can improve a researcher's ability to measure and predict phenomena. Highly reliable scales with good validity are more likely to predict relevant outcomes than scales with low reliability and poor validity. Thus, development of (high-quality) scales can improve our ability to predict cognition, emotions, and behavior, thereby contributing to our understanding of psychological processes and behavior.

Third, development of high-quality tools and scales can inspire other researchers to begin studying a topic in new ways and different contexts. As an example, research on time orientation has exploded since the introduction of scales to assess individual differences in concern with future consequences (Strathman, Gleicher, Boninger, & Edwards, 1994, reviewed in this chapter) and time orientation (Zimbardo & Boyd, 1999).

Finally, scale development papers provide tools researchers can often directly use in their studies—for specific hypothesis testing or for exploratory purposes. Over the longer term, scale development papers receive a fair amount of empirical attention and impact, especially when published in top-tier journals. This can help a researcher establish a name for himself or herself in a field and launch a long and productive line of research, with significant impact—if the instrument indeed proves to be valuable.

COSTS OF DEVELOPING INDIVIDUAL DIFFERENCE TOOLS

As we have just noted, developing tools to assess individual differences can be rewarding, but it can also involve some costs, including significant time and effort. To develop a good scale or instrument takes a great deal of work. One must think very carefully about the construct, develop and refine items to tap that construct, and establish its validity. Often, this can take several years, many data collections, and some significant financial investments even before the paper goes out for its first round of reviews.

Another drawback is that the "burden of proof" for researchers introducing a new scale is high. What we mean is that because there is already a large collection of scales in existence, reviewers can sometimes be wary of a new one and may assume that the new scale is nothing more than a new set of items tapping an existing construct. Because reviewers would prefer not to have the same construct floating around under two (or more) different names, reviewers may be reluctant to publish a new scale out of concern that it is unnecessary and may lead to confusion. This does not necessarily preclude developing a new scale, but it does mean the researcher who wants to introduce a new scale should be prepared to clearly explain how his construct is different than existing scales and provide empirical data supporting his or her scale's discriminant and predictive validity (as defined earlier).

Illustrations

GRIT: PERSEVERANCE AND PASSION FOR LONG-TERM GOALS

In 2007, Duckworth, Peterson, Matthews, and Kelly introduced a scale to measure Grit, which the authors defined as "perseverance and passion toward long-term goals" (p. 1087). The authors opened their article with an intriguing quote from William James (1907), who suggested that "compared to what we ought to be, we are only half awake" (p. 322). The implications of this quote for the article are immediately clear: As researchers, we should aim to identify factors that allow people to reach their full potential. Duckworth and colleagues noted that much research addressing this question has focused on the role of IQ, but relatively little has focused on what differentiates people of equal IQ. In an effort to answer that question, Duckworth and colleagues focused on factors that are "essential to success no matter the domain" (p. 1087), in particular, the construct they called Grit. After reviewing past research on factors that predict achievement, including the Big Five taxonomy, the authors concluded that "Grit may be as essential as IQ to high achievement" (p. 1089).

After establishing the importance of Grit, the authors reviewed existing measures that may be able to assess the construct. The authors were very clear that any such measure should be brief and should meet four specific criteria. Specifically, it should have good psychometric properties, have face validity with adolescents and adults, not be susceptible to ceiling effects in high achievers, and accurately reflect the Grit construct. The authors pointed out that many existing measures that might be relevant fail to meet all four of these criteria, establishing the need to develop a new scale to measure Grit.

In their first study, the authors generated an initial pool of 27 items on the basis of interviews with various groups of successful people, which they administered to a large sample of adults. Through exploratory and confirmatory factor analyses, the authors arrived at a reliable and valid 12-item, two-factor solution, with factors assessing "consistency of interests" and "perseverance of effort." Supporting the predictive validity of the Grit, results also showed that Grit scores were higher among respondents with more education and those who are older. A second study showed that these relationships held even after controlling for Conscientiousness, the Big Five trait most highly correlated with Grit, whereas a third study showed that Grit predicted GPA over and above SAT scores, even among an elite sample of undergraduates.

To further evaluate the predictive validity of the Grit, in Study 4, the authors used the Grit to predict whether West Point cadets would make it through a challenging summer training course. Results showed that Grit predicted retention better than trait self-control and incoming composite candidate scores. Grit also predicted the cadets' 1-year "military performance score" above and beyond trait self-control and incoming candidate scores. In Study 5, the authors showed that Grit predicts summer training retention over and above Conscientiousness.

In their final study, the authors showed that Grit predicts how well children ages 7 through 15 perform in a National Spelling Bee championship. Results showed that Grit predicted performance over and above trait self-control and IQ (especially at the highest levels of performance) and that amount of time studying and previous participation in spelling bees mediated that relationship.

Duckworth and colleagues' paper has several features that make it a very nice model for scale development: Grit is couched in the context of the Big Five; Grit predicts achievement over and above conceptually related constructs such as conscientiousness, self-control, and IQ; and the authors used novel, interesting, and practical achievement outcomes, including completion of a rigorous summer training camp among freshman West Point cadets and success within the Scripps National Spelling Bee competition. These favorable properties, and the relevance of Grit for many domains of performance, help to explain why the Grit paper has already had a sizable impact on the field.

NEED FOR COGNITIVE CLOSURE

In 1994, Webster and Kruglanksi introduced an individual difference construct known as the *need for cognitive closure* (NFC), which they defined (p. 1049) as "a desire for '*an* answer on a given topic, *any* [italics in original] answer . . . compared to confusion and ambiguity' (Kruglanski, 1990, p. 337).'" Webster and Kruglanski developed a 42-item scale to measure individual differences in NFC and reported six studies on over 850 participants demonstrating its measurement properties and validity. Considering its large number of citations, Webster and Kruglanski's paper clearly made a significant contribution to the literature. As we illustrate next, much of this impact is due to the quality of their original paper and the relevance of the NFC construct for a wide range of motivated social cognitive processes (e.g., person perception).

One of the key strengths of Webster and Kruglanski's (1994) paper is that it grounded individual differences in NFC within earlier work showing that people varied in the need for closure based on the situation. As the authors noted, the NFC was originally treated as a manipulation check rather than an individual difference variable. For example, prior research had shown that various features of the situation (e.g., time pressure, noise) temporarily increased people's desire for cognitive closure. Building on this work, Webster and Kruglanski hypothesized that in addition to being susceptible to situational manipulation, the NFC might also represent an individual difference variable, with some people predisposed toward a high need for closure and others predisposed toward a low need for closure. Given this, Webster and Kruglanski set out to measure individual differences in NFC and show that individual differences in NFC had the same effect on judgments and behavior as did features of the situation. As the authors clearly articulated (p. 1050), development of an individual difference measure of NFC had three advantages. Briefly stated, it could (a) establish the generalizability of these effects and thereby provide even stronger evidence for the more global NFC construct, (b) provide a deeper appreciation for the different ways NFC is expressed, and (c) allow researchers to explain more variance in relevant outcomes based on the main and interactive effects of trait NFC.

With motivation for the construct established, the authors set out to develop and validate the NFC scale. The authors first defined five key dimensions of the construct (e.g., preference for order and structure, discomfort with ambiguity) and then generated a diverse set of items corresponding to the five dimensions. Following a process of item purification (based on item analyses), the 42-item NFC was formed.

Webster and Kruglanski (1994) first demonstrated the factor structure, internal reliability, and temporal stability of the NFC scale using college students and a broader sample of the population. They then considered the convergent and discriminant validity of the scale, showing that it overlaps with (but is not identical to) related constructs such as authoritarianism, dogmatism, cognitive complexity, the need for structure, and the need for cognition (but not social desirability). As a second form of validity, the authors used the known-groups comparison approach by comparing the NFC scores of two groups that should, in theory, differ on the NFC (i.e., conventional vs. artistic types). As expected, conventional types (accounting majors) scored significantly higher than artistic types (studio-art majors) on the NFC scale.

Although the first three studies provided good evidence for the reliability and validity of the scale, Webster and Kruglanski (1994) were not done. Building on their initial findings, the authors believed it important to establish that individual differences in NFC had the same effects on judgments and behavior as did prior situational factors that temporarily increased NFC. Accordingly, Webster and Kruglanski demonstrated that people scoring high on the NFC scale were more likely to (a) show primacy effects (Study 4; i.e., better recall for information at the beginning of a list), (b) fall prey to the correspondence bias (Study 5; i.e., the tendency to view behavior as corresponding with or being caused by the person), and (c) resist persuasive appeals when they felt they had enough initial information to make a judgment (Study 6).

In sum, Webster and Kruglanski (1994) made a contribution by introducing a theoretically grounded individual difference variable that could affect a wide array of motivated social cognitive judgments and behaviors and by providing a compelling series of studies validating the NFC scale.

TIGHTWADS VERSUS SPENDTHRIFTS

In 2008, Rick, Cryder, and Loewenstein reported a series of studies validating their new scale assessing individual differences in the tendency to be a spendthrift (a person who finds it difficult to control spending money) versus a tightwad (a person who has difficulty spending money). The Spendthrift–Tightwad (ST-TW) scale is a face-valid, 4-item scale with higher values reflecting a tendency to be a spendthrift. As we explain, the scale possesses good reliability and good convergent validity and is able to predict financial outcomes (e.g., credit card debt and amount of money saved)—all good properties, to be sure, but what makes this scale really novel is its theoretical basis.

As the authors discussed, standard economic models of decision making assume that people make choices between options on the basis of anticipated consequences (i.e., decision making is "consequentialist" in nature). For example, one consequence people might consider when deciding whether or not to buy a new car is how that car will make them feel in the present and what opportunities they may be missing out on in the future as a result of that decision (e.g., forgoing a vacation). As the authors noted, although consumers could consider such future "opportunity costs," research has suggested that they do not do so spontaneously. This, then, raises the question: If consumers do not consider future opportunity costs, why should consumers show any restraint? Indeed, as the authors stated, "If people relied solely on cognitively nebulous representations of forgone consumption, most people would likely spend compulsively" (Rick, Cryder, & Loewenstein, 2008, p. 768). Despite this, some consumers do control their spending. The next question is, why?

To answer that question, Rick and his colleagues (2008) suggested that consumers may control spending by relying on the "immediate pain of paying." As preliminary support for this idea, the authors cited a study by Knutson, Rick, Wimmer, Prelec, and Loewenstein (2007). In that study, participants made choices about whether to purchase a series of consumer products while having their brains scanned in an fMRI machine. Results indicated that, just before choosing *not* to purchase a certain product, there was heightened activity in the insula, a part of brain associated with pain detection. This suggested that the immediate experience of "pain of paying" could serve as a potential deterrent to spending.

Building on this idea, Rick et al. (2008) set out to develop and validate a scale to measure the "pain of payment." The authors' focus on the "pain of paying" is what makes this article so interesting, because validating the construct required novel approaches, as we explain next.

The authors began by reporting exploratory and confirmatory factor analyses supporting the presence of one factor. The authors then discussed differences on the ST-TW scale between arguably different segments of the population (readers of *Globe and Mail* and the *New York Times*, and viewers of NBC). As expected, ST-TW scores tended to be lower among older and more educated respondents. After next establishing the reliability and stability of the scale, the authors explored the discriminant validity of the ST-TW scale by correlating it with a range of similar constructs. The highest correlation emerged with the intuitively related (but conceptually distinct) concept of frugality (–.46). To establish the ST-TW's discriminant validity with respect to frugality, the authors first reported a confirmatory factor analysis showing that a two-factor model fit better than a one-factor model combining the frugality and pain of paying items. To provide a stronger test of the scale's discriminant validity, the authors then used both scales to predict responses to two statements: Spending money is painful for me; saving money is pleasurable for me. As expected, when both predictors were entered into the model, the ST-TW scale was the only unique predictor of pain of paying, and frugality was the only unique predictor of pleasure of saving. In short, the ST-TW predicted what it should (pain of paying) and not what it shouldn't (pleasure of saving). The authors then showed that their scale predicted real-world outcomes, including credit card debt and amount of savings.

The authors next reported experiments designed to assess the construct validity of their scale. In the first experiment, participants imagined they were buying a DVD box set and could get it overnight for a fee. Participants were told the fee was a "$5 fee" or a "*small* $5 fee." The phrase *small fee* was intended to reduce the perceived pain of paying. As expected, tightwads were significantly less likely than spendthrifts to pay the standard $5 fee. But when presented with a "small" fee, tightwads' willingness to pay the fee increased and was not significantly different from that of spendthrifts. In the second experiment, participants were asked if they would be willing to spend $100 for a massage that was either motivated by their desire for pleasure (hedonic) or recommended by their physician (utilitarian, reducing the pain of paying). Paralleling their earlier findings, the authors found that tightwads were less likely than spendthrifts to purchase the hedonic massage but that tightwads showed a significant increase in willingness to pay when the massage was utilitarian and were as likely as spendthrifts to pay in this condition.

In conclusion, Rick and colleagues (2008) made a contribution by grounding their new construct within a meaningful theoretical context and providing compelling evidence for its predictive and construct validity (the pain of paying). This, combined with the brevity and face validity of the scale, will likely to make the ST-TW scale popular for years to come.

COMPULSIVE BUYING TENDENCIES

In 2008, Ridgway, Kukar-Kinney, and Monroe published an article titled, "An Expanded Conceptualization and a New Measure of Compulsive Buying." After highlighting the importance of compulsive buying, Ridgway and her colleagues spent the remainder of their introduction couching compulsive buying within the broader framework of two related psychological disorders, including obsessive–compulsive and impulse control disorders, arguing that compulsive buying tendencies contain elements of both disorders. Accordingly, the authors defined *compulsive buying* as "a consumer's tendency to be preoccupied with buying that is revealed through repetitive buying and a lack of impulse control over buying" (p. 622).

To make the case for a new measure, the authors clearly articulated problems with several existing compulsive buying measures. For example, many measures assess the consequences of compulsive buying (e.g., large credit card balances, bounced checks). As the authors noted, this confounding has the potential to categorize people as compulsive buyers only if their compulsive buying leads to financial problems. This, in turn, could lead researchers to underestimate the prevalence of compulsive buying within more affluent populations (and overall). According to the authors, existing compulsive buying scales have several other limitations, including the fact that all focus on either compulsive or impulsive behavior (but not both), some require a prior psychiatric diagnosis, some focus on shopping (as opposed to buying), and some possess unfavorable reliability and validity. One feature of this article that makes it somewhat unique is that the authors provided a very detailed table summarizing the strengths and limitations of existing scales, reinforcing the authors' argument that a new scale was needed.

To develop the new scale, the authors first gathered and generated a large number of relevant items and asked experts to review them for their clarity and how well they matched the construct definition. Exploratory and confirmatory factor analyses were used to reduce the resulting 15 items down to 6 items that load on two correlated factors (obsessive-compulsive buying and impulsive buying).

In Study 2, the authors collected additional data to validate the scale on a broader sample and compare it to the compulsive buying screener (Faber & O'Guinn, 1992). To explore the overall construct of compulsive buying, the authors first averaged the compulsive-buying and impulsive-buying subscales into a global compulsive-buying index (CBI). To test the nomological validity of the CBI, the authors correlated the CBI with variables shown in past research to predict compulsive buying tendencies (e.g., materialism, depression, anxiety) or be predicted by compulsive buying tendencies (e.g., positive postpurchase emotions, hiding purchases, family arguments, credit cards close to their maximum limit). Supporting the discriminant validity of the scale, the authors also established that their new CBI was not too strongly correlated with the more general obsessive–compulsive disorder. Supporting the incremental validity of the CBI over the earlier compulsive buying screen, multiple regressions showed that the CBI was more highly correlated with a range of relevant precursors and consequences of compulsive buying. Interestingly, the authors then helped readers understand the critical point at which compulsive-buying tendencies become highly problematic by looking for a large jump (or step) in four different variables (e.g., negative feelings, arguing with family) as a function of the CBI. Finally, the authors showed that, relative to the compulsive-buying screener, their new CBI classifies a higher number of people as compulsive buyers, primarily because it does not confound compulsive-buying tendencies with financial consequences of those tendencies.

In their final study, the authors examined whether their new CBI would predict actual (and self-reported) spending. As expected, the CBI predicted self-reported spending. More impressive, the CBI predicted actual online spending.

In sum, several features of this article make it a nice example of the scale development paradigm. First, the authors spent a great deal of time carefully defining compulsive buying and locating it within the context of related problems (obsessive–compulsive and impulse-control disorders). Second, they provided a detailed analysis of the limitations of past compulsive buying measures to highlight the need for a new measure. Finally, the authors provided clear evidence for the nomological, discriminant, and incremental validity of their scale and showed that their measure is able to predict actual online purchases.

BRAND ENGAGEMENT IN THE SELF-CONCEPT

In 2009, Sprott, Czellar, and Spangenberg introduced a new marketing construct called *brand engagement in self-concept* (BESC), which they defined as "an individual difference representing consumers' propensity to include important brands as part of how they view themselves" (p. 92). Sprott and colleagues subsequently developed an 8-item scale to measure BESC and reported six studies validating the scale. As we explain next, a close look at the development of the BESC provides an excellent illustration of how scholars can make a contribution by introducing and measuring a novel individual difference construct.

To begin, it was necessary for the authors to lay the groundwork for the novelty of the BESC construct and the need for a new measure to assess BESC. Prior to the BESC, marketing researchers had been keenly interested in the role of the self in consumer behavior, and research had already shown that consumers who had strong self-brand connections held more favorable brand attitudes. However, as Sprott and colleagues (2009) noted, prior research had focused more narrowly on connections between a consumer and specific brands, whereas their BESC construct represented a more general tendency for consumers to include (various) brands in their self-concept (e.g., not only a single brand, such as Nike, but a large number of other brands, such as Apple, Starbucks, and Subaru). Moreover, although two prior scales seemed to tap a similar construct (self-brand connections—Escalas, 2004; and attachment-to-possessions scale—Ball & Tasaki, 1992), both prior scales were, as Sprott et al. noted, distinct from their BESC construct.

Having drawn the key distinction between BESC and prior constructs, Sprott and colleagues (2009) proceeded to item development, drawing on Nunnally and Bernstein's (1994) method of reviewing the relevant literature, forming a larger pool of 32 items and asking experts to review the items for their appropriateness to the BESC construct. The pool of 32 items was, through standard item purification techniques, reduced to the final 8-item BESC scale.

One of the interesting features of the article is that details about the development of the measure (e.g., factor analyses) are provided in a web appendix, freeing the authors to spend the majority of their time validating the scale (i.e., demonstrating its construct and predictive validity). After exploring the nomological validity of the scale (i.e., assessing the relationship between BESC and a variety of scales that should be related and not related to BESC), the authors turned their attention to the validity studies.

The six validity studies are an impressive and persuasive collection of studies for several reasons. First, the studies demonstrate the relevance of the BESC for a variety of different consumer-related outcomes (self-brand associations, attention to/identification of brands, brand recall, brand attitudes and intentions, price sensitivity, and willingness to wait for a branded product). Second, the first three studies, designed to demonstrate the simple effect of BESC, tap different methods (e.g., Implicit Association Test, recalling products in one's pantry, person evaluation based on presence of brands). Third, the final three studies move beyond the main effect of BESC to test for theoretically meaningful interactions (e.g., BESC × presence/absence of a brand logo × brand attitudes; BESC × price; BESC × waiting time). Fourth, four of the six studies were able to yield meaningful results, even though BESC was assessed several weeks prior to the main study. Fifth, all totaled, the measurement and validity studies were conducted on over 2,000 participants, and the studies yielded a very consistent pattern of findings in support of the BESC. Finally, the general discussion does a nice job of highlighting the theoretical implications of the work for research on branding and the self-concept, pointing out future research directions and outlining the managerial implications of the findings, a somewhat challenging task when the variable of interest is an individual difference construct.

In sum, Sprott and colleagues (2009) made a contribution by arguing persuasively for the uniqueness of the BESC construct, situating the construct within a well-recognized framework (self-brand connections) and amassing an impressive collection of integrated and well-rounded validity studies that had important theoretical and practical implications.

CONSIDERATION OF FUTURE CONSEQUENCES

In 1994, Strathman, Gleicher, Boninger, and Edwards published a paper detailing the development of the consideration of future consequences (CFC) scale. The authors defined *CFC* as "the extent to which people consider the potential distant outcomes of their current behaviors and the extent to which they are influenced by these potential outcomes" (p. 743) and present a 12-item scale to measure the construct and several studies supporting its validity.

From the outset of their article, it is clear that the authors viewed the construct as having important implications across a range of domains, noting that it often takes many years for the problems associated with many risky behaviors (smoking, alcohol use) to emerge. Within this context, the authors stated that their research "starts with the notion that there are clear and reliable individual differences in the extent to which individuals are likely to consider distant outcomes in choosing their present behavior" (Strathman et al., 1994, p. 742). The authors went on to differentiate between high CFCs (those who consider future outcomes important and are willing to sacrifice immediate outcomes in the interest of long-term outcomes) and low CFCs (those who consider immediate outcomes important and are unconcerned with the costs or benefits of actions that may not occur for many years). The authors reviewed prior conceptualizations of "future time orientation," noting that most had failed to provide a consistent pattern of results across studies. The authors also highlighted that their new CFC scale was conceptually distinct from previous time orientation constructs, which tended to focus on "preoccupation with present and future time."

The authors began by refining an initial set of 24 items down to the 12 best items and established the scale's reliability using seven samples of students from three universities. Results consistently indicated that the scale has a desirable internal reliability and showed good test–retest reliability, supporting its temporal stability.

The authors next turned to their validity studies. They began by assessing the scale's convergent validity, showing that it correlates in the expected direction with related constructs, including delay of gratification, locus of control, and future time orientation. Although significant, the modest size of the correlations (all < .50) suggests that the CFC scale is assessing a novel construct, supporting its discriminant validity. To further evaluate the validity of the scale, Strathman et al. (1994) used the known-groups method, showing, as expected, that students involved in various social causes (which require long-term commitment and thinking) scored higher than students not involved in such causes.

As another demonstration of validity, the authors reported an experiment in which they assessed (UCLA) students' support for offshore oil drilling. In this study, they manipulated the short-term versus long-term costs and benefits of offshore oil drilling. Overall, high CFCs were less supportive of drilling than low CFCs. Arguably more interesting was the theoretically meaningful interaction. As predicted, low CFCs were more supportive when benefits were immediate and costs were delayed, and high CFCs were more supportive when costs were immediate and benefits were delayed.

A final study provided support for the incremental validity of the CFC scale. In short, CFC predicted environmental concern, health concern, and cigarette use over and above four related scales (conscientiousness, hope, optimism, and future orientation).

Since its introduction, the CFC scale has been applied in a wide range of domains, including health psychology, environmental decision making, organizational behavior, and interpersonal relationships (for a review, see Joireman, Strathman, & Balliet, 2006). The wide scope of relevant contexts and the large number of citations generated by the CFC scale attest to its importance and impact. In sum, development and validation of the CFC scale provides an excellent illustration of how scholars can make an impact by introducing an important and theoretically rich individual difference construct.

Conclusion

As the papers highlighted in this chapter illustrate, scale development papers often take somewhat different approaches. An author's end goal, however, is the same: namely, to articulate the need for a new individual difference construct; base the construct in the context of relevant theory and past research; show that the measure in question can be reliably measured; and provide compelling evidence for the measure's convergent, discriminant, predictive, and construct validity using a systematic series of studies that often draw on novel as well as theoretically and practically relevant outcomes.

Author Interviews

Highlighted Author

What is your advice for publishing high-quality research that is likely to have impact?

What "individual difference measure" paper would you recommend and why?

Angela Duckworth
Assistant Professor, Department of Psychology, University of Pennsylvania, Philadelphia

I do a lot of talks for teachers and parents. Their common-sense questions point me in the direction of what is useful and important to a broader range of people than just my immediate scholarly peer group. If you listen to what people want to know, including nonexperts, you will learn very quickly the difference between a high-impact research question and a low-impact one.

I recommend Gross and John's (2003) paper in which they develop a scale to assess two emotion regulation strategies (reappraisal vs. suppression). More broadly related to individual differences, I really like the Roberts and DelVecchio (2000) meta-analysis of personality change. This is a highly cited paper because it establishes the empirical fact that personality demonstrates both stability and change all through the life course.

Arie Kruglanski
Distinguished University Professor, Department of Psychology, University of Maryland, College Park

Have an interesting theory and an interesting way or ways of testing it.

A paper my colleagues and I published in the *Journal of Personality and Social Psychology* detailing the development of a scale designed to measure individual differences in two tendencies critical to successful self-regulation, including assessment (evaluating goals and assessing progress) and locomotion (initiating and maintaining movement toward a goal; Kruglanski et al., 2000). Results showed that assessment and locomotion are largely independent factors that are related to distinct task orientations and motivational processes.

Highlighted Author

Nancy Ridgway
Professor of Marketing, Robins School of Business, University of Richmond, Richmond, VA

What is your advice for publishing high-quality research that is likely to have impact?

I would tell scholars that hope to produce high-impact research that they need to ask important questions. A simple correlation between two variables (even if it is put in the form of a model with moderating variables) is just not "big" enough to be high impact. For example, in my paper, I developed not only a strong theoretical base but also solid design, analysis, and results. An example of solid design is that I collected data using three different samples. That way, the Compulsive Buying Scale could be evaluated on a wide variety of consumers. Finally, I serve as a reviewer of a lot of papers submitted to journals. What I have discovered is that most papers do not ask big questions. They ask small iterative-type questions that do not really add much to our literature base. The other major problem I see in the papers I review is that the results do not work out as hypothesized. If you know the literature extremely well, your hypotheses should be very clear, and your results should confirm those hypotheses.

What "individual difference measure" paper would you recommend and why?

I would recommend that those interested in producing a high-impact scale read two papers in the *Journal of Consumer Research:* "A Consumer Values Orientation for Materialism and its Measurement: Scale Development and Validation," by Marsha L. Richins and Scott Dawson (1992), and its follow-up paper, "The Material Values Scale: Measurement Properties and Development of a Short Form," by Marsha L. Richins (2004). Both papers are very thorough in terms of scale development, and the first paper, especially, is very rich theoretically. The analysis of the second paper is a good model for scale development.

Scott Rick
Assistant Professor of Marketing, Ross School of Business, University of Michigan, Ann Arbor

There are so many routes to impact, it's hard to be dogmatic here. I've tried to address questions or problems that are of interest to both academics and nonacademics. I think it's better to chip away at a big question than to completely answer a micro question. Joe Alba's (2012) discussion of the benefits of "bumbling" is a must-read for anyone interested in answering big, meaningful questions.

Shane Frederick's (2005) Cognitive Reflection Test (CRT) has been hugely impactful. Decision-making researchers had long been interested in the operation of System 1 (quick, automatic) and System 2 (effortful, deliberative) processes, and correctly answering the CRT items requires the operation of both systems (System 2 must override System 1). Thus, it naturally appealed to many decision-making researchers, and the test's simplicity (three items) further stimulated wide usage. It sparked (or perhaps rekindled) a lot of interest in the role of cognitive ability in decision making.

Highlighted Author

What is your advice for publishing high-quality research that is likely to have impact?

What "individual difference measure" paper would you recommend and why?

David Sprott
Boeing/Scott and Linda Carson Chaired Professor of Marketing, Associate Dean for Graduate, International and Professional Programs, Department of Marketing, Washington State University, Pullman

As with this paper, I believe that contributions must be judged and grounded in the extant literature. Since the time of our paper's publication, there has been a huge amount of work studying how consumers relate to brands (e.g., in terms of brand attachment or brand love), and the nature of our contribution is somewhat different today as judged by this new work.

There are a number of good papers out there that develop measures of individual difference variables; too many to recommend just one. For me, the best papers to consider are those that follow traditional methods associated with developing reliable and valid measures per basic psychometric theory. No matter the area, a good measure is important for quality research.

Alan Strathman
Teaching Professor, Department of Psychological Sciences, University of Missouri–Columbia

Read broadly and look for related ideas in other areas of psychology and other disciplines entirely.

John Cacioppo and Rich Petty's (1982) Need for Cognition Scale. I recommend it for two reasons. One is that the scale taps an individual difference that helps explain much daily behavior. Second, they did a thorough job validating the scale and then found interesting ways to examine the effects of need for cognition on judgment and behavior.

Introduce an Innovative New Method 10

Background

This chapter is about publishing an article that draws on a sophisticated, novel, and/or intriguing method or dependent variable that makes readers shake their heads, drop their jaws, and say, "Wow, I wish I had thought about that." This chapter is also about blood, sweat, and tears. To develop a truly innovative method often requires a willingness to abandon one's typical methodological routine; think more creatively than usual; and exert significant effort in experimental design, execution, and data collection. At the end of the day, however, we believe that you will find the endeavor is well worth your effort and enjoyable, and it can even reignite or enhance your passion for research.

http://dx.doi.org/10.1037/14525-011
How to Publish High-Quality Research, by J. Joireman and P. A. M. Van Lange
Copyright © 2015 by the American Psychological Association. All rights reserved.

WHAT IS AN INNOVATIVE METHOD?

Innovative methods come in a variety of forms. Innovative methods can involve an *independent variable* such as subliminally priming people with PC versus Mac logos or exposing people to violent video games; a *data collection method*, such as a reaction time measure (e.g., the Implicit Association Test [IAT], Stroop task), a physiological measure (e.g., heart rate, galvanic skin response), a behavioral measure (e.g., walking speed, eye contact), or a brain scan (e.g., an fMRI); or a *sophisticated data analytic technique* such as hierarchical linear modeling, or moderated mediation (see Chapter 8). Second, although researchers can develop interesting self-report methods, innovative methods almost always involve an actual behavioral context (vs. a hypothetical scenario) or an actual behavioral outcome (vs. a self-report). Third, and relatedly, an innovative method deals with real-life (e.g., actual consumption of snack foods) or subtle, yet important, cognitive/emotional/behavioral processes that had heretofore been difficult to study (e.g., implicit attitudes). Fourth, innovative methods are novel (or in the case of data analytic methods, cutting edge). Fifth, innovative methods help shed light on important practical and theoretical questions. Sixth, these methods can be either subtle or blatant and oftentimes deal with something we have long taken for granted. Seventh, innovative methods have the potential to advance research in many different domains. Finally, innovative methods are stimulating, fun to read about, and enhance the overall story underlying a paper.

BENEFITS OF DEVELOPING INNOVATIVE METHODS

At this point, readers may be thinking: Sure, research methods can be exciting, novel, and even "sexy," but is this really necessary in order to make a meaningful contribution? The simple answer to this question, of course, is no. It is not necessary to use or develop an exciting method to make a contribution. There are plenty of well-worn methods that can still address interesting and fundamentally important research questions. Moreover, one could argue that it may be a little irresponsible to make the entire focus of a research project about figuring out how to use a "sexy method," just for the sake of using such a method. Indeed, the fields of social psychology and consumer behavior have recently witnessed a number of scholars who seemed so bent on telling a good story that they fabricated their data or engaged in questionable screening techniques. In sum, it is important to recognize, in this context, that the "tail should not wag the dog." Rather, an innovative method should support, bring excitement to, and clarify a fundamental research question and should never be the sole goal or an enticement to engage in unethical research practices.

With those caveats expressed, there at least five reasons for using an innovative method. First, reviewers, editors, and your broader readership enjoy a good story (e.g., Peracchio & Escalas, 2008). Again, the story should not become so important that it leads one astray, but a good story can play a pivotal role in sharing one's contribution, and one important part of that story is the method. In fact, many Method and Results sections can be a bit dry, so adding a little jazz can improve readers' enjoyment of the paper. Second, as we noted earlier, an innovative method often deals with real life. As such, it usually enhances the practical implications of your work. Third, an innovative method, when paired with more traditional methods, can enhance the generalizability and impact of your work. For example, readers may be quite likely to see value in your method for their own research, adopt your method, and cite you as a result. Fourth, investing the effort to develop a novel new method may give you new insights into the problem itself (e.g., leading to advances in your theoretical reasoning). Finally, developing a new method can be fun. If you feel stuck in a rut, it can reenergize your enthusiasm for a given topic; even if you are not stuck in a rut, it can enhance your existing excitement for research. In sum, using an innovative method should not be motivated by a desire to use such a method, per se, but rather, by a desire to enhance the quality and impact of your research.

COSTS OF DEVELOPING AND USING INNOVATIVE METHODS

There always seems to be room for novel research methods. After all, no single method is perfect. But might there be costs associated with new methods as well? One potential concern is that a particular line of research may get a little "carried away" with primary or exclusive use of a particular method, thereby sometimes neglecting the broader scientific goals it seeks to accomplish. To some degree, this happened in "old" research on the prisoner's dilemma, where specific aspects of the method received so much attention that researchers tended to overlook the broader scientific goals they sought to accomplish (for a discussion, see Pruitt & Kimmel, 1977). When findings become too "method bound," there is a possibility of a problem—that researchers would spend too much time on the specifics of the methods rather than addressing the broader scientific goals. We deliberately use the term *possibility*, because sometimes the specifics of a method uncover a major theoretical issue. For example, in research on the classic prisoner's dilemma, people have generated new questions by addressing the issue of noise or unintended errors (Van Lange, Ouwerkerk, & Tazelaar, 2002) or by extending the paradigms in ways that led to some key insights.

An important case in point is research in which participants were able to punish (or reward) one another, which demonstrated the benefits of having sanctioning systems that the group members themselves could use (see Fehr & Gächter, 2002)—and that later also uncovered important cultural influences (see Herrmann, Thöni, & Gächter, 2008). Other methods, including the IAT (Greenwald & Banaji, 1995), have yielded similar discussions. But like the prisoner's dilemma, the IAT has yielded scientific progress. Not only did it contribute immensely to the toolbox of measures, it also helped to promote a theoretical distinction between explicit and implicit attitudes and social cognition—with implicit processes referring to mechanisms that largely or completely escape from our conscious attention. Next, we discuss six articles that highlight different aspects of the innovative method paradigm.

Illustrations

DO WOMEN WHO ARE OVULATING PURCHASE SEXIER CLOTHING?

In 2011, Durante, Griskevicius, Hill, Perilloux, and Li published a three-study paper examining the ovulatory shift hypothesis, the idea that "natural selection may have shaped aspects of women's psychology to shift during the brief window within each cycle when conception is possible" (p. 922). More specifically, Durante and her colleagues were interested in how, why, and when women's product choices are influenced by hormonal fluctuations associated with ovulation. Building on evolutionary social psychology and past ovulation research, the authors hypothesized that women who are ovulating would be more likely to select products that enhance their sexual appeal and attractiveness. By setting consumer behavior within an evolutionary social psychology framework, exploring the impact of a biological marker for sexual reproduction on women's choice of sexy products, and adding an element of competition for mates, the authors quickly gain the attention and interest of their readers. We know that this is going to be a fascinating read.

In each study, Durante and her colleagues asked women to select 10 clothing and accessory items from a larger array of items presented on a simulated shopping website. Half of the products had been pretested as sexy; the other half were matched products that had been pretested as less sexy. The dependent variable in each study was the percentage of sexy items chosen. The simulated website and nature of the clothing (sexy vs. not) are two of the features of the article that make it "sexy" (and novel).

Another key feature of Durante and colleagues' work that helps it stand out from the pack is the independent variable, namely, whether women make their choices when they are or are not ovulating. As the authors clearly explained, just before women ovulate, they experience a spike in the luteinizing hormone. Using careful and painstaking procedures (repeated urine tests), the researchers were able to tell when women were or were not ovulating. They then tested women under these conditions. The first two experiments use a within-subject design, testing women at two times of the month. The final experiment uses a between-subjects design, testing half of the women when they are ovulating and the other half when they are not.

A final feature of the paper that adds to its appeal is its theoretically meaningful and intriguing results. In Experiment 1, the authors began by testing the basic hypothesis, namely, that women would select a higher percentage of sexy products when they were ovulating than when they were not. Results supported this prediction. More important, from a theoretical perspective, the authors were interested in why and when this might be most likely to happen. As noted, using an evolutionary framework, the authors argued that ovulating women select sexy products to enhance their attractiveness and help them compete against rivals for available suitors. To test this hypothesis, in Experiment 2, Durante and colleagues exposed women to pictures of attractive local females, unattractive local females, attractive local men, or unattractive local men. They reasoned that ovulating women would only be more likely to select sexy products when earlier exposed to meaningful rivals (attractive local women). Indeed, results supported this hypothesis. Finally, in Experiment 3, the authors were interested in testing their hypothesis in a somewhat different manner. Specifically, they reasoned that other attractive women would not represent rivals if those women were not local. Consistent with this hypothesis, Durante and her colleagues found that ovulating women were only more likely to choose sexy products than nonovulating women when first exposed to local attractive women but not when exposed to unattractive local or distant women, or significantly, to attractive distant women.

In sum, the theoretical intrigue, novel (and labor intensive) independent variable, realistic and sexy dependent variable, and the fascinating storyline all combine to help make this an outstanding illustration of the innovative method paradigm.

HOW MUCH WOULD YOU PAY FOR AN ATTRACTIVE AND SUCCESSFUL MATE?

In their 2002 paper, Li, Bailey, Kenrick, and Linsenmeier set out to resolve a paradox in the mating literature: Although research had shown that men value physical attractiveness more than women, and women value status more than men (e.g., Buss, 1989), neither sex rated these traits as especially important, leading the researchers to wonder, "Do the sexes differ in characteristics that do not really matter?" (p. 947). To address this question, it was necessary to develop a new method for assessing mating preferences. The problem with previous methods, the authors pointed out, is that those methods put no constraints on the trade-offs between different traits, essentially giving people an "unlimited budget" to "pay for" desired traits. Because traits like physical attractiveness and status can be satiated once they reach a certain threshold, people may seek out other complementary traits. This, in turn, might make attractiveness and status appear somewhat unimportant, overall.

To address this limitation, Li and colleagues developed two novel methods. In the first method, used in Studies 1 and 2, participants were given "mating dollars" and asked how they would spend those dollars on different traits as they attempted to design their ideal marriage partner. More specifically, for each trait, participants indicated which percentile they wanted their ideal mate to fall into, and each percentile was translated into a dollar amount (e.g., indicating that one would want a partner to be in the 70th percentile on status would "cost" the participant $7.00). To gain greater insight into whether certain characteristics were necessities versus luxuries, participants were asked to allocate mating dollars under three different budgets (low, medium, high). If men consider physical attractiveness a necessity, and women consider status a necessity, the largest sex difference in dollars allocated to these two traits should emerge when people face a low budget (because when people have limited resources, they first allocate money to necessities).

In Study 1, participants recruited at Chicago's O'Hare International Airport were asked how they would allocate mate dollars to 10 traits when designing their ideal marriage partner under low ($20), medium ($40), or high ($60) budgets. When faced with a low budget, men spent the highest percentage of their budget on physical attractiveness (and significantly more than women), while women spent the highest percentage of their budget on intelligence and yearly income (with both expenditures significantly higher than those of men), confirming the expected sex differences. Interestingly, under high budgets, men and women did not differ in the percentage of mate dollars allocated to physical attractiveness or yearly income.

In Study 2, the authors aimed to replicate their findings using college students, a more limited number of traits, and a new allocation method that eliminated the possibility of a ceiling effect potentially present in Study 1. Once again, when faced with a limited budget, women spent the highest percentage of their mating dollars on status (and significantly more than men), whereas men spent the majority of their mating dollars on physical attractiveness (and significantly more than women). Moreover, as before, these sex differences became less pronounced when participants were working with a larger budget.

In Study 3, the authors introduced a second novel technique for assessing which traits represent priorities for men and women. Participants were told they would be evaluating the suitability of 30 targets as long-term marriage partners. Participants were told the targets had been ranked on five traits including physical attractiveness and status. Using their computer mouse, participants could find out more information about each target on any of the five characteristics. The primary dependent measure was the mean number of times a trait was chosen as the first trait viewed. In line with Studies 1 and 2, men were most likely to view information about physical attractiveness first, whereas women were most likely to view information about status first (and men and women differed on both measures).

In sum, Li and colleagues (2002) used two novel methods to resolve an intriguing paradox: Although past research showed that men and women differed on the importance of physical attractiveness and status, neither considered such traits especially important (under an unconstrained budget). By examining how participants allocated mating dollars under various budgets, Li and colleagues were able to demonstrate that men treat physical attractiveness and women treat status as necessities. Moreover, using a second creative method, Li et al. provided further evidence that men and women differentially prioritize physical attractiveness and status. Many elements of this article highlight the use of highly novel and sexy methods for addressing theoretically rich and practically important questions.

CAN EATING THANKSGIVING DINNER SAVE YOU MONEY?

In 2010, Mishra and Mishra published an intriguing article suggesting that eating Thanksgiving dinner just may save consumers money by reducing the likelihood that they will engage in impulsive buying. Good news for turkey-filled consumers looking to save a buck, bad news for post-Thanksgiving retailers looking to make a buck.

Readers wondering how Mishra and Mishra got from Thanksgiving dinner to impulsive buying are in for a treat. Indeed, the authors illustrated the sexy method paradigm in a delightful and unexpected way by linking turkey consumption to increases in tryptophan and the neurotransmitter serotonin, which prior research has shown reduces a variety of impulsive behaviors as well as compulsive buying. In accordance with this research, the authors predicted that people who consume high levels of tryptophan would show lower tendencies to engage in impulsive buying. Moving beyond this main effect, the authors also predicted that the tendency for tryptophan to reduce impulsive buying would be stronger among consumers high in trait impulsivity. To gain more insight into the underlying mechanism, Mishra and Mishra also explored the effects of tryptophan on impulsive responding, in general. In line with their earlier predictions, they hypothesized that consumption of tryptophan-rich foods would reduce impulsive responding (in general). The authors reported two studies testing their hypotheses.

In Study 1, the authors surveyed respondents immediately after Thanksgiving dinner (from 7 p.m. to 11 p.m.) and identified two groups of people: those who ate a traditional Thanksgiving dinner (with turkey and carbohydrates, which should lead to higher levels of serotonin because of the tryptophan) and those who did not (e.g., those who ate pizza, salmon, burritos). Because alcohol leads to a focus on immediate outcomes and diminished decision making, respondents who had consumed alcohol were eliminated from the study. Participants completed a trait impulsivity scale, a measure of mood, and responded to an impulsive buying scenario. Specifically, participants rated the likelihood that they would buy a new Dell computer for "just $499.00 + Free Shipping + FREE printer." As predicted, results showed that participants who ate a traditional Thanksgiving meal stated weaker intentions to make an impulsive consumer choice than those who did not eat such a meal and that this effect was stronger among those high in trait impulsiveness (as predicted). Results also indicated that this effect could not be explained by differences in mood between the two groups.

Because many factors may vary along with turkey consumption, and because the researchers did not have full control over exactly what consumers ate, the authors complemented their initial findings in a second study in which they experimentally manipulated serotonin levels by giving participants a chocolate shake high in tryptophan, or with no tryptophan. Given that it takes time for tryptophan to increase serotonin levels, participants were required to return 2.5 hours after they had ingested the shake. At that time, participants first completed a go/no task designed to test impulsive responding (Newman, Widom, & Nathan, 1985). Participants then imagined that they were thinking about buying a big screen TV and were considering two payment options: either buying the TV immediately and paying for it on a credit card with a high interest rate or putting the TV on a 3-month layaway and paying three regular payments but no interest. Results from both dependent measures revealed that those who consumed high levels of tryptophan were less impulsive.

The idea of tying Thanksgiving dinner to impulsive choices (in light of Black Friday) through levels of serotonin is very creative and sophisticated. Moreover, highlighting the role of neurotransmitters in impulsive buying has the potential to open up and inspire many new and exciting directions for future research. In short, Mishra and Mishra's

(2010) paper provides a nice illustration of how the innovative method paradigm can address interesting real-world problems and inspire new directions of research.

Using Cortisol Responses to Assess Social Identity Threat Within Women

In 2011, S. S. M. Townsend, Major, Gangi, and Mendes published a paper examining how women respond to social identity threat (SIT), which the authors defined as "the psychological state that occurs when people are aware that they have the potential to be viewed negatively or devalued because of their membership in a particular social group" (p. 151; cf. Steele, Spencer, & Aronson, 2002). As the authors noted, SIT in women may result from features of the situation (e.g., a sexist boss), features of the person (e.g., chronic perceptions of sexism), or both. Central to the mission of the paper, SIT is assumed to be stressful and to subsequently interfere with various dimensions of functioning, but prior studies using self-reported stress have not consistently supported this prediction. Given these puzzling findings, the authors argued for the use of more indirect measures of stress responses that "get under the skin."

In making a case for the link between SIT and stress responses, the authors first reviewed research showing that SIT elicits heightened arousal, heart rate, blood pressure, and a variety of symptoms linked to stress, including headaches, depression, and nausea. The authors also pointed out that despite these insights, little research had examined how SIT impacts the hypothalamic-pituitary-adrenal cortical (HPA) axis. Activation of the HPA axis results in the release of the stress hormone cortisol and a range of other negative consequences, including impaired cognition and mental and physical problems. Although at least one prior study had demonstrated that SIT leads to heightened cortisol levels, the authors extended this research by exploring the role of individual differences in chronic perceptions of sexism (CPS) and also within the context of an interaction with an out-group member (sexist male) with the strong potential to heighten SIT. To test their hypotheses, they used two creative studies drawing on both a realistic face-to-face interaction and the sophisticated dependent measure of cortisol.

In Experiment 1, women first completed a scale to measure CPS and several other measures that could covary with CPS. Once they arrived at the lab, a male experimenter explained that the participant and a second "participant" (confederate) would be interviewed by a third male "participant" (confederate) for the chance to join the interviewer on a task to win $50. Participants were led to believe that the other applicant was either male or female. Participants then recorded a video introducing themselves to the others. Participants were then informed that the (male) interviewer had chosen the other male applicant for sexist reasons (i.e., the participant is too "emotional") or the other female applicant for merit-based reasons (i.e., based on a "leadership questionnaire"). Participants then delivered a 5-minute speech for the job, provided self-reported stress, and gave three saliva samples poststressor to assess cortisol levels. Results revealed no significant effects of the stressor on self-reported stress but did show a positive relationship between the trait of CPS and changes in cortisol levels (vs. baseline), but only in the sexist condition, as expected.

In Experiment 2, the authors aimed to enhance the generalizability of their findings within a new context. Women pretested on CPS were led to believe that a male ostensibly high or low in sexist attitudes (based on responses to a questionnaire) would evaluate the participant's suitability as a coworker or a supervisor on the basis of their performance on a cognitive task. Saliva samples were taken at two times poststressor. Results again revealed no effect on self-reported stress, but a positive relationship between CPS and changes in cortisol levels (vs. prestressor baseline), which was not, in this case, moderated by the sexist versus nonsexist condition.

In sum, the authors used two realistic contexts and one sophisticated outcome measure to gain greater insight into the effects of SIT on stress responses in women. Each method required a large investment of time, resources, and effort, which together significantly enhanced the external validity of the study's findings. Moreover, the use of cortisol responses allowed researchers to detect an effect that would likely have been overlooked if the authors had only relied on self-reports (which showed no significant effects in either study). These features of the paper provide an excellent illustration of the innovative method paradigm.

DO MEN WHO FEEL LINGERIE WANT IMMEDIATE GRATIFICATION?

In 2008, Van den Bergh, Dewitte, and Warlop published an article titled, "Bikinis Instigate Impatience in Intertemporal Choice." Even before diving into the details, readers are keenly aware that this is going to be a "sexy study." The reader grins, anticipating the ultimate conclusion: Show (heterosexual) men sexy stimuli and they'll want immediate gratification. The storyline is intuitive, but nevertheless intriguing. Readers want to learn more. And as we explain, they will not be disappointed.

In Experiment 1a, heterosexual men rated 15 pictures of attractive females (i.e., in bikinis or lingerie) or 15 pictures of landscapes. Next, participants completed a delay discounting task to measure the extent to which they discounted the value of future monetary outcomes—in short, to measure the extent to which they were "present oriented." In Experiment 1b, heterosexual men rated women's bras or T-shirts and then completed the same delay discounting task. Results in both studies clearly showed that those in the sexy stimuli condition were more likely than those in the control condition to engage in temporal discounting. In short, exposure to sexy stimuli made men impatient and lean toward immediate gratification.

In Experiment 2, with the basic effect established, the authors next considered whether a theoretically relevant individual difference variable might moderate the impact of sexy stimuli on temporal discounting. Heterosexual men were exposed to a video of bikini-clad women running across fields, hills, and beaches, or a video of men running through scenery. Next, participants completed the delay discounting task, a measure designed to rule out an alternative explanation (distraction), and a personality scale assessing sensitivity to reward. The key result indicated that the effect of the sexy stimuli on discounting was moderated by individual differences in sensitivity to reward, such that the effect only emerged among men high in sensitivity to reward (as expected).

Finally, in Experiment 3, the authors sought to evaluate whether the interaction obtained in Experiment 2 would be most pronounced among men who were "deprived" and, further, would be eliminated among men who had been "satiated." Heterosexual men first rated bras or T-shirts, as in Experiment 1B. Participants then indicated how much money they had in their checking account. To manipulate deprivation versus satiation, the authors assigned participants different rating scales (cf. L. D. Nelson & Morrison, 2005). Participants in the satiation condition rated their savings using a scale with a maximum of 400 euros, whereas those in the deprivation condition rated their savings using a scale with a maximum of 400,000 euros. Next, participants rated their mood and completed an expanded version of the delay discounting task, which assessed not only discounting of monetary rewards, but also discounting of candy and soda, to enhance the generalizability of the results. As predicted, results revealed that sexy stimuli led to discounting of the three types of rewards among one specific group of participants: namely, those high in sensitivity to reward who had not been satiated.

Through its focus on sexy stimuli, Van den Bergh, Dewitte, and Warlop's (2008) paper clearly illustrates the innovative method paradigm. It is important to recognize, however, that several other features of the paper make it even stronger. First, the authors used multiple methods (exposure to attractive women in advertisements, bras, and videos). Second, they used various types of temporal discounting (money and hedonic food products). Third, the authors built on their key result by highlighting the role of a theoretically meaningful individual difference variable (sensitivity to reward) and, further, a theoretically meaningful three-way interaction with satiation. Thus, the contribution of the paper is a combined result of the method, measure, and systematic progression from a simple situational effect through a theoretically meaningful (and practically important) three-way interaction.

THE SOCIAL MINDFULNESS PARADIGM: LEAVING OTHERS THE OPPORTUNITY TO CHOOSE

In 2013, Van Doesum, Van Lange, and Van Lange introduced the social mindfulness (SoMi) paradigm, a novel method designed to assess a new construct they called *social mindfulness*, defined as the extent to which people "safeguard other people's control over their own behavioral options in situations of interdependence" (p. 86). To illustrate the concept of social mindfulness, assume two siblings are staring at a candy jar containing two popcorn-flavored Jelly Bellies and one coconut-flavored Jelly Belly. Further assume that the siblings must choose in order, and the first sibling prefers coconut-flavored over popcorn-flavored Jelly Bellies. In this situation, in contrast to his or her initial (self-interested) preference, the socially mindful sibling would choose a popcorn-flavored Jelly Belly, as this would allow the second sibling an opportunity to choose between popcorn and coconut-flavored Jelly Bellies.

To develop the SoMi concept, the authors drew on interdependence theory (Kelley & Thibaut, 1978), self-determination theory (Deci & Ryan, 2012), and work on empathy (Davis, 1983). Within the framework of interdependence theory, SoMi represents an inclination to maximize another's well-being. In the framework of self-determination theory, SoMi represents an awareness that people have a fundamental need for autonomy. With these frameworks as a backdrop, the authors then suggested that SoMi should be most likely when people have the *skill* to recognize others' needs (perspective taking) and the *will* to act on that recognition (empathic concern). This framework sets up several testable hypotheses, namely that SoMi should be more likely when people are in an "other-oriented" frame of mind, when people possess a prosocial value orientation, and when people are high in empathy. Assuming SoMi may also serve as a social signal of one's prosocial intentions, observers should form more favorable impressions of those who make socially mindful choices. The idea is that even if one may not always recognize it when they are choosing, observers will see it quite readily.

To test these hypotheses, the authors conducted seven studies using their new SoMi paradigm. Although the choices varied between studies, the basic setup was the same. Participants were informed that they were interacting via computer with another person whom they would not meet, and they would make a series of choices between three options (e.g., two green pens and one blue pen) across a range of product categories (e.g., pens, baseball hats, jams).

In Study 1a, Dutch participants were randomly assigned to one of three "mind-set" conditions in which they were instructed to either (a) keep the other's perspective in mind, (b) keep the other's best interest in mind, or (c) think about their own preferences. A fourth (control) condition received no instructions. The researchers also assessed individual differences in prosocial (vs. proself) value orientations. The key dependent measure was the proportion of socially mindful choices (i.e., picking the more prevalent option, thus leaving the partner a choice between the two remaining [distinct] options). Results revealed that participants in the two "other-minded" conditions (a and b) made more socially mindful choices than those instructed to consider their own preferences (c) or those in the control condition, with the latter two conditions not differing significantly. Results also showed that those with a prosocial value orientation made more socially mindful choices than those with a proself value orientation.

In Studies 1b and 1c, the authors addressed two alternative explanations for their initial findings (using an American sample). In Study 1b, participants completed the same SoMi paradigm but were informed that they would not learn of the other's choices. In Study 1c, participants again completed the SoMi paradigm, but in this case, half of the participants were told the other person would not be able to see their initial choice. Both studies replicated the findings from Study 1a, suggesting that social mindfulness was not due to a desire to learn about the choices of the other person (Study 1b) or make a good impression (Study 1c).

Building on their initial studies, the authors next explored whether those who make socially mindful choices are perceived more favorably. In Study 2a, Dutch participants were assigned to the role of observer or recipient within the SoMi paradigm. Observers were led to believe they were watching two others interact in the SoMi paradigm, whereas recipients believed they were actually interacting with another person in the SoMi paradigm (and were the second person to choose, thus making them the "recipient" of the other's choice). Using preprogrammed choices, the "other" player made either zero, one, or two (out of two) socially mindful choices. Results revealed that perceptions of the other player were more favorable when the player made at least one socially mindful choice, and the effect did not depend on whether the participant was simply an observer or a recipient of the other's choices. Study 2b, using a slightly different method (e.g., dropping a filler task) revealed identical results.

In Study 3, the authors explored whether facial expressions conveying trustworthiness impact choices in the SoMi paradigm. To accomplish this, prior to making choices in the SoMi paradigm, participants viewed pictures of their supposed partner that had previously been shown to be low versus high in trustworthiness. As predicted, participants made more socially mindful choices when their partner appeared high in trustworthiness.

Study 4 explored links between choices in the SoMi paradigm and theoretically relevant personality traits. As predicted, those high in empathy, honest/humility, and concern for others (prosocials) made more socially mindful choices in the SoMi paradigm. The significant correlations were of intermediate magnitude (sharing about 9% of the variance) across the various measures, suggesting shared and unique underlying constructs. Both are important in terms of progress in theory and methods.

In sum, Van Doesum and colleagues introduced the novel new construct of social mindfulness and a simple, yet elegant, method of measuring it. Using a series of studies, the authors explored how a constellation of related constructs (other-oriented mindset, prosocial orientation, empathy, and honesty/humility, trustworthiness of the partner) predicted choices in the SoMi paradigm and how choices in the SoMi paradigm are perceived, providing a well-rounded exploration of this new (and timely) construct.

Conclusion

The goal of the innovative method paradigm is to use a novel, intriguing, and/or sophisticated independent or dependent variable, or data analytic technique, that provides unique theoretical and practical insights and will very likely make for a more compelling and interesting story. As the articles reviewed in this chapter indicate, there is a lot of exciting and innovative research going on across a range of disciplines. We believe future researchers aiming to develop novel methods can profitably use this chapter's illustrations as an inspiration and guide for taking a creative approach to the study of human behavior.

Author Interviews

Highlighted Author

Kristina Durante
Assistant Professor,
Department of
Marketing, University
of Texas at San
Antonio

What is your advice for publishing high-quality research that is likely to have impact?

First, always be thinking about your research. My best ideas are taken from my everyday social interactions. Second, have a strong theoretical framework supporting your research predictions. Third and most important, have a research idea that is counterintuitive at first blush, yet surprisingly straightforward when given a second thought.

What "innovative/sexy method" paper would you recommend and why?

This is a difficult question, as there are a great number of papers that I believe have used an "innovative/sexy method." I'll compromise and only talk about two papers that I recently read that fit this bill. The first is a paper in *Psychological Science* by Carin Perilloux, Judy Easton, and David Buss (2012) titled, "The Misperception of Sexual Interest." As part of the study, the researchers set up a live speed-dating event that had men and women interacting with each other as potential dating partners. Perilloux and colleagues found that contrary to intuition, unattractive men were more likely to misperceive (or overperceive) that attractive women are interested in them as romantic partners. The other paper is also in *Psychological Science* (2011), authored by Jonah Berger and titled, "Arousal Increases Social Transmission of Information." Berger predicted that arousal should speed the transmission of information (or word of mouth). He had participants complete a task in which they would become emotionally (Study 1) or physically (Study 2) aroused (watching an emotional film clip and jogging in place). Indeed, physiological arousal led to increases in the spread of information such as news and other stories. Both of these papers use innovative and "sexy" methods to move beyond measures of preferences and examine real behavior.

Highlighted Author

Norman Li
Associate Professor of
Psychology, School
of Social Sciences,
Singapore Management
University, Singapore

What is your advice for publishing high-quality research that is likely to have impact?

Become knowledgeable in theories and empirical work outside of your main area and, ideally, outside of your field. Models or frameworks that are used in seemingly unrelated areas or fields may be importable and applicable to problems that cannot otherwise be solved with local tools.

What "innovative/sexy method" paper would you recommend and why?

One such paper is Townsend and Levy's (1990) *Journal of Psychology* paper. Mate preference researchers have historically relied on people indicating the importance of descriptors such as "good looks" and "earning prospects." However, Townsend, an anthropologist, argued here and elsewhere that especially for college students, these notions aren't vivid or concrete enough to evince the strong underlying sex differences in preferences. To more realistically represent key constructs, they used a sexy method by bringing in male and female models varying in physical attractiveness and having them dress up in costumes ranging from a Burger King uniform to a suit and Rolex watch. This allowed for an ecologically valid depiction and manipulation of key traits and a more valid test of sex-differentiation in mate preferences.

Arul Mishra
David Eccles Faculty
Fellow and Associate
Professor of Marketing,
David Eccles School of
Business, University of
Utah, Salt Lake City

Something that has worked for me and many of my coauthors is to look at an idea from different angles, sometimes even unconventional methods. That helps enhance the richness of one's work.

There are many memorable papers that have used interesting and sexy methods. The types of studies that I think tend to be remembered more are field studies in the real world. Such studies do a very elegant job of not only testing an idea but also clearly showing its actual implications. One pioneering article that comes to my mind is Nisbett and Kanouse's (1969) *Journal of Personality and Social Psychology* paper titled, "Obesity, Food Deprivation, and Supermarket Shopping Behavior."

Highlighted Author

Sarah Townsend
Assistant Professor
of Management and
Organization, Marshall
School of Business,
University of
Southern California,
Los Angeles

What is your advice for publishing high-quality research that is likely to have impact?

I would encourage researchers to seek out diverse perspectives: Read something outside of your area of expertise, discuss your research with people outside of your discipline (or people who are not in the academy!), and attend talks or conferences outside of your discipline. Most important, follow your passions, not the areas that are currently "hot" in the field—people typically do their best, most innovative work when they are passionate about the problem they study.

What "innovative/sexy method" paper would you recommend and why?

There are several papers I admire for introducing an "innovative/sexy method" to the field. One that immediately comes to mind is "The Subtle Transmission of Race Bias via Televised Nonverbal Behavior" by Weisbuch, Pauker, and Ambady (2009). This paper reports a series of innovative studies showing that many American television programs contain nonverbal race bias and that even though people are unable to detect this bias, exposure to these programs influences their implicit and explicit racial attitudes. How were the researchers able to measure the existence of nonverbal race bias when people are unable to recognize it? In a very inventive study, the researchers edited clips from 11 popular television shows, removing the audio and the focal character. Participants watched the edited clips and rated how other characters responded to this unseen focal character. Results showed that White focal characters received more favorable nonverbal responses than Black focal characters. In subsequent studies, Weisbuch and colleagues went on to show that watching programs with this race bias increased viewers' own bias. I find these methods "sexy" for two reasons. They are not only a rigorous way to measure the bias contained in cultural products (i.e., television programs) but also an empirical way to demonstrate how such products can transmit their bias onto viewers.

Highlighted Author

Bram Van den Bergh
Assistant Professor,
Department
of Marketing
Management,
Rotterdam School of
Management, Erasmus
University Rotterdam,
Rotterdam, the
Netherlands

What is your advice for publishing high-quality research that is likely to have impact?

I was exposed to the Wilson and Daly findings at a conference (Human Behavior and Evolution Society conference) that has no affinity with marketing research whatsoever. I am convinced that scholars should adopt an open-mind perspective and read journals outside of their field and attend conferences outside of their core discipline. This maximizes the likelihood of exposure to novel and inspiring findings, spurring creative research hypotheses that make contributions across disciplines. I tend to believe that my findings are of interest not only to consumer behavior scholars, but to psychologists and economists as well.

What "innovative/sexy method" paper would you recommend and why?

One of the most interesting and sexy papers that I read recently is a *Psychological Science* article by Crum and Langer (2007) titled, "Mind-Set Matters: Exercise and the Placebo Effect." The authors show that physical exercise affects health in part or in whole via the placebo effect. In a study with female room attendants in several hotels, half of the attendants were informed that the work they do (cleaning hotel rooms) is "good exercise and satisfies the Surgeon General's recommendations for an active lifestyle." The control group did not receive this information. It turns out that the informed group showed a decrease in weight, blood pressure, body fat, waist-to-hip ratio, and body mass index. This paper uses an intervention that is easy to implement (i.e., receiving info or not) to document a mind-blowing effect (i.e., the effect of physical exercise depends on one's mind-set) that is fascinating from a theoretical perspective (i.e., placebo). The authors use real people (i.e., no university students), look at real outcomes (i.e., no surveys using hypothetical questions), and address an important societal problem (i.e., health).

Highlighted Author

Niels Van Doesum
PhD student,
Department of Social
and Organizational
Psychology, VU
University, Amsterdam,
the Netherlands

What is your advice for publishing high-quality research that is likely to have impact?

At least in social psychology, I believe that high-impact research always builds on what is already available in some way or other and is able to combine new insights with a certain degree of synthesis while putting things in a broader perspective that has implications beyond its own specific field or focus. Another factor is that it usually represents the zeitgeist rather well, which makes it "click" or feel right to many people. Without the current focus on mindfulness, for instance, our paper on *social* mindfulness might not have found the place it has right now. That being said, I don't know if there really is a recipe for high impact per se, and I also don't know if it should be a goal in itself; maybe it's better to simply aim for high quality and hope that the field will agree that what you are doing fits the qualifications.

What "innovative/sexy method" paper would you recommend and why?

I have always been intrigued by the effectiveness of the Cyberball game developed by Kip Williams and colleagues (e.g., Williams, Cheung, & Choi, 2000). The basic and simple computer animations have shown over and over again to be very effective in manipulating ostracism, making it widely and easily useable in both laboratory and Internet research. This for me is a good example of how a concept can be boiled down to its essence while making successful use of new media that are developing at that time.

Venture Into the Real World

11

Background

In the previous chapter, we discussed how researchers can introduce a novel method or measurement technique. In this chapter, we discuss a related paradigm, namely, conducting research in the "real world" (i.e., in the field). Though surveys and lab experiments with college students are quite common, relatively easy, and useful, much can be gained by complementing such methodologies with data collected in the field.

BENEFITS OF VENTURING INTO THE REAL WORLD

There are a number of benefits associated with conducting research in the real world. To begin, as we noted in our discussion of the TAPAS system (Chapter 2), application is a fundamental goal of theory testing and development. Conducting research in the real world, with more representative samples,

http://dx.doi.org/10.1037/14525-012
How to Publish High-Quality Research, by J. Joireman and P. A. M. Van Lange

can help researchers evaluate the generalizability of their findings in more realistic and perhaps "noisy" situations. This, in turn, offers researchers an opportunity to test the practical usefulness of their theories outside the sterile confines of the lab.

Conducting research in the real world can also provide insight into potential boundary conditions for an effect, based either on the unique features of the situation or the sample. Identifying boundary conditions, in turn, can help researchers refine their theories and may suggest new directions for future research that had not been previously considered.

Another reason for venturing into the real world is that it forces researchers to think carefully and creatively about how their key constructs might be operationalized in more realistic settings. This process has at least two benefits. First, it may suggest the need to refine one's definition of the theory's key constructs. Second, although it is often challenging, generating a creative method is often also a stimulating and rewarding exercise that can make the research process more enjoyable.

A final reason for conducting research in the real world is that if done right, it can significantly increase the likelihood that your manuscript will be accepted in a good outlet and, once published, have higher impact. Indeed, reviewers appreciate and respect the effort that goes into real-world studies, and readers can immediately see the relevance of a study conducted in the real world. Colloquially speaking, real-world studies can give you "street credibility."

COSTS OF VENTURING INTO THE REAL WORLD

Not surprisingly, real-world research also comes with some costs. Given the nature of the manipulations, gaining approval from your institutional review board may take more time, as you may be seeking to waive consent (for publically observable behavior) or to collect data among vulnerable populations (e.g., prisoners). Finding a willing field partner can also be challenging and time consuming. For example, an organization may be reluctant to "try out" a new employee motivational program, unless they have some guarantee that it won't hurt production. On a related note, simply executing research in the real world will often involve significant time, personnel, and financial resources. Another challenge with real-world studies is that control over confounds and extraneous variables may be more difficult. As an example, in quasi-experimental designs, in which individual participants cannot be randomly assigned to conditions, it is possible that the treatment conditions may vary (before the manipulation) on theoretically relevant variables, and these preexisting differences could potentially explain the results. Schools, for example, could be randomly assigned to one of two learning strategies, but it may not be possible to randomly assign the individual students in each school to the conditions. Thus, careful thought needs to go in to selecting locations that are matched on key variables that could influence the outcomes or collecting variables that could potentially represent confounds. Finally, in a real-world setting, where the outcome of interest is simply observed behavior, it is challenging at best to measure intervening mechanisms (e.g., state mood). Nevertheless, if done right, we have found that benefits of such applied research nearly always outweigh the costs.

CREATIVE APPROACHES TO CONDUCTING RESEARCH IN THE REAL WORLD

As the articles highlighted in this chapter illustrate, there are a variety of creative ways a researcher can conduct research in the real world. For example, a researcher may be interested in conducting an intervention study aimed at changing behavior (while also testing a theoretical proposition). Good examples of this approach include Bateson, Nettle, and Roberts's (2006) research exploring whether a visual cue suggesting one is being watched (i.e., a pair of eyes) can increase cooperation rates (i.e., contributions to an honor box) in an employee break room, and Berger and Rand's (2008) work exploring whether posters linking alcohol consumption with a "dissociative reference group" (graduate students), hung in campus dorms, can reduce self-reported alcohol consumption among undergraduates. Another approach is to simulate a real-world setting in the lab. Berger and Rand's first study, in which they simulate a retail store in the lab, provides a good illustration of this technique. A third approach is to stage an interaction between the participant and a trained confederate of the experimenter. Here, readers will find two illustrations inspiring, including Argo, Dahl, and Morales's (2008) work on positive contagion in a retail setting and Bushman and Anderson's (2009) work exploring how exposure to violent media impacts prosocial behavior. Another creative approach is to explore how a naturally occurring feature of the environment impacts behavior. Readers interested in this approach can profitably consult Kramer and Weber's (2012) work exploring how winter weather reduces financial risk-taking, and Bushman and Anderson's second study exploring how moviegoers' willingness to intervene in an emergency is affected by the (violent vs. nonviolent) nature of the movie they just watched at a real-world theater. Finally, a researcher may considerably strengthen his or her findings by observing real behavior (in the lab or the field), often following an experimental manipulation. Several of the articles discussed in this chapter illustrate this approach, including Mogilner's (2010) third study exploring how thoughts of money reduce actual time socializing (vs. working) in a café, Berger and Rand's second study exploring whether linking junk food consumption with graduate students impacts the foods undergraduates actually select in a campus eatery, Bushman and Anderson's research exploring how exposure to violent media impacts real prosocial behavior, and Bateson et al.'s work exploring how cues of being watched impact actual donations to an honor box. Researchers may also find it helpful to conduct a diary study, as illustrated in Little, McNulty, and Russell's (2010) research exploring whether frequent and highly satisfying sex may buffer the negative relationship between insecure attachment and relationship satisfaction (described in Chapter 8).

Although the six approaches just described are not exhaustive, these techniques (and the illustrations described in this chapter) can serve as inspiring examples of what researchers can achieve when they venture out into the real world. Additional inspiration will no doubt be gained by consulting the articles our highlighted authors recommend.

TIPS FOR CONDUCTING RESEARCH IN THE REAL WORLD

Before describing the illustrations of the real-world paradigm, we offer tips researchers should consider before venturing out in the real world. Each of these tips bears on the validity of the study.

First, real-world studies often involve more noise than is present in the carefully controlled lab. Given this, it is valuable, if possible, to establish the basic effect in the lab first, and then assess the power of the manipulation. Building in sufficient power, in turn, can overcome the additional noise present in the real world and increase the likelihood of detecting a real effect.

Second, real-world studies do not always offer the opportunity for pure random assignment to conditions. Rather, many real-world experiments are more appropriately characterized as quasi-experimental designs in which locations (e.g., stores, schools) are randomly assigned to a condition but individual participants are not. This introduces the possibility that some feature of the setting, which is not of interest to the researcher, will systematically vary with the focal manipulation, making it difficult to firmly establish causation. Being aware of potential confounds can help the researcher attempt to reduce differences between conditions as much as possible before the study and/or collect personal (or environmental) measures that can be used as control variables in subsequent statistical analyses.

Third, on a related note, if a researcher plans to use confederates in the real world, the confederates should be carefully trained to ensure, as much as possible, identical interaction patterns (within conditions), to avoid potential confounds. In addition, the confederates should be blind to the experimental manipulation to avoid the possibility of experimenter expectancy effects.

Finally, if a researcher plans to use observation, a carefully designed coding protocol should be developed, and multiple observers should be used to enhance the validity of the coding by checking for interrater reliability.

Although the tips just offered are not exhaustive, they do capture the essence of many of the key issues researchers face when venturing into the real world. Researchers interested in a more complete discussion of the issues involved in applied research may wish to consult a number of good sources on experimental design (e.g., Shadish, Cook, & Campbell, 2002) and applied psychological research (e.g., Sadava & McCreary, 1997; Schultz & Oskamp, 2000).

Illustrations

POSITIVE CONSUMER CONTAGION: SHOPPERS LIKE PRODUCTS TOUCHED BY ATTRACTIVE OTHERS

In 2008, Argo, Dahl, and Morales reported a series of three creative field studies in retail settings exploring how consumers' evaluation of products is impacted when an attractive other has first touched the product. As the authors noted, "when it comes to physical touch in retail settings, consumers are faced with a paradox" (p. 690). This paradox is a result of two opposing tendencies: Namely, consumers like to touch products before buying them, but as Argo, Dahl, and Morales (2006) had previously shown, consumers are also often disgusted when other shoppers touch and thus "contaminate" the product through negative contagion. Although negative contagion clearly occurs, the authors questioned whether negative contagion is universal and, moreover, whether there may be circumstances under which positive contagion will occur.

To build their case for the possibility of "positive contagion," the authors first noted that many ads draw on beautiful models, and certain retail outlets, such as Abercrombie & Fitch, have policies of hiring attractive employees, both of which "hint at an important role for beauty and attractiveness in the retail context" (Argo et al., 2006, p. 690). Drawing on anthropological work on sympathetic magic and its corresponding law of contagion, the authors next outlined theory and research suggesting that when a source touches an object, people appear to believe the "essence" of the source has transferred to the object, even if the source is no longer touching the object. As a result, when the source is negative, evaluations of the object become less favorable. However, when the source is positive, evaluations of the object could become positive.

As such, the authors hypothesized that when an attractive other touches a product in a retail setting, evaluations of that product should increase (the *positive consumer contagion effect*). On the basis of past cross-gender interaction research, the authors also predicted that positive contagion should be stronger when the "other" is of the opposite sex. Finally, the authors argued that the positive contagion effect occurs because consumers believe some physical essence of the source has transferred to the product (i.e., a physical model of the contagion effect).

To test their hypotheses, the authors conducted three field experiments. In Study 1, male and female college students were instructed to walk through their campus bookstore for several minutes, ostensibly to get a feel for the store, and then contact a salesperson in the clothing section to try on a specific T-shirt. Once each student embarked on his or her tour of the store, the researcher told the salesperson via text message that the participant was walking toward the salesperson. As the participant arrived in the clothing section, the salesperson informed the participant that he or she only had one more T-shirt left and that somebody else was trying it on. The salesperson then directed the participant to the dressing room area. At that point, a second (female) confederate walked out of the dressing room, leaving the target T-shirt in the dressing room and leading the participant to believe that the confederate had just tried on the T-shirt. The confederate was either a highly attractive and well-dressed professional model or another college student of average attractiveness. Once this confederate had left the dressing room, the participant tried on the T-shirt and then evaluated the T-shirt, indicated his or her intention to purchase the shirt, and said how much he or she would be willing to pay for the shirt. Results were in line with the hypothesized (cross-sex) positive contagion effect: Male participants expressed more favorable evaluations, higher purchase intentions, and a willingness to pay higher prices for the shirt when they had been led to believe that a highly attractive (vs. a moderately attractive) female had previously touched the product; by contrast, the attractiveness manipulation had no impact on these outcomes among female participants.

In Study 2, the authors used an identical protocol but included male and female confederates to formally test their (cross-sex) interaction hypothesis. Results supported the cross-gender positive contagion effect: Male shoppers expressed more favorable product evaluations, higher purchase intentions, and higher willingness to pay for the shirt when an attractive female (but not male) confederate had first tried on the shirt; similarly, female shoppers showed higher product evaluations, purchase intentions, and willingness to pay when an attractive male (but not female) confederate had first tried on the shirt.

Study 3 was designed to test the hypothesis that a physical contagion model explained the data. The procedure was similar to Study 1, with two exceptions. To begin, there was no second shopper; rather, the physical attractiveness manipulation was conducted by varying the attractiveness of the (female) salesperson (highly attractive vs. average attractiveness). Second, the authors varied whether the contagion was physical or nonphysical. To accomplish this, the salesperson informed each participant that the store had only one T-shirt and that she had tried the shirt on the day before. Participants in the physical contagion condition were then handed the T-shirt on a hanger, whereas those in the nonphysical condition were handed the T-shirt in a dry cleaning bag and told the shirt had just been dry cleaned (thus "cleansing" it of any possible contagion). Results revealed higher product evaluations and purchase intentions when the salesperson was highly attractive (vs. average in attractiveness), but only when the T-shirt had not been dry cleaned, thus supporting a physical model of contagion.

Argo and colleagues' (2008) article provides a nice model of how to conduct carefully controlled experiments in realistic field settings, complete with actors/confederates and a realistic (shopping) task. Although it may have been possible to observe similar effects using a written (or perhaps videotaped) scenario, the authors greatly improved the ecological validity and practical implications of their study by conducting it within a real-world setting. Moreover, through their clever "dry cleaning" manipulation, in Study 3, the authors were able to provide clear evidence for their argument that a physical model underlies the positive contagion effect.

CUES OF BEING WATCHED PROMOTE COOPERATION

In 2006, Bateson, Nettle, and Roberts published an elegant real-world experiment designed to test the hypothesis that environmental cues suggesting that one is being watched can increase cooperation in a naturalistic setting. Prior to their study, theory and research had suggested that cooperation can be enhanced via rewards and punishments administered by one's immediate interaction partners and by a desire to maintain a reputation as a cooperative person. On the basis of this framework, prior lab-based research had examined whether subtle cues suggesting that one was being monitored could increase cooperation in anonymous economic games (e.g., Haley & Fessler, 2005). Building on this work, Bateson et al. (2006) set out to examine whether subtle reminders of reputation may also enhance real-world cooperation, thereby also addressing the practical implications of reputational concerns in a real-life context.

To test their hypothesis, the authors set up a 10-week intervention study within a break room located in their university. The break room contained an "honesty (or honor) box" in which 48 faculty and staff were expected to deposit money for any tea, coffee, and/or milk they used. Prior to the study, employees had been regularly reminded of the payment policy, and a clear payment norm had been established. Reinforcing this norm, on a cupboard above the honesty box and drink preparation area was a medium-size (148 mm × 210 mm) sign reminding employees of the payment policy. However, because of the setup of the break room, it was very unlikely that donation behavior would be observed, making it effectively anonymous.

To manipulate "cues of being watched," the authors varied the picture on the sign above the honesty box and preparation area. On odd numbered weeks, the sign had a picture of a person's eyes; on even numbered weeks, the sign had a picture of flowers. Multiple pictures were used to enhance the generalizability of the findings beyond a single picture or expression.

At the end of each week, the authors measured how much money was donated per liter of milk consumed. The authors reported their results in an "eye-catching" graph, where they showed contribution rates for each week, alongside the picture placed on the sign for that week. Consistent with their hypothesis, results revealed a large and significant effect of the sign intervention, with donations nearly three times higher when the sign above the donation box contained a picture of human eyes rather than flowers.

Bateson et al.'s (2006) paper is noteworthy for a number of reasons. First, it is a perfect illustration of using a creative method to test an important theoretical and practical question. Second, it uses a creative method for manipulating "reputational concerns" and pays careful attention to design issues (e.g., making sure that the environment, in fact, allowed each participant to actually see the sign). Third, it reports very strong results (a nearly three-fold increase in donations) and displays those results in a manner that grabs the reader's attention and is very easy to understand. Finally, it addresses alternative explanations in the discussion and helps readers appreciate the broader theoretical and practical implications of the findings.

RISKY BEHAVIORS CAN BE REDUCED BY LINKING THEM WITH AN OUTGROUP

In 2008, Berger and Rand drew on the idea of "identity signaling" to explore whether health behaviors (i.e., healthy eating and reduced alcohol consumption) can be promoted when the unhealthy alternatives (i.e., junk food and binge drinking) become associated with an outgroup that an individual would prefer to not be associated with (i.e., a *dissociative reference group*). To motivate their topic, the authors first noted that people often engage in unhealthy behaviors, despite the negative consequences, which suggests that health behavior interventions may need to go beyond simply stressing the future consequences of one's actions. The authors then illustrated their alternative (identity signaling) approach using a real-world example. Specifically, they observed that many undergraduates (at Stanford University) prefer to not wear bicycle helmets because they associate wearing helmets with graduate students, a group they do not necessarily dislike but nevertheless consider awkward and too intense. As a result, the authors stated, "identity trumped safety" (p. 509).

To build their theoretical argument for identity signaling, the authors first reviewed research indicating that consumer behavior is often driven by "symbolic concerns" and the desire to communicate a certain identity about the self to others. Moreover, people often purchase products (and engage in behaviors) in an attempt to model the behavior of aspirational reference groups and avoid products (and behaviors) that are connected to dissociative reference groups. It is important, the authors argued, that perceptions of which products and behaviors are associated with which reference groups can shift over time. This suggests that interventions aimed at reducing unhealthy behaviors might aim to convince the target audience (e.g., undergraduates) that those unhealthy behaviors are linked with a group that the target does not wish to be confused with (e.g., graduate students). From a practical perspective, the authors further argued that such "identity-avoidance manipulations . . . must extend beyond the context in which the intervention materials are presented" (Berger & Rand, 2008, p. 510). This, in turn, sets up the need for real-world studies assessing the power of identity-avoidance manipulations to elicit real behavior change in naturalistic settings. To that end, the authors conducted one lab-based (junk food) study establishing the basic effect in a simulated retail setting, a quasi-experimental study aimed at reducing alcohol consumption, and a randomized field experiment aimed at encouraging healthy eating.

In Study 1, the Junk Food Study, undergraduates first read an article indicating that junk food consumption was especially high among undergraduates, or graduate students, depending on the condition. Validating this manipulation, pretesting indicated that graduate students did, in fact, represent a dissociative reference group (a group that undergraduates did not dislike but also did not want to be confused with). Next, ostensibly as part of a different study, participants made choices between actual healthy and unhealthy food options in a different room set up to simulate a retail setting. Participants made these choices in groups and were informed that other participants would be forming impressions of them on the basis of their choices. Results revealed that when junk food consumption had been linked with graduate students (vs. undergraduates), participants were less likely to select junk food, consistent with an identity-signaling approach.

In Study 2, the Alcohol Study, the researchers posted flyers in bathrooms and on bulletin boards in two different freshman dorms. The two dorms were carefully selected to be as similar as possible to minimize the possibility that preexisting differences would be confounded with the key message manipulation. In the control condition dorm, the flyer stressed the negative consequences of drinking too much alcohol (such as impaired cognitive functioning). In the outgroup signal condition, the flyer linked heavy alcohol consumption with graduate students and stated "nobody wants to be confused with this guy." After 2 weeks, participants self-reported their alcohol consumption. As expected, results revealed that alcohol consumption was 50% lower when the flyers suggested that heavy alcohol consumption was linked with graduate (as opposed to undergraduate) students. Supporting their conceptual argument, additional analyses revealed that the effect of the flyer was only significant among those students who indicated that they did not want to be confused with a graduate student.

In Study 3, the Restaurant Study, the researchers first asked people entering an on-campus eatery to complete a "media perception survey." In the survey, participants read one of two magazine articles designed to manipulate identity signaling and completed a self-monitoring scale. Participants in the control condition read an article about politics, while those in the outgroup signal condition read an article linking junk food consumption with another out-group (online gamers). Without the participant's knowledge, a researcher inside the restaurant recorded which foods the participant selected. Two coders later rated how healthy the meal was perceived to be, and the researchers calculated for each patron the percentage of calories from fat based on their food selections. Results revealed that those in the out-group signal condition chose foods that were rated as healthier and had fewer calories from fat but (as predicted) that this effect only occurred among those high in self-monitoring (who were more concerned about adjusting their behavior to match public expectations).

Berger and Rand's (2008) paper illustrates the power of using the real-world paradigm. Across three experiments, and two health behaviors, the authors combined the strengths of the lab (with a real, behavioral choice) with the strengths of quasi-experiments and true field experiments, using both self-reports and observed behavior, to produce a compelling case for their argument that health behavior can be promoted by linking the opposing unhealthy behaviors with a dissociative out-group. Especially creative, in our view, was the decision in Study 3 to record and code each patron's actual food choice on perceived healthiness and the meal's percentage of calories from fat (an objective measure of the meal's healthiness). Future research modeling this three-step approach in new contexts would no doubt be an effective strategy.

EXPOSURE TO VIOLENT MEDIA REDUCES PROSOCIAL BEHAVIOR

In 2009, Bushman and Anderson published a paper combining lab and field methodologies to test the hypothesis that exposure to violent media (violent video games and films) reduces prosocial behavior. To develop their hypothesis, the authors extended the general aggression model to desensitization effects by proposing that exposure to violent media leads to desensitization to violence, which in turn leads to decreased attention to violent events, empathy for victims, perceptions of injury, and negative attitudes toward violence, and to heightened belief that violence is normal, which in turn increases aggressive behavior and reduces prosocial behavior. As the authors noted, although prior research had shown that playing violent video games reduces arousal in response to real-world violence (cf. Carnagey, Anderson, & Bushman, 2007), studies had not yet shown that exposure to violent media reduces prosocial behavior.

To test their hypothesis, the authors conducted two studies. In Study 1, a laboratory experiment, college students were randomly assigned to play either a violent video game or a nonviolent video game for 20 minutes, while the experimenter ostensibly went to a different building to "code some data." After they had played their assigned video game, participants rated the video game on a number of dimensions, wrote down their favorite type of video game, and then completed a long questionnaire designed to keep them in the lab for the next phase of the study. Shortly after the participant had completed his or her video game, the experimenter, located outside the participant's room, played an audio recording of an argument between two college students (matching the participant's gender). Participants were led to believe that the argument escalated into a fight, that one of the students was groaning and had injured his or her ankle, and that the other student had left the scene. The experimenter then timed how long it took for the participant to come out and help the assumed victim (up to a 3-minute maximum).

Results revealed that those who had played a violent video game were less likely to hear the fight, judged the fight to be less severe, and took 4.5 times longer to intervene than those who had played a nonviolent video game.

To test the generalizability of their findings, Bushman and Anderson (2009) conducted a second study in the real world in which they assessed how long it would take moviegoers to help a victim who had ostensibly dropped her crutches outside a movie theater. Two (between-participant) variables were manipulated, including the timing of the staged emergency (before vs. after the movie) and the type of movie people were planning to watch or had just watched (nonviolent vs. violent).

Results confirmed the authors' earlier findings. When the emergency was staged after the movies, those who had watched the violent movie were significantly slower to intervene than those who had watched a nonviolent movie. However, when the emergency was staged before the movie, moviegoers who had showed up to watch a violent movie were as quick to help the victim as those who had showed up to watch the nonviolent movie, indicating that it was the type of movie people actually watched, as opposed to the type of movie people were planning to watch, that impacted helping response times.

Bushman and Anderson's (2009) paper is an excellent illustration of how researchers can use strong theory and the real-world paradigm to publish high-quality research. The authors concisely reviewed past research on exposure to violent media, clearly identified an important gap in that literature, and showed how they would fill it. The authors then outlined their desensitization model and helped readers appreciate the various ways exposure to violence could interfere with the decision to help a person in need (e.g., by reducing the likelihood of noticing an emergency, interpreting an event as an emergency), which nicely set up their key dependent variables. The authors consequently used two different forms of violent media, two different settings, and a variety of behavioral measures to establish clear support for their hypothesis that exposure to violent media reduces the likelihood of engaging in prosocial behavior. And, in Study 2, in which random assignment to movies was not possible, the authors took care to design their field study in such a way as to avoid a possible confound between type of movie seen and personal characteristics that might predispose movie goers to see certain movies—namely, by showing that helping times prior to the movies were unaffected by the type of movie people planned to watch, but helping times were significantly longer after people had seen a violent versus a nonviolent movie.

WINTER LEADS PEOPLE WITH SEASONAL AFFECTIVE DISORDER TO BECOME RISK AVERSE

In 2012, Kramer and Weber published an intriguing paper aimed at evaluating whether winter leads people with seasonal affective disorder (SAD) to show increased risk aversion in financial decision making. The authors motivated their study by first reviewing studies showing increased risk aversion in financial markets during the fall and winter (vs. spring and summer). Despite this suggestive (market level) evidence, the authors noted that financial economists were "skeptical of psychological mechanisms for market dynamics, [making] the 'SAD' explanation for what looks like risk aversion in winter . . . hotly contested" (p. 193). The authors then outlined competing theories for how mood (driven by season) might impact risk aversion. According to the affect infusion model (Forgas, 1995), negative mood should increase risk aversion via mood-congruent thoughts; by contrast, according to the mood maintenance hypothesis (Isen, Nygren, & Ashby, 1988), negative mood should reduce risk aversion, as people take risks to attempt to get out of their negative mood. Comparing the two models, the authors logically argued that the former is more likely to apply to (relatively) stable mood states, such as SAD. Accordingly, they predicted that those suffering from SAD should be more risk averse than those not suffering from SAD, most notably, during the winter months.

To test this hypothesis and gain deeper insight into the possible psychological mechanisms underlying heightened risk aversion during the winter months, the authors conducted a real-world longitudinal study assessing financial risk aversion over the course of the summer of 2008, winter of 2008–2009, and summer of 2009. Participants completed a diagnostic measure of SAD, and then during each of the three waves, reported their level of depression and completed the safe asset vs. risky (SAVR) task, a behavioral measure of risk aversion designed by the authors. During each stage, participants were paid $20. Participants could then elect to keep their money, or direct some percentage of it into a "risky investment" that had the potential to yield a higher payment. For example, in the low-risk option, participants could direct 10% of their $20 into an investment that had a 50:50 chance of resulting in $22.20 or $18; by contrast, in the high-risk option, participants could direct 100% of their $20 into an investment that had a 50:50 chance of resulting in $42 or $0. The authors then converted participants' choices into a risk-aversion index, which constituted their primary dependent measure.

Consistent with the authors' hypothesis, those suffering from SAD were more risk averse than those without SAD, but only during the winter months; though directionally more risk averse during the summer, the differences between SAD and non-SAD participants were not significant outside the winter wave. Additional results, within the winter wave, showed that depression mediated the impact of SAD on financial risk aversion (SAD → depression → financial risk aversion).

Kramer and Weber's (2012) paper is a novel illustration of how researchers can capitalize on naturally occurring events to test a hypothesis with theoretical and practical implications. Prior to their study, previous aggregated financial data had suggested increased risk aversion during the winter months, but evidence for the psychological mechanism was lacking. By exploring how a dispositional tendency toward SAD moderated the impact of season on financial risk aversion in an experimental task, the authors were able to offer "the first and only direct test of the psychological mechanisms hypothesized to drive a robust and controversial effect in financial markets" (p. 196), as well as an excellent illustration of the real-world paradigm for publishing high-quality research.

THINKING ABOUT MONEY REDUCES
TIME SPENT SOCIALIZING

In 2010, Mogilner published a series of three studies testing the hypothesis that thinking about money (vs. time) leads people to spend less time on the fulfilling activity of socially connecting with others. Mogilner motivated her study by first observing that although many people believe that money is associated with happiness, the link between money and happiness is far weaker than people think. Building on these findings, she posed the intriguing question "How can researchers reconcile the general belief that money and happiness are closely associated with the empirical demonstration that the two are largely unrelated?" (p. 1347).

To address this question, she suggested that working hard to earn more money carries a cost—namely, a reduction in the time available to engage in gratifying social interactions that are associated with greater happiness. Mogilner then argued that although money is often a driving force in Americans' search for happiness, redirecting Americans' attention from thoughts of money to thoughts of time could lead to less time working, more time socializing, and thus greater happiness.

Mogilner (2010) tested this hypothesis in two lab studies and an elegant real-world study set within a café. In Study 1a, a national sample of Americans completed one of three scrambled sentence tasks designed to direct their attention to time, money, or neither. Half of the participants then indicated the likelihood that they would engage in a number of different activities over the subsequent 24-hour period (i.e., socialize, engage in intimate relations, work, commute). The other half of the participants made predictions for how likely others would be to spend time on the same activities. All participants also rated how happy each activity would make them (or others). Results revealed that among those predicting their own future behavior, participants primed with money planned to spend more time working and commuting, and less time socializing and engaging in sex, compared with those primed with time. By contrast, the prime had no effect on ratings of how likely others would be to engage in the same behaviors. In Study 1b, Mogilner replicated these findings within a low-income population to establish the generalizability of her findings within a population in which money is limited, and daily activities are heavily impacted by the need to make money. In the field experiment (Study 2), patrons about to enter a café first completed one of the three scrambled sentence tasks used in the previous studies. Once patrons entered the café, a second researcher observed how much time the participant spent working and socializing. Consistent with her earlier findings, Mogilner found that those primed with money spent a larger percentage of their time working than those primed with time, whereas those primed with time spent a larger percentage of their time socializing than those primed with money. Moreover, those primed with money spent more time working than socializing, and those primed with time spent more time socializing than working.

Mogilner's (2010) paper serves as a nice example of how researchers can establish an interesting effect in the lab with self-reports and "seal the deal" with a final real-world experiment set in a realistic setting that involves observation of actual behavior. The paper also addresses a fascinating puzzle and serves as an example of how researchers can challenge existing (lay) assumptions—in this case, about the assumed positive link between money and happiness. As noted, results revealed that when primed with money, people planned to, and actually did, spend less time socializing, whereas when primed with time, people were more likely to spend time socializing. It is important that results also revealed that people believed and actually reported they were happier when they spent more time socializing (vs. working). Future researchers hoping to make a meaningful contribution would be well advised to consider the theoretical and methodological strategy pursued by Mogilner.

Conclusion

One of the most common criticisms we see in the review process is that the researchers have relied completely on self-reports. In this chapter, we highlighted a paradigm that addresses this key limitation and consequently adds significant depth to a research paper. When an effect can be demonstrated in the field, using observational data, confederates, and/or a meaningful intervention, reviewers will have more confidence in the relevance of the findings. Moreover, once published, the media and general public will likely be better able to appreciate the relevance of the work and potentially put it into practice, adding to the paper's impact. The illustrations described in this chapter serve as excellent models of how researchers can creatively use the real world to test theoretically relevant and practically important hypotheses and ultimately publish in their fields' best journals.

Author Interviews

Highlighted Author

What is your advice for publishing high-quality research that is likely to have impact?

What "real-world" paper would you recommend and why?

Jennifer Argo
Professor, Department of Marketing, Business Economics and Law, Alberta School of Business, University of Alberta, Edmonton, Alberta, Canada

Examining consumer behavior in the appropriate experimental venue is important. We were interested in understanding how a relatively subtle gesture could impact consumer evaluations, and so we felt the best place to capture the effects was in the real world. We were not convinced that merely asking people to imagine that touch had transpired would be sufficient to capture the effects. Often people do not (a) realize how easily they are impacted and/or (b) want to admit that they have been impacted. As such, assessing behaviors in a real-world context alleviates these problems.

Ariely and Levav's (2000) paper in which they study how individuals make a decision in a group setting using real-world choices. It is very difficult to be able to understand how others around us influence our choices, and so I am not optimistic that they would have obtained the same results if they had asked people to imagine the situation. They use a clever setup to examine a complex decision situation.

Melissa Bateson
Professor of Ethology, Centre for Behaviour and Evolution Institute of Neuroscience, Newcastle University, Newcastle Upon Tyne, UK

I think that one of the reasons that our paper has been so successful is that it is remarkably short and simple. I also believe that the figure is extremely powerful. I think it is worth investing some time producing visual representations of data that tell your story clearly.

I recommend a paper by Keizer, Lindenberg, and Steg (2008) published in *Science* titled, "The Spreading of Disorder." It's great because it shows experimental evidence for the broken-windows hypothesis.

Highlighted Author

Jonah Berger
James G. Campbell
Associate Professor
of Marketing,
The Wharton
School, University
of Pennsylvania,
Philadelphia

Brad Bushman
Professor of
Communication and
Psychology at The Ohio
State University,
Columbus, and
Professor of
Communication
Science at the VU
University, Amsterdam,
the Netherlands. He
holds the Margaret
Hall and Robert Randal
Rinehart Chair of Mass
Communication.

What is your advice for publishing high-quality research that is likely to have impact?

Field work is almost always more impactful. It doesn't have to be a field experiment; even archival data are good. Field work helps people outside the discipline see that certain effects are not just things that can be conjured in the lab under ideal conditions but are also processes that actually affect important, measurable behaviors in the field. Always bottle the phenomenon if you can.

High-impact research is almost always grounded in theory. Often it also tests hypotheses deduced from theories in a novel or even paradoxical manner. It helps if the topic has applied significance. I like to do research where I test the same hypothesis in the laboratory first, then in the real world. Many people criticize laboratory studies of aggression as "trivial" and "artificial," but the same effects we observe in the laboratory we also observe in the real world.

What "real-world" paper would you recommend and why?

Salganik, Dodds, and Watts (2006). Stellar paper. We all know conformity happens, but showing how this process affects collective outcomes is amazing. Also, and I'm biased: Berger, Bradlow, Braunstein, and Zhang (2012), a paper in which we explore how certain baby names become popular due to the popularity of related names in preceding years.

My honors student Stacey Sentyrz conducted a series of studies for her undergraduate honors thesis showing that the presence of a mirror reduces consumption of high-fat foods (Sentyrz & Bushman, 1998). On the basis of self-awareness theory, she predicted that the presence of a mirror would cause people to focus on internal standards (e.g., being thin and healthy), and would therefore influence people to avoid fatty foods. The first study was conducted in a lab, with participants seated at a table facing a one-way mirror. Hungry college students participated in what they thought was a taste-test study. They were given a plate of minibagels and three types of cream cheese to put on the bagels—full fat, reduced fat, and nonfat. They rated the cream cheese on several dimensions (e.g., texture, taste). By the flip of a coin, the one-way mirror they were facing was either covered with a curtain or not covered. As expected, people who saw their reflection in the mirror ate less full-fat cream cheese (but not less reduced-fat or fat-free cream cheese) compared with those who did not see their reflection in the mirror. Stacey replicated this study in a real-world setting—a supermarket. She set up a taste-test table in which shoppers could sample full-fat, reduced-fat, and fat-free margarine spread on bread. The researcher flipped a coin during the day to determine whether the table top was an uncovered or covered mirror. As in the lab experiment, the mirror reduced consumption of full-fat margarine (but not reduced-fat or fat-free margarine). This research not only tests self-awareness theory in a novel way, but it has real-world significance. If people put a mirror on their fridge, they might eat less fatty food.

Highlighted Author

Lisa Kramer
Associate Professor of Finance, University of Toronto, Toronto, Ontario, Canada

What is your advice for publishing high-quality research that is likely to have impact?

My best advice is to work on problems that strike a personal chord. If a researcher herself isn't passionate about a research question, she can't expect her planned audience to be interested. The urge to satisfy one's personal curiosity can provide essential momentum for pursuing a difficult research question. It is also important, of course, to pursue topics that others will likely find interesting, but often it is hard to predict which topics those will be, so from my point of view the most important factor is a deep sense of personal inquisitiveness with respect to a particular question.

What "real-world" paper would you recommend and why?

Thaler and Benartzi's (2004) article titled, "Save More Tomorrow: Using Behavioral Economics to Increase Employee Saving." In this article, the authors build on the established finding that people exhibit time inconsistency—for instance, preferring not to make the consumption sacrifices their current selves would have to make in order to save for retirement the way their future selves would prefer. The authors devised a clever tool (called Save More Tomorrow™, or SMarT), whereby individuals can commit today to save in the future whenever they get a raise at work. This innovation helps individuals overcome their natural tendencies (to the benefit of the individuals' future retired selves). Thaler and Benartzi test the efficacy of the SMarT tool with real individuals making real retirement savings decisions, and they show those who are offered access to the SMarT tool save significantly more than those who are not. This clever study is one of the earliest demonstrations that "nudging" or "libertarian paternalism" can work in practice.

Highlighted Author

Cassie Mogilner
Assistant Professor
of Marketing,
The Wharton
School, University
of Pennsylvania,
Philadelphia

What is your advice for publishing high-quality research that is likely to have impact?

Test research questions that you personally think are interesting and that you would be excited to go home and tell your family about. If it takes more than three sentences to convey to your mom why it's interesting, you either need to think more about how to pull out and better communicate the essence of the question, or you need to reconsider how interesting the question is. Although an interesting research question is a requirement, it also helps to test the question in a compelling way. In addition to highly controlled lab experiments that nail down the effect and potential process, try to think of a way to go out into the "real world" to demonstrate the basic effect observing people's actual behavior.

What "real-world" paper would you recommend and why?

The paper by one of my advisors, Sheena Iyengar, and Mark Lepper titled, "When Choice is Demotivating: Can One Desire Too Much of a Good Thing?" (2000; *Journal of Personality and Social Psychology*), served as my guide for an ideal lineup of studies. It tested an interesting question (even your mom would think so) and demonstrated the effect in a combination of lab and field experiments.

Explore the Role of Culture 12

Background

In the previous chapter, we considered the value of conducting research in the "real world," which, among other things, helps to establish the generalizability of one's findings to settings outside the lab. In this chapter, we turn our attention to a final and related paradigm, namely, exploring the role of culture. Like the real-world paradigm, exploring the role of culture is aimed, in large part, at establishing the (cross-cultural) generalizability of principles initially established within a more limited (and mostly Western) cultural context. As the illustrations we have selected will show, this cultural-research paradigm is theoretically rich and can be applied using a wide variety of creative approaches. Before discussing those illustrations, we briefly consider some major historical milestones that shaped the field and outline some of the main conceptual and methodological issues facing researchers interested in the role of culture.

http://dx.doi.org/10.1037/14525-013
How to Publish High-Quality Research, by J. Joireman and P. A. M. Van Lange

HISTORICAL ROOTS

Cultural approaches to human behavior have a long history in social and behavior sciences, going back to classic contributions by Margaret Mead and other influential cultural anthropologists (for reviews, see Adamopoulos & Lonner, 2001; Jahoda & Krewer, 1997). Within psychology, the field of cross-cultural psychology developed rapidly in the 1960s and became institutionalized in the early 1970s with the establishment of the *Journal of Cross-Cultural Psychology* in 1970 and the formation of the International Association for Cross-Cultural Psychology in 1973. Since that time, a number of well-recognized lines of cross-cultural research have been developed, including research on cross-cultural differences in values (Hofstede, 1980; Schwartz, 1992), individualism–collectivism (Triandis, 1995), interdependent versus independent views of the self-concept (Markus & Kitayama, 1991), and the "culture of honor" in the Southern part of the United States (Nisbett & Cohen, 1996). More recently, Henrich, Heine, and Norenzayan (2010) highlighted that cultures differ not only on the interpersonal or social domains but also on motivation, cognition, and even the heritability of IQ. As will become clear, many of these "classics" relate directly to the more recent illustrations we discuss in this chapter.

CROSS-CULTURAL AND CULTURAL PSYCHOLOGY

Researchers interested in "exploring the role of culture" may adopt one of several approaches, each with its own unique set of assumptions, goals, and methodologies. Two of the most frequently recognized approaches are cross-cultural and cultural psychology. These approaches differ in many respects. One of the most basic differences is the extent to which each approach is interested in identifying universal principles of behavior that may transcend culture versus understanding behavior within a specific cultural context.

One of the most common approaches to studying the role of culture is *cross-cultural (or comparative culture) psychology*. According to Berry, Poortinga, Segall, and Dasen (2002), cross-cultural psychology is "the study of: similarities and differences in individual psychological functioning in various cultural and ethnocultural groups; of the relationships between psychological variables and socio-cultural, ecological and biological variables; and of ongoing changes in these variables" (p. 3). Cross-cultural psychology typically treats culture as an antecedent, a mediator, or a moderator of behavior and focuses largely on examining cultural differences in thought, feelings, and behavior using quantitative methods. Cultures are compared with the dual goals of establishing the generalizability of findings from one culture to another and exploring and explaining differences between cultures in search of a more universal or panhuman psychology (Berry, Poortinga, & Pandey, 1997).

A second approach is *cultural psychology*. Whereas cross-cultural psychology is comparative in nature, cultural psychology focuses more on "understanding the person in a historical and sociocultural context" and discovering "how mind and culture define and constitute each other in specific contexts" (Adamopoulos & Lonner, 2001, p. 20). Cultural psychology views culture and behavior as "indistinguishable" (Greenfield, 1997, p. 306) and assumes that culture resides *within* the individual. Thus, rather than viewing culture as an antecedent, mediator, or moderator of behavior—as in cross-cultural psychology—cultural psychology focuses on culture as a *process* and typically adopts a more eclectic array of methods, including qualitative and quantitative methods.[1]

As readers will see, the illustrations in this chapter fall primarily within the realm of cross-cultural psychology. With that being said, the illustrations also highlight the value in paying attention to the unique features of the cultures in question, collaborating with scholars familiar with the cultures in question, and advancing theoretically derived hypotheses concerning the nature of the cross-cultural differences in question. This suggests that the illustrations can, in many ways, be viewed as integrating elements of the cross-cultural and cultural psychology perspectives.

ECOCULTURAL FRAMEWORK

As noted, researchers adopting the cross-cultural approach typically view culture as an antecedent, a mediator, or a moderator of behavior. Within this perspective, one comprehensive framework used to understand the role of culture is Berry, Poortinga, Segall, and Dasen's (1992) *ecocultural framework*. The ecocultural framework is an interactive-process model that links population-level background variables (i.e., ecological and sociopolitical context) with individual-level psychological outcomes (i.e., observed behavior and inferred characteristics) via a variety of intermediary processes including biological and cultural adaptation, ecological influences, genetic and cultural transmission, and acculturation.

Each of the illustrations chosen for this chapter fit well within the ecocultural framework. Herrmann, Thöni, and Gächter (2008), for example, explored how differences in the sociopolitical climate (e.g.,

---

[1]Two additional approaches are indigenous psychology and psychological anthropology. *Indigenous psychology* assumes that work should be undertaken by scholars within the culture of interest and for the benefit of the people residing in that culture, and that "home-grown" theories and methods should be developed on the basis of knowledge of the unique functioning of the culture in question. *Psychological anthropology*, by contrast, aims to integrate social, behavioral and anthropological perspectives to describe universal principles about human behavior that are not necessarily based on a priori assumptions. Readers interested in a complete review of these four approaches may consult Adamopoulos and Lonner (2001).

norms of civic cooperation, rule of law) might explain cultural differences in cooperation and antisocial punishment; Leung and Cohen (2011) investigated interactions between culture, personality, and the situation within face, honor, and dignity cultures; Miyamoto, Nisbett, and Masuda (2006) studied the connection between the built (ecological) environment and basic cognitive/perceptual processes; Monga and John (2007) tested interactions between culture and brand-extension fit in predicting brand evaluations; Schaller and Murray (2008) examined how cultural differences in susceptibility to infectious diseases adaptively shaped emergence of cultural differences in basic personality traits; and Shen, Wan, and Wyer (2011) showed how the differential weight placed on the reciprocity norm across cultures can explain cultural differences in willingness to accept a small gift.

BENEFITS OF STUDYING BEHAVIOR ACROSS CULTURES

Exploring the role of culture has several benefits. To begin, it is clear that cultural differences play an important role in behavior. Thus, studying behavior across cultures helps to determine the extent to which principles in one culture emerge in other cultures and the degree to which principles must be adapted and refined to form a more complete picture of the phenomenon in question. As such, culture has become a field on its own, while remaining closely connected to other fields of psychology. Culture has also become an important part of theorizing in psychology and other fields, addressing issues such as the evolution of culture.

Second, studying behavior across cultures may point to a useful theory that can be generalized to people. A good example can be seen in work on cross-cultural differences in individualism–collectivism (Triandis, 1995), which correspond closely to individual differences in independent versus independent views of the self-concept (Markus & Kitayama, 1991).

A third benefit is that a researcher may recognize a novel process or phenomenon in a culture outside her own and bring that principle back to her country of origin. Finally, researchers who explore the role of culture can open up new collaborative relationships, which bring with them opportunities to explore new cultures (in person) and expose the researcher to novel ideas and approaches for studying the phenomenon in question.

METHODOLOGICAL ISSUES AND CHALLENGES

Researchers interested in exploring the role of culture face a range of methodological issues and challenges. First and foremost, the cross-cultural researcher must be sensitive to cultural differences and subtleties. Language and norms must be carefully considered in designing and implementing cross-cultural studies. Questionnaires should be translated and back translated with care, to ensure that the original meaning of the items is clearly conveyed. And norms and regulations regarding data collection and privacy should also be understood. Another major issue has to do with the quasi-experimental nature of cross-cultural comparisons, as we detail next.

Earlier, we noted that cross-cultural psychology typically treats culture as an antecedent variable that predicts variation in observed behavior (e.g., returning a favor) and inferred characteristics (e.g., values, personality traits). Within an experimental framework, a cross-cultural study can be viewed as a *quasi-experimental design*, where the researcher has control over selection of the groups or conditions but cannot randomly assign participants to the conditions (i.e., cultures). This poses problems for the interpretation of cross-cultural differences. Most notably, because culture is composed of a complex constellation of values, beliefs, norms, and behavioral logics (e.g., see Honor, Face, and Dignity Cultural Logics section below), many variables "covary" (or are confounded) with the primary predictor of culture. As a result, cross-cultural differences are open to a wide range of alternative (or rival) interpretations.

Researchers interested in conducting cross-cultural comparisons can address the potential "confound problem" methodologically and statistically. When designing the study, researchers should attempt to equalize the samples from different cultures as much as possible on variables that do not represent the primary focus of the comparison (e.g., compose samples equal in terms of age and gender). In addition, they should carefully consider collecting relevant covariates that might covary along with culture. These covariates may be of central interest to the theoretical framework (e.g., a mediator of culture's impact) or may reflect processes relevant to alternative interpretations. Once the data are collected, these primary process variables and tangential covariates can be used in the statistical analysis. For example, tangentially related potential confound variables can be entered on Step 1 of a hierarchical regression analysis, and culture can be entered on Step 2. If the cultural differences remain, even after controlling for the potential confounds, a researcher is in a stronger position to rule out certain rival explanations. On the other hand, if the covariates serve as theoretically relevant mediators, cultural differences may disappear after controlling for the covariates (e.g., see Herrmann, Thöni, & Gächter, 2008).

Another methodological solution to the confound problem is to directly manipulate the presumed mediating process, once the basic cross-cultural difference has been observed. The articles by Monga and John (2007) and Miyamoto, Nisbett, and Masuda (2006) summarized in this chapter provide excellent illustrations of this approach. The remaining illustrations in this chapter provide additional insight into the myriad of creative methods cross-cultural researchers use to explore the role of culture.

Illustrations

CULTURAL DIFFERENCES IN THE LIKELIHOOD OF PUNISHING COOPERATORS

In 2008, Herrmann, Thöni, and Gächter published a study exploring cross-cultural differences in the prevalence of antisocial punishment (i.e., punishing "overcooperators," or group members who show higher than average levels of cooperation). Although many studies had previously shown that people will punish group members who fail to cooperate at sufficient levels (i.e., free riders), little was known about the phenomenon of antisocial punishment. As the authors noted, their interest in antisocial punishment was grounded, more broadly, in their interest in understanding cross-cultural differences in cooperation and punishment.

To explore this question, the authors conducted a four-person, 10-trial public goods dilemma experiment within 16 cultures. On each trial of the public goods dilemma, college students were given 20 tokens each and had to decide how many (if any) of the tokens to contribute to a public fund. Each token contributed was worth 1.6 tokens to the group and was divided equally among the group members (i.e., paid back to each group member 0.4 tokens each), regardless of the group members' contributions. Thus, it was possible to "free ride" on the contributions of others. This arrangement created a (give-some) social dilemma in which the option that produced the best outcome for the individual (keeping all the tokens and benefitting from others' contributions) would lead to lower outcomes for the group.

At the end of each trial, (anonymous) group members received feedback about the contributions of their other group members. Subsequently, half of the participants (those in the punishment condition) were allowed to give away some of their tokens to "punish" other group members; for each token contributed to a given target's punishment fund, the targeted group member would lose three tokens (up to a maximum of 10 tokens). The remaining participants were never allowed to punish their fellow group members.

Results revealed several interesting patterns. To begin, participants in all cultures paid, on average, approximately 3.5 tokens to punish group members who had made below-average contributions. This provides evidence for the generality across cultures that people are quite willing to punish free riders at quite a cost to themselves. Although cultures differed somewhat in the tendency to punish these free riders, cultural differences were much more apparent in antisocial punishment, or the tendency to punish group members whose contributions were above (or even at) the average level of the group. For example, whereas participants from the United States (Boston) and Australia (Melbourne) donated, on average, less than one antisocial punishment token, those from Greece (Athens) and Oman (Muscat) donated, on average, between three to four tokens to punish the overcooperators.

Additional results revealed that cooperation was higher when participants were given the opportunity to punish other group members. When free riders were punished, they typically increased their subsequent contributions, but this effect was not significant in cultures that tended to engage in higher levels of antisocial punishment (e.g., it did not emerge in Greece, Saudi Arabia, Belarus, Ukraine, or Oman). In addition, when punishment was allowed, cooperation was negatively related to the level of antisocial punishment (suggesting that highly cooperative group members reduced their contributions after finding themselves the target of antisocial punishment). Here again, however, response to (antisocial) punishment varied by culture, only emerging in about half of the cultures studied.

To gain additional insight into the underlying causes for the cross-cultural differences, the authors next used measures gathered by the World Values Survey (*norms of civic cooperation*; e.g., the importance of paying taxes) and the World Bank (*rule of law*; e.g., perceived fairness of law enforcing institutions) to predict the likelihood of punishing free riders and antisocial punishment. When both predictors were entered into the model simultaneously, punishment of free riders was positively associated with norms of civic virtue, whereas antisocial punishment was negatively associated with norms of civic virtue and rule of law.

Herrmann, Thöni, and Gächter's (2008) paper provides a nice model of how to combine a macrolevel approach to cultural differences (including 16 cultures) with a more fine-grained analysis of the social (and psychological) mechanisms that can potentially explain those differences (e.g., linking different types of punishment with societal norms). The authors' careful attention to design issues (e.g., selecting equivalent samples, of college students, to rule out potential confounds due to demographic differences), use of secondary data (e.g., World Values Survey and data from the World Bank), and detailed analyses further illustrate the many necessary ingredients for an excellent article.

HONOR, FACE, AND DIGNITY CULTURAL LOGICS: A CULTURE × PERSONALITY × SITUATION (CuPS) MODEL

In 2011, Leung and Cohen advanced a model to understand both within- and between-culture variation in behavior. The model proposes that many behaviors can best be understood to be a function of the dynamic interaction between Culture, Personality, and Situations (CuPS). The authors developed their CuPS approach to address several shortcomings in research on cultural and individual differences: Most notably, many cross-cultural studies tend to overlook variability among people within a given culture, and many individual difference studies tend to overlook the impact of culture. The model assumes that people vary in the extent to which they endorse (or reject) their culture's dominant logic, which the authors defined as an integrated set of "scripts, behaviors, practices and cultural patterns [which] revolve around [a] central theme" (p. 508). In the present paper, the authors focused on how individuals who endorse or do not endorse the logics of honor, face, and dignity cultures behave in situations that "call for" returning favors and behaving honestly.

Honor, face, and dignity cultures differ with respect to the way they deal with the problems of social order (e.g., cooperation and aggression) and valuation (the source of a person's worth). More specifically, honor, face, and dignity cultures vary in the way they define "morality, exchange, reciprocity, punishment, and the inalienable versus socially conferred worth of the individual" (Leung & Cohen, 2011, pp. 508–509). *Honor cultures* revolve around an individual's "claim to pride" and stress the importance of positive and negative reciprocity. In these cultures, a person gains honor by returning favors and punishing noncooperators, behaviors that demonstrate one's trustworthiness and intolerance to being exploited. *Face cultures* revolve around maintaining status (saving face) in the context of well-established hierarchies and promoting harmony. Humble behavior that shows respect for hierarchy and promotes harmony is encouraged (cf. Kim & Cohen, 2010). When behavior falls short of this standard (e.g., a person causes another to "lose face"), direct retaliation is shunned, as it would lead to a disruption of social harmony. Face-losing victims, instead, rely on others within the system to punish the noncooperators (i.e., indirect reciprocity). Finally, *dignity cultures* emphasize the inalienable worth of each individual, which is not dependent on the opinions of others. Within a dignity culture, good behavior comes from an inner core of integrity and a system of direct reciprocity and individual rationality (e.g., economic exchange guided by rational self-interest tempered by tit-for-tat reciprocal strategies).

With the three cultural logics defined, Leung and Cohen (2011) next turned to how people who endorse or do not endorse those logics vary in situations that involve repaying favors (Study 1) and behaving honestly (Study 2). Rather than comparing different countries, the authors focused on how Americans who endorse these respective cultural logics vary, with Asian Americans representing face cultures, Southerners and Latinos representing honor cultures, and Northern Anglo Americans representing dignity cultures.

One of the more interesting arguments in the paper is the idea that certain cultural logics may lead people to behave in apparently contradictory ways in different situations. For example, those steeped in the culture of honor adhere to the idea that aggression should be repaid with aggression, an "eye for an eye" philosophy reflecting a form of negative reciprocity designed to protect one's honor (i.e., honor violence). After observing this retaliatory behavior, a person from a different culture may be inclined to believe that all members of an honor culture are highly aggressive. Consequently, the outside observer may be surprised to learn that the same honor-culture actor who is ready to repay aggression with aggression is equally likely to repay favors with favors, a form of positive reciprocity. Leung and Cohen (2011) resolved this apparent contradiction by explaining that repaying aggression and repaying favors are part of the broader cultural logic within an honor culture, which stresses the importance of reciprocity (in general). Restated, within an honor culture, a person who appears highly aggressive in one context and highly cooperative in another context is actually displaying a high degree of consistency that is guided by the same, broader underlying logic (reciprocity).

In contrast to honor cultures, dignity and face cultures do not emphasize reciprocity (as much) and thus do not connect positive and negative reciprocity as part of a broader cultural logic. As a result, people from nonhonor cultures who endorse aggression and negative reciprocity in one situation may be less likely to return a favor in another situation, because endorsement of aggression is guided by a different logic (i.e., it is a sign of weak self-control or a lack of concern with protecting others' face).

Combining these lines of reasoning, the authors arrived at the prediction that members of an honor culture who strongly endorse the notion of honor violence will be *more likely* to repay a favor than those who do not endorse it, whereas in face and dignity cultures, those who strongly endorse honor violence should be *less likely* to repay a favor than those who do not endorse it. Moreover, when there is no favor to repay (i.e., a person is simply in need of help but has not previously performed a favor for the target), members of both cultures should respond similarly, regardless of their endorsement of honor violence. Taken together, these predictions led the authors to expect a three-way

Culture (honor vs. nonhonor cultures) × Personality (low vs. high personal endorsement of honor violence) × Situation (favor to repay vs. no favor to repay) interaction (i.e., CuPS).

Using a similar line of reasoning, the authors next make a complementary set of CuPS predictions comparing dignity to nondignity cultures. To recall, dignity cultures stress an individual's inalienable worth and promote the belief that good behavior comes from an inner core of integrity. In nondignity cultures (honor and face), good behavior is instead motivated by a concern with the responses of and impact on others. This suggests that when there is a favor to repay, members of dignity and nondignity cultures will respond differently, depending on how strongly they endorse their own cultural logic. In particular, within dignity cultures, people should be more likely to return a favor if they strongly endorse the dignity logic (inalienable worth) than if they weakly endorse this logic; by contrast, within honor and face cultures, people should be more likely to return a favor if they strongly endorse the logic that the source of a person's worth is socially determined. Finally, when there is no favor to repay, members of dignity and nondignity cultures should not differ. When combined, these predictions led the authors to predict a second three-way Culture (dignity vs. nondignity cultures) × Personality (endorsement of inalienable worth vs. socially conferred worth) × Situation (favor to repay vs. no favor to repay) interaction (i.e., CuPS).

To test these predictions, the authors conducted an experiment involving an elaborate and creative procedure involving two trained confederates and a "mini-odyssey through the psychology building" (Leung & Cohen, 2011, p. 511). The study was run using college students representing face (Asian Americans), honor (Southerners and Latinos), and dignity (Northern Anglos) cultures. The participant and two confederates arrived at the lab at the same time and first rated their (a) endorsement of the actions in a series of film clips depicting honor violence (e.g., a male college student who was being bullied punches the bully) and (b) endorsement of the belief that a person's worth is inalienable versus socially conferred. Prior to viewing the movies, one of the two confederates offered the participant some candies; in some cases, the confederate who offered the candies would later require a favor (returning a computer disk), whereas in other cases, the confederate who offered the candies would simply serve as a distractor in the broader script. Following the movie and a fake debriefing, the "disk confederate" pulled out a computer disk and left it on a table outside the lab, while the "distractor confederate" engaged the true participant in casual conversation. Through a carefully staged script, the disk confederate made it clear that he or she was heading to Room 25 of the Psychology Department building and then left the lab, apparently forgetting the computer disk. If the real participant did not notice the disk, the distractor confederate made sure that the real participant was aware of it, but indicated that he or she could not return it to the disk confederate. Following this elaborate interaction, the researchers coded whether (and to what extent) the participant would attempt to return the disk. Because the signs in the building were confusing, and the "disk confederate" had apparently moved from Room 25 (in the basement) to Room 841 (on the 8th floor), returning the disk was a significant undertaking. "Helping points" were given on the basis of how far the participant went in returning the disk (e.g., 0 for not trying, 1 for going to Room 25, 2 for going to 8th floor, 3 for waiting on the 8th floor for someone to show up at Room 841).

Consistent with the authors' hypotheses, results revealed the predicted three-way interactions between Culture, Personality, and the Situation. Focusing on the first predicted interaction: When there was no favor to return, results revealed no significant differences between cultures or individual differences in endorsement of honor violence. However, when the disk confederate had offered the participant some candies (there was a favor to return), results revealed the predicted Culture × Personality interaction: Specifically, within honor cultures, helping was positively related to endorsement of honor violence, whereas in nonhonor cultures, helping was negatively related to endorsement of honor violence. In sum, results revealed that the same personal disposition (endorsement of honor violence) had opposite effects on reciprocity in honor and face/dignity cultures.

Results also supported the second interaction prediction. Within the dignity culture, when there was a favor to repay, helping was related to stronger endorsement of the belief that a person's worth is inalienable (endorsement of the dignity cultural logic), whereas within honor/face cultures, helping was related to stronger endorsement of the belief that worth is socially conferred.

In a second experiment, the authors applied their CuPS model to understanding the conditions under which members of face, honor, and dignity cultures would be more likely to cheat on an exam. The authors manipulated the salience of the honor culture (via film) and whether the experimenter offered the participant gum, and they used a clever method for assessing cheating. Consistent with their reasoning, within honor cultures, priming the honor culture led those who endorsed the honor culture logic to become more honest, whereas it led those rejecting the honor culture more likely to cheat. Within nonhonor cultures, by comparison, cheating was higher among those endorsing honor violence, and this relationship did not depend on whether the honor culture logic had previously been primed via watching a movie. In addition, within dignity cultures, when the experimenter offered the participant a piece of gum, thereby providing the opportunity to return the favor, those who more strongly endorsed a belief in inalienable worth were less likely to cheat, a finding consistent with the result from the first experiment.

In sum, Leung and Cohen (2011) proposed a comprehensive model to account for meaningful interactions between culture, personality, and situations, and they tested that model within honor, face, and dignity cultures. One of the paper's main contributions was to highlight that the same disposition in one culture (e.g., endorsement of honor violence) carries much different meanings in different cultures and can, as a result, lead to counterintuitive results. In nonhonor cultures, endorsement of honor violence implies a lack of self-control and belief in aggression, in general, and thus leads to a reduced willingness to return favors. By contrast, within honor cultures, the notion of honor violence (negative reciprocity) is closely linked with the idea of returning favors (positive reciprocity); as a result, within honor cultures, endorsement of honor violence is (perhaps counterintuitively) positively associated with the tendency to return favors. Researchers interested in a broad framework for integrating culture, personality, and social situations will find this article a helpful guide in formulating nuanced and potentially counterintuitive predictions.

CULTURAL DIFFERENCES IN THE BUILT ENVIRONMENT SHAPE PERCEPTION

In 2006, Miyamoto, Nisbett, and Masuda set out to understand how the *built environment* (i.e., complexity and density of buildings in a city) may shape cultural differences in perceptual processes. The authors first reviewed a number of studies indicating that people from Eastern Asian cultures are more likely than those from Western cultures to think holistically and pay attention to background/contextual information, whereas those from Western cultures are more likely than those from East Asian cultures to think analytically and pay attention to the information in foreground (e.g., Masuda & Nisbett, 2001). As the authors noted, although evidence for such processing differences had been growing at the time of the study, little attention had been paid to identifying a mechanism to explain those differences. One approach had been to suggest that differing socialization processes, and corresponding individual differences (e.g., in individualism vs. collectivism), may account for cultural differences in perceptual processing. In contrast to this approach, the authors turned to the built environment as an explanation. Specifically, the authors proposed that people from East Asian cultures may be more likely to pay attention to contextual/background information because East Asian cities are more complex than Western cities, thus visually "affording" (or encouraging) a more holistic perspective.

To test their hypothesis, the authors conducted three experiments. The first two experiments were designed to determine whether East Asian cities were, in fact, visually more complex than Western cities. The third experiment was designed to test whether exposure to scenes from East Asian cities (vs. Western cities) led people to pay more attention to information in the background of a scene.

In Study 1a, the authors took a large number of pictures near schools, post offices, and hotels in small, medium, and large cities in Japan and the United States. Locations and frames of reference for the various pictures were carefully matched. American and East Asian students (at the University of Michigan) were subsequently shown a subset of those pictures and rated how complex, ambiguous, and disorganized (chaotic) they were. Results showed, as predicted, that the Japanese cities were perceived as more complex than the American cities.

In Study 1b, the authors validated their findings using sophisticated computer software that was able to compute the number of distinct objects in a scene. Consistent with their initial findings, results revealed that the pictures from Japanese cities contained more objects than the pictures from American cities.

In Study 2, the authors sought to explore how exposure to scenes from the different environments might affect the extent to which perceivers paid attention to information in the foreground (vs. background) of a scene. Participants were first exposed to a subset of the pictures used in Study 1a. Next, participants were shown a series of two videos and asked to identify all differences between the videos (i.e., to assess change blindness). As predicted, participants identified significantly more changes in the background of the target pictures after being exposed to Japanese, as opposed to American, cities.

Miyamoto, Nisbett, and Masuda's (2006) work is an interesting and creative example of cross-cultural research. Whereas many cross-cultural studies have compared individuals from different cultures on an outcome of interest (e.g., holistic vs. analytic thinking), Miyamoto and her colleagues compared the visual complexity of two relevant cultures and further explored how exposure to these different visual environments shaped (afforded) previously established culture differences in perception (i.e., the tendency for people from East Asian cultures to pay more attention to information in the background of a scene). Researchers focusing on the role of culture who are striving to "think outside the box" will find this paper an inspiring example.

CULTURAL DIFFERENCES IN RESPONSE TO BRAND EXTENSIONS

In 2007, Monga and John published a paper examining cultural differences in how consumers evaluate brand extensions. As the authors noted, although a large number of studies had shown that consumers evaluate brand extensions more favorably when the extension is viewed as a good fit with the parent brand, few studies had attempted to determine whether this finding applies to "consumers around the globe" (p. 529). To address that gap, the authors explored how cultural differences in Western/analytic versus East Asian/holistic processing might impact responses to brand extensions. The authors hypothesized that because holistic thinkers are more likely than analytic thinkers to see connections between objects, people from East Asian cultures should perceive a higher fit between a parent brand and its brand extension and, consequently, evaluate brand extensions more favorably. To test this and a number of related hypotheses, the authors conducted three studies.

In Study 1a, the authors asked college students at a U.S. university to evaluate one of three brand extensions that had previously been shown to be of very low fit (Kodak shoes), low fit (Kodak filing cabinet), or moderate fit (Kodak greeting cards). Approximately half of the students were Americans, whereas the other half were from India and had been in the United States for less than 3 years. Preliminary analyses revealed that the American students were more analytical in their thinking than the Indian students. As expected, the primary analyses revealed that the Indian students evaluated each of the three brand extensions more favorably than did the American students. Similarly, subsequent analyses showed that those scoring low in analytic thinking evaluated the brand extensions more favorably than those high in analytic thinking.

In Study 1b, the authors aimed to extend the generalizability of their findings and determine whether extremely high fit extensions would eliminate the cross-cultural difference observed in their first study. American and Indian college students evaluated one of four brand extensions for McDonalds, including products representing a very low fit (razor), a low fit (chocolate bar), a moderate fit (omelet), or a high fit (onion rings). Confirming their earlier findings, the authors found that Indian students evaluated the first three extensions more favorably than American students. However, students from the two cultures evaluated the high-fit extension equally, thus establishing a boundary condition for the cross-cultural difference.

In Study 2, Monga and John (2007) set out to determine whether they could reverse the observed cultural difference by leading American students to think holistically and Indian students to think analytically. To accomplish this, the authors first led half of the participants to adopt an independent self-view (related to analytic thinking) and the other half to adopt an interdependent self-view (related to holistic thinking) by having participants read a paragraph and circle pronouns consistent with the independent self (e.g., I, me) or the interdependent self (e.g., we, us); a separate pretest validated the manipulation, such that those in the independent condition scored higher on a test of analytic thinking than those in the interdependent condition. Subsequently, participants evaluated the low-fit extension from Study 1a (Kodak filing cabinet).

The primary results revealed several important patterns. First, as expected, the authors found that American students scored lower in holistic thinking than the Indian students. Second, when students had not been led to adopt the thinking style of their own culture, Indian students perceived a higher brand fit and evaluated the brand extension more favorably than American students, confirming the authors' earlier findings. In contrast, when students were led to adopt the thinking style of the other group's culture (Americans were led to think holistically, Indians were led to think analytically), the American students evaluated perceived a higher brand fit and evaluated the brand extension more favorably than the Indian students. Finally, when Indians and Americans were primed with the same style of thinking, the cross-cultural differences in brand extension responses were eliminated, which again shows that the authors' results are due to underlying differences in style of thinking across cultures.

Monga and John's (2007) paper serves as a clear illustration of how researchers can identify the need for a cross-cultural comparison and use strong theory to make predictions for the cross-cultural comparison. The paper also provides an interesting demonstration of how researchers can effectively "reverse" the group-level difference by manipulating the mechanism assumed to underlie the cross-cultural difference (e.g., leading Indian students to think analytically and American students to think holistically). This clean and well-organized approach can serve as a useful template for researchers interested in understanding the nature of cross-cultural differences in a given domain.

DIFFERENCES IN DISEASE PREVALENCE PREDICT CULTURAL VARIATIONS IN PERSONALITY TRAITS

In 2008, Schaller and Murray proposed and tested several intriguing hypotheses linking disease prevalence to cross-cultural variation in sociosexual style (restricted vs. open), extraversion, and openness to experience. As the authors noted, although a certain degree of cross-cultural variation in personality may be traced back to the unique histories of certain cultures, such (idiosyncratic) historical events and conditions do not allow for more broadly generalizable conclusions on the origins of cross-cultural differences in personality. To address this problem, the authors put forth an integrative framework explaining how "basic human tendencies, operating in conjunction with varying ecological conditions, can produce cross-cultural differences" (p. 212).

The authors built their argument by first reviewing research suggesting that suspicion about, and a lack of openness to, out-groups (e.g., in-group bias and xenophobia) can be viewed, in part, as "disease-avoidant psychological processes" (p. 213). Extending this argument, the authors next argued that similar disease-avoiding processes might apply, more generally, to a host of unfamiliar objects in a person's environment. As a consequence, the authors proposed that an incautious personality may be especially costly in regions characterized by a high prevalence of disease. This line of reasoning leads to the authors' three hypotheses: namely, disease prevalence should be associated with three traits especially relevant to one's openness to and interaction with others (and consequently, their vulnerability to disease). Specifically, disease prevalence should be associated with a less open sociosexual style, lower extraversion, and lower openness to experience.

To test their hypotheses, Schaller and Murray (2008) used medical atlases and epidemiological sources to code the prevalence of seven diseases (e.g., malaria, leprosy, and typhus) for 71 geographical regions around the world. They then correlated these prevalence estimates with scores on sociosexual style and the Big Five personality traits, previously reported by other researchers.

Consistent with their hypotheses, results revealed that disease prevalence was negatively related to sociosexual style (especially among women), Extraversion, and Openness to Experience. Disease prevalence was not, however, systematically related to the remaining Big Five traits of Conscientiousness, Agreeableness, and Neuroticism.

Additional analyses ruled out a number of alternative explanations for the results. In particular, the authors demonstrated that their results could not be explained by regional variation in life expectancy, economic development, variations in individualism/collectivism, or climate (e.g., latitude and temperature).

Schaller and Murray's (2008) paper illustrates how a well-grounded theoretical framework can be combined with meaningful secondary data to test a number of interesting hypotheses concerning the origins of culture. Their paper also shows how collecting data to rule out alternative explanations further strengthens the conclusions from cross-cultural comparisons. Consequently, cross-cultural researchers interested in understanding the intersection between personality, culture, and the environment would find this article of great interest.

DIFFERING IMPORTANCE OF THE RECIPROCITY NORM EXPLAINS CULTURAL DIFFERENCES IN WILLINGNESS TO ACCEPT A SMALL GIFT

In 2011, Shen, Wan, and Wyer reported a series of studies aimed at understanding cultural differences in the willingness to accept a small gift. The authors motivated their study by first highlighting the possible misunderstandings that can arise when people of different cultural backgrounds exchange gifts. Although gift exchange between friends is likely to be viewed by all cultures as a form of affection, and thus open to misunderstanding based on culture, gift exchange between acquaintances may be interpreted in different ways if the gift giver and gift recipient are from different cultures. More specifically, because people from East Asian cultures are more likely than those from Western cultures to adopt an interdependent self-construal, and adhere to a reciprocity norm, it is likely that gift recipients from East Asian cultures will be more likely than those from Western cultures to view a gift as requiring reciprocity. This, in turn, is likely to lead to gift recipients from East Asian cultures to experience heightened feelings of indebtedness and lower feelings of appreciation for the gift, feelings that should consequently reduce East Asians' willingness to accept a free gift.

To test their hypotheses, the authors conducted eight studies. The first four (Studies 1a–1d) used a scenario methodology to provide initial support for the (cultural difference and mediation) hypotheses. In Study 1a, students from Hong Kong were less likely than those from Canada to accept a friend's offer to pay for a taxi ride to the airport. In Study 1b, students from Hong Kong were less likely than those from Canada to accept a salesperson's offer of a free sample of soup in a supermarket, and this difference was mediated by feelings of indebtedness and appreciation for the gift. In addition, students from Hong Kong were more concerned with "losing face" if they accepted the offer and did not reciprocate, which in turn was positively related to feelings of indebtedness. In Study 1c, students from Hong Kong and Canada imagined they bumped into a past college classmate at the airport who offered to buy the participant a coffee. In line with Studies 1a and 1b, students from Hong Kong were less likely than students from Canada to accept the offer, and this difference was mediated by feelings of indebtedness and appreciation. In addition, students from Hong Kong were less likely to believe the classmate's offer to buy coffee was sincere, which in turn predicted reduced feelings of appreciation. Finally, in Study 1d, the authors showed that the previously established cultural differences were observed (eliminated) when participants were instructed to respond in a manner that made them feel better (would be polite), thus ruling out the possibility that the authors' initial findings were due to Hong Kong students' desire to behave in a polite manner.

Studies 2 through 4 built on the authors' initial findings. In Study 2, the authors explored how Hong Kong and Canadian students responded to a gift (free coffee at the airport) given in the context of an exchange relationship (from a casual acquaintance) versus a communal relationship (from a close friend). In line with the authors' reasoning, students from Hong Kong were only less likely than Canadian students to accept a free gift when the gift was from an acquaintance. When the gift was from a close friend, students from both cultures were equally likely to accept the gift, supporting the argument that gift exchange in the initial studies was interpreted in the context of an exchange (as opposed to communal) relationship.

In Study 3, female Canadian and Chinese students at a Canadian university were recruited to complete a short or a long survey. Following the survey, participants were told the researchers had some candy bars available, and participants could take as many as they wanted. Consistent with the argument that the reciprocity norm is stronger for those from East Asian cultures, Chinese students took more candy bars after completing the long (vs. short) survey, whereas length of survey had no impact on the number of candy bars taken by Canadian students.

In Study 4, Shen and colleagues (2011) first had (female) students from Hong Kong and Canada take part in a series of distractor studies. Subsequently, the experimenter running the study asked participants if they would be willing to complete another short (vs. long) study in the future as part of the experimenter's dissertation. Once participants had signed up (or not), the experimenter told participants there were some candies left over from a previous study, and participants could take as many as they desired (from a cup of 10). As expected, students from Hong Kong took fewer candies after deciding not to participate than to participate, whereas Canadian students did not base the number of candies taken on whether they agreed or did not agree to participate.

In Study 5, North American and Asian (female) students at a Canadian university were offered some candies on campus, ostensibly as part of an Easter celebration. Participants were then asked to complete a survey gauging "responses to gifts." Consistent with the earlier findings, Chinese students took fewer candies than the North American students and reported greater feelings of indebtedness and less appreciation after taking the candies. Moreover, Chinese students were more likely to complete the survey if they had taken a large number of candies, whereas the number of candies taken had no impact on willingness to complete the survey among North American students.

Taken together, Shen and colleagues used a variety of methods to show consistent and meaningful cross-cultural differences in willingness to accept a free gift from an acquaintance. In sum, people from East Asian cultures are less likely than those from Western cultures to accept free gifts from acquaintances, because East Asians are more likely to adhere to the norm of reciprocity and thus feel more indebted and less appreciative of the free gift. Researchers interested in understanding the mechanism underlying cross-cultural differences could profitably use Shen and colleagues' paper as an effective model.

Conclusion

Broadly framed, the primary goal of cross-cultural psychology is to "extend the range of variation of psychological functioning" (Adamopoulos & Lonner, 2001, p. 15) beyond what Berry et al. (1997) referred to as WASP (Western academic scientific psychology). This chapter's illustrations highlight the range of creative methods researchers use to meet this goal. The illustrations reflect collaboration between researchers from different cultures; exploration of cross-cultural differences between and within countries; use of mixed (correlational and experimental) methods; use of methods designed to reduce potential confounds; and collection and/or manipulation of societal-level and individual-level ecological, sociopolitical, and psychological antecedents and mediating process variables. As a result, the illustrations provide readers interested in exploring the role of culture with a creative and informative source of ideas for expanding our understanding of behavior across the full spectrum of human experience.

Author Interviews

Highlighted Author

Simon Gächter
Professor of the
Psychology of
Economic Decision
Making, University
of Nottingham
School of Economics,
Nottingham, England

What is your advice for publishing high-quality research that is likely to have impact?

Be ambitious and enthusiastic about your research! Try to work on fundamental research questions, not on the low-hanging fruit. Being grounded in relevant theory is important, but keeping an open mind and eye to observe reality around you can be very inspiring as well. For example, our research on antisocial punishment did not start with any theoretical hypotheses but with a conjecture by Benedikt Herrmann, nurtured by personal experience of life in Russia, that cooperation and punishment are very different in Russia than in Switzerland. When Benedikt first told me his conjecture, I was skeptical but intrigued. So we decided to follow up on his hunch by designing new experiments to see whether Benedikt's intuition would be true. It was—we uncovered antisocial punishment, which we deemed an important phenomenon because of its detrimental consequences for cooperation.

By definition, high-impact research is interesting for many people over long periods of time. Therefore, think hard about what would make your paper interesting for many people, ideally, and for very high-impact papers, necessarily outside your own field. Whether people find a paper interesting has a lot to do with how fundamental the research question is, how surprised and intrigued readers are by your findings, and how strong the evidence is. Care for the big picture surprises, but also try to get all details right, and provide enough data. A surprising result based on slender data may get you some initial interest, but people may sooner or later discard

What "cross-cultural" paper would you recommend and why?

Henrich, Heine, and Norenzayan's (2010) paper titled, "The Weirdest People in the World?" published in *Behavioural and Brain Sciences*. This paper is an important contribution about the necessity of cross-cultural work to prevent overly strong claims about human nature based on data collected only in WEIRD (Western, educated, industrialized, rich, and democratic) societies.

your paper as being unconvincing. Provide data and experimental protocols, if asked, in a timely and well-documented way. After all, one way to become influential is if people want to replicate and extend your findings in new directions.

Producing a good paper requires almost 24/7 thinking about it. Try to put yourself into the shoes of critical referees (and hopefully many other future readers) and challenge yourself by taking the perspective of critics on all aspects of your paper. You have to be fully immersed in your paper while working on it. It is a good idea to present papers at seminars, conferences, and workshops to get people's reactions fairly early on. This has helped us a lot in seeing what worked and what didn't, and sometimes comments inspired new experiments to make the paper stronger. Collect enough data, and do careful analysis according to the state of the art (of your own discipline and the target audience). Try to think about good figures that convey the main results in an easily accessible and therefore memorable way. Invest a lot of time in writing, and be prepared to rewrite a few times. Do not oversell, because this undermines your credibility (but underselling is a problem too). Be patient and submit only once you are truly convinced (beware of self-deception) that you can't do more to make the paper better.

Highlighted Author

Angela Leung
Associate Professor,
School of Social
Sciences, Singapore
Management
University, Singapore

What is your advice for publishing high-quality research that is likely to have impact?

They should have a good grasp of the theoretical and empirical background of the related topic, but they need not fully immerse themselves in the prior literature by exhausting the reading list. Reading "too much" can sometimes impose structures or confines to how we approach the research problems. Instead, reading sufficiently but not overdoing it may help lift up the lens others used to view the problem and lead to a new perspective others cannot see otherwise. Researchers can start formulating their research ideas once they have sufficiently explored the literature and then go back to visit the literature to fill in gaps and make connections. This is likely to be an iterative process of developing and refining the research ideas. Also, be prepared to keep up with new methodological tools and trends. Quite often, interdisciplinary collaborations provide the opportunity to bridge methodological conventions and create new tools that contribute in important ways to high-impact research. For example, novel methodologies such as online experimental social science, mining of online data, computational simulations and modeling, and the analysis of big data are getting increasingly popular in psychology. Researchers of high-impact research are receptive to these new opportunities for broadening their methodological bandwidth.

What "cross-cultural" paper would you recommend and why?

I have had the pleasure of working with an excellent team of collaborators on a paper related to multicultural experience and creativity (Leung, Maddux, Galinsky, & Chiu, 2008) published in *American Psychologist*. Rapid globalization has drastically increased the frequency and intensity of intercultural contacts. What does it take to thrive in a multicultural and cosmopolitan environment? With the triangulation of diverse methodological approaches, this research is the first systematic empirical investigation of this timely topic, bringing the psychological studies of multiculturalism and creativity to a new direction. In this review paper, we documented a series of empirical studies to demonstrate the enduring benefit of creativity as one psychological ramification of multicultural experiences. Further, we set out to systematically reveal *how* and *when* individuals can capitalize on their intercultural contacts to instigate their creative capability.

Highlighted Author

Yuri Miyamoto
Associate Professor,
Department of
Psychology,
University of
Wisconsin–Madison

**Alokparna
(Sonia) Monga**
Associate Professor
of Marketing, Darla
Moore School of
Business, University
of South Carolina,
Columbia

What is your advice for publishing high-quality research that is likely to have impact?

Reach outside your own field of expertise. I took classes and read books on architecture and urban engineering when I was working on this project. It not only helped me generate ideas but also informed the methodology.

I realized that by thinking deeper and deeper about branding and culture, I was able to come up with new connections that had not been made earlier. Therefore, I would encourage scholars to specialize in one area of research. By doing so, they would easily be able to identify big questions that have not been examined. I would also encourage scholars to read widely in many different journals to identify novel factors that could offer insights into their specialty area.

What "cross-cultural" paper would you recommend and why?

There are so many significant cross-cultural studies that it is hard to pick one, but if I were forced to do so, I would recommend Kitayama, Markus, Matsumoto, and Norasakkunkit (1997). They showed how daily situations that exist in each culture can play a role in shaping and maintaining culturally specific psychological processes. This paper had a large impact on the formulation of our paper (Miyamoto, Nisbett, & Masuda, 2006).

The Nisbett, Peng, Choi and Norenzayan (2001) article is an excellent paper to read. It is a review paper that summarizes and connects all the research that has been conducted on cross-cultural differences in analytic–holistic thinking. It questions the long-held view that cognitive processes are similar across cultures. It also traces various experimental findings back to the differences in the social systems of the ancient Greek and Chinese civilizations. This is a riveting article for culture researchers.

Highlighted Author

Mark Schaller
Professor, Department
of Psychology,
University of British
Columbia, Vancouver,
British Columbia,
Canada

What is your advice for publishing high-quality research that is likely to have impact?

Whenever you develop a research project, ask this question: "Who cares?" I mean that literally. Exactly *who* are the people who might realistically find the research results to be useful and relevant to their own pursuits? Your research is likely to have greater impact if it addresses topics that are of intellectual interest to a larger number of people. It is also likely to have greater impact if that set of people includes folks from multiple subdisciplines within psychology, and it will probably have even greater impact if it also includes folks working in other disciplines too.

What "cross-cultural" paper would you recommend and why?

My favorite articles in cultural psychology are those that illustrate deeper, more universal processes lurking beneath the ethnographic dazzle of cross-cultural differences. For this reason, I think anybody with an interest in cultural psychology would benefit from reading a paper that two colleagues of mine—Ara Norenzayan and Steve Heine—published in *Psychological Bulletin* a few years back (2005). The article explores, in a very thoughtful way, how cross-cultural research can be used to identify specific psychological phenomena that are, or aren't, universal across humans everywhere.

Hao Shen
Associate Professor,
Department of
Marketing, Chinese
University of Hong
Kong, Shatin, NT,
Hong Kong

We spent 3 to 4 years working on this project. It is not easy to establish a theoretically interesting story based on the effect we get. So I suggest other authors can make the research more theory driven when they start to work on an idea. That is, they can first consider the theoretical contribution of an idea and then apply the idea in real life. This can make it easier to understand the process that drives the effect and also tell a story about the work.

I recommend a paper by Torelli and Shavitt (2010). I think this paper provides intriguing insights into how the conceptualization of power differs across cultures. For example, vertical individualism is more associated with personalized power (power is for status and personal achievement), whereas horizontal collectivism is more associated with socialized power (power is for helping and taking care of others). These findings make a good theoretical contribution to the understanding of the relationship between culture and power.

CONCLUSION III

A Process Model for Publishing High-Quality Research

13

O ur goal in this book has been to illustrate eight paradigms for publishing high-quality research; to show how those paradigms contribute to theory development and testing; to provide guidance on to how generate ideas, write a strong first draft, and successfully navigate the revision process; and to emphasize the importance of ethics throughout the entire process. This chapter has two principal purposes. First, we highlight several key themes of this book. Second, on the basis of insights gleaned from the recommendations of the authors we highlight herein, we develop a process model for publishing high-quality research.

http://dx.doi.org/10.1037/14525-014
How to Publish High-Quality Research, by J. Joireman and P. A. M. Van Lange

Key Themes

Throughout this book, we have emphasized several key themes that support high-quality research. Briefly put, researchers should start with a great idea, frame that idea in the context of a meaningful theory, write and navigate the revision process effectively, and pay careful attention to ethical issues throughout the entire process.

IT ALL STARTS WITH A GREAT IDEA

At the heart of every high-quality paper is a great idea. This "nugget" gives rise to your paper's key contributions and is pivotal for getting readers interested and on board with your paper. In Chapter 1, we discussed 16 different strategies authors can use to start the idea-generating process. Some strategies involve interacting with peers both within and outside your discipline. Others require paying attention to interesting and important phenomena in the real world. And yet others involve taking a fresh look and often challenging intuitions, conventional wisdom, or long-held existing assumptions. We encourage readers to pay careful attention to the origins of the ideas in the papers they are reading to gain additional insight into this critical stage of the research process.

THE IMPORTANCE OF THEORY

In our experience as authors, reviewers, and editors, it is clear that one of the most important factors that affects whether a manuscript is accepted or rejected at a high-quality journal is the value of the manuscript's contribution. The manuscript's contribution, in turn, rests heavily on the extent to which the manuscript is theoretically grounded and addresses a meaningful gap in the literature, a position expressed by many of our highlighted authors as well.

With this in mind, in Chapter 2, we considered what theory is and what theory is not, and described a system for evaluating theories. The TAPAS (truth, abstraction, progress, and applicability) system (Van Lange, 2013) proposes that good theories pursue truth (using sound reasoning and methods), are abstract (articulate broad, generalizable principles that go beyond a particular setting), result in progress (build on past theory and research, extending what we already know), and are applicable (e.g., outside the lab). To refine your skills in theory development and testing, we encourage you to keep these criteria in mind and to carefully consider how theoretical arguments are developed in other high-quality papers you admire. Certainly, the papers highlighted in this book represent an excellent place to start.

THE PARADIGMS SUPPORT THEORY
DEVELOPMENT, THEORY TESTING, AND TAPAS

Another important theme running throughout this book is that each of the eight paradigms for publishing high-quality research supports the development and/or testing of theory and the TAPAS system. Bridging disciplines supports building comprehensive/integrative theories and applying theories developed in one domain to phenomena in a different domain to establish abstract and applicable principles. Meta-analysis helps to bring order to a large literature and can be used to test, refine, or develop theories. Launching a paradigm shift contributes to progress by pushing theoretical boundaries and challenging existing assumptions. Combining mediators and moderators helps in the search for underlying mechanisms and boundary conditions. Developing a new tool for assessing individual differences, or a new innovative method, supports the search for truth and application via better measures and methods. Venturing into the real world supports the application of theory in realistic settings. And exploring the role of culture helps test the extent to which theories can generalize or must be adapted across settings.

STRONG WRITING AND A QUALITY REVISION
CAN MAKE OR BREAK YOUR CONTRIBUTION

Knowing the eight publication paradigms, using them to test theory, executing them successfully, and obtaining high-quality results are all important, but they represent only the first step in publishing high-quality research. Once the data are in, it is critical to share and publish your contribution in an influential or excellent journal, which rests largely on your ability to submit a strong initial manuscript and successfully navigate the review and revision process. To facilitate that process, we emphasized three broad principles: striving for perfection, objectively reflecting on the quality of your writing, and gathering and responding to feedback from other scholars before submitting. We then discussed a number of more specific strategies, including leading your reader by the hand, thinking carefully about the organization of your paper, providing overviews, using effective transitions, using straightforward language, making sure each sentence adds value, and avoiding (unnecessary) redundancy. We also provided suggestions for tackling the Introduction, Method, Results, and Discussion sections. In the final part of Chapter 4, we reflected on the revision process, where we emphasized the value of a 3R approach, which suggests you should be reflective, rational, and respectful during the revision process. We also provided specific tips for a successful revision process: namely, don't fool yourself or try to pull the wool over the reviewers' eyes, do respond to each comment (in a respectful manner), and produce a clear and detailed response letter (often called a cover letter).

Beyond these strategies, we recommend paying careful attention to the way high-quality papers and arguments are structured, recognizing patterns in each section of the paper, and aiming to model your writing after papers you view as especially well written. In our opinion, the papers illustrated in this book, and the papers recommended by the highlighted authors, provide multiple examples of these "best practices."

ON THE IMPORTANCE OF ETHICS

Needless to say, all of the advice we have offered must rest on a strong, ethical foundation. In Chapter 3, we considered a number of reasons for conducting research in an ethical manner and summarized key ethical principles concerning the execution of research and the analysis and reporting of data. As noted, a number of fields, including social psychology and consumer behavior, have recently uncovered researchers who have either completely fabricated their data or engaged in highly questionable "screening" of the data. It is often important to think carefully before conducting the studies whether the goal is testing and improving measurement techniques and procedures ("piloting") or examining relationships among variables to develop initial ideas or hypotheses (exploratory research). Both of these more exploratory approaches to research precede hypothesis-testing research and often help identify which variables to include in your research (and why) and how precisely you want to use them later on (after the data are collected). And arguably, the most important principle when it comes to an ethical treatment of data is transparency in the collection of data, the screening of data, and the actual analysis of data.

A Process Model for Publishing High-Quality Research Grounded in Our Highlighted Authors' Key Insights

The preceding section summarizes broad themes that we have highlighted in the book. When asked what advice they would give other scholars hoping to publish high-quality research that is likely to have an impact, our highlighted authors echoed a number of these themes and shared many additional valuable insights. In this section, we summarize their suggestions and organize them, along with some of our own ideas, within a five-stage process model, as shown in Figure 13.1. We also direct readers to the applicable chapters in the present book. This process model was designed to be useful for both scholarship and training. Insights from each and every highlighted author were essential in building this model, and we would like to thank them for taking the time to reflect on this issue and share their wisdom. Certain unique phrases or terms that were offered by a single highlighted author are recognized in Figure 13.1 with an asterisk.

STAGES IN THE PROCESS

Stage 1 (the motivational sphere) captures the essential objectives and motivations that can guide and inspire researchers to conduct the highest quality research. One theme expressed by many of our highlighted authors was that researchers should pursue a topic they are passionate about, and that can sustain their interest for an extended period of time. Equally important, researchers should keep in mind that "there are several roads to Rome" (as discussed in Chapter 1). An additional recommendation was that researchers should not chase the "dragon of impact" per se (Griskevicius, Tybur, & Van den Bergh, 2010; Chapter 5) but should instead seek to engage in high-quality research and effectively "let the chips fall where they may." This is good advice for at least two reasons. First, many factors can ultimately affect whether a certain paper has an impact. Second, pursuing interesting and high-quality research increases the likelihood of enjoying the journey and ultimately having an impact. Finally, as noted, an overarching objective should always be to maintain integrity and transparency throughout the publication process.

With objectives and motivations clearly defined, researchers can engage in an initial set of activities that promote the development of critical abilities and skills, which in turn support the ability to execute and ultimately publish high-quality research.

Stage 2 (initial activities) can be divided into two categories. *Mental preparation* is a broad term we use to represent an important but perhaps overlooked part of the creative, idea-generating process. Here, our highlighted authors encouraged readers to "think big" (Vohs, Chapter 5), "avoid low-hanging fruit" (Gächter, Chapter 12), and pursue groundbreaking contribution, rather than more incremental contributions. A majority of our highlighted authors also stressed the importance of observing (and engaging with) the real world as a source of inspiration for ideas and focusing on "problems of everyday life" (Schaller, Chapter 12) that people from all walks of life would

FIGURE 13.1

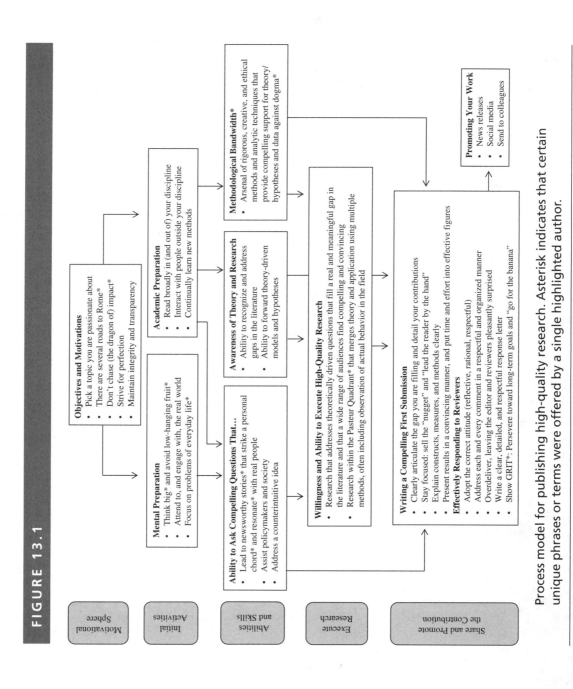

Process model for publishing high-quality research. Asterisk indicates that certain unique phrases or terms were offered by a single highlighted author.

find interesting. If the question is of interest to one's friends, family, and/or coworkers, it is likely to be of interest to a much wider array of audiences.

Clearly, a second set of vital initial (and ongoing) activities falls under the umbrella of academic preparation. Numerous highlighted authors encouraged readers to read broadly, both within and outside their area and discipline, and to consciously seek out people in other disciplines (e.g., attend conferences outside one's own discipline). Another recommendation was to be continually updating one's knowledge of new methods and statistical techniques.

Stage 3 (abilities and skills) follows from the initial mental and academic preparation activities. The creative process of mental preparation, for example, directly supports the ability to ask compelling (and often counterintuitive) questions that "strike a personal chord" (Kramer, Chapter 11), which could lead to "newsworthy stories" (Rindfleisch, Chapter 5) that "really resonate with people" (Paharia, Chapter 8), and that policymakers, granting agencies, and society would find useful. Another critical skill at this stage is to develop an awareness of theory and research, which positions researchers to recognize significant gaps in the literature and forward theory-driven models and hypotheses. Finally, academic preparation supports the development of a useful and creative toolbox of research methods, thereby expanding a researcher's "methodological bandwidth" (Leung, Chapter 12), which facilitates the ability to provide persuasive support for one's hypothesis and, when tackling a potentially controversial issue, to "use data against dogma" (Joseph & Newman, 2010; Chapter 6).

Stage 4 (execute research) focuses on the willingness and ability to conduct high-quality research. When one focuses on interesting, theoretically driven questions one is passionate about, and pairs that motivation with a solid grounding in theory, research, and methods, it is possible to execute high-quality research. By including the term *willingness*, we recognize that to pursue the big, groundbreaking questions and avoid the low-hanging fruit, it is essential to set a high standard for the project and be dedicated to the collection of compelling data, which often involves significant work on the front end (carefully designing the study), during execution (collecting the data), and when analyzing the data (e.g., coding real behavior from a field experiment). To use Duckworth's construct (Chapter 9), skills and abilities must be combined with "Grit" to see a project through to the end.

As many of our highlighted authors have noted, when it comes to execution, it is often useful to conduct research within the "Pasteur quadrant" (Luszczynska, Chapter 8), where theory and application are joint objectives. With this in mind, many authors also emphasized the value of conducting theoretically grounded research in real-world settings.

Stage 5 (sharing and promoting the contribution) focuses on *effectively communicating* the contribution to reviewers, editors, and increasingly, the public. Before delving into recommendations for this stage of the process, it is important to comment on the direct paths from abilities and skills (Stage 3) to sharing the contribution (Stage 5). These direct paths indicate that writing (and revising) are significantly influenced by (a) a researcher's ability to ask interesting questions (which enhances the ability to hook the reader), (b) a researcher's awareness of theory and research (which enhances the ability to articulate a meaningful gap and frame the contribution), and (c) a researcher's methodological bandwidth (which enhances the ability to convey, with appropriate research and data analytic methods, the key findings of the research). With this in mind, we turn next to a summary of the tips on writing and revising.

When *writing the initial submission*, it is essential that researchers clearly (and explicitly) identify a real and important gap in the literature and help reviewers understand how their manuscript fills that gap and consequently contributes to the literature. Staying focused and well organized, selling the nugget, and leading the reader by the hand are critical at this stage, as is a clear definition of constructs, measures, and methods. In addition, results should be presented in a convincing manner, often with great attention to detail (e.g., in the figures), and the discussion should help readers appreciate the goals, findings, theoretical and practical implications of the paper, as well as interesting directions for future research. Indeed, as Schaller (Chapter 12) noted, often a manuscript's most important contribution is its ability to raise more fundamental questions about the phenomenon under investigation.

Once the reviews are in, a researcher needs a good strategy for *responding to reviewers*. Here, authors must take care to prepare the revision according to the 3Rs (be reflective, rational, and respectful). Each comment should be addressed in a polite and organized manner, and you should seek to overdeliver and even aim to delight reviewers with the care and effort you put into the revision. A clear and detailed response letter is also vital at this point. Finally, and perhaps especially in the face of challenging reviews, researchers should show "Grit" (Duckworth, Chapter 9), by persevering, focusing on long-term goals (Strathman, Chapter 9), and—as one gets closer to the final goal—"going for the banana," as we explain in Chapter 14.

A final component of the process involves *promoting the work* via news releases (often encouraged by one's university), social media (e.g., ResearchGate), and sending your article to colleagues. Taking a proactive approach, even after the paper has been published, can significantly increase your paper's impact (both within and outside your discipline).

BENEFIT OF THE MODEL

Although the stage model we have developed may seem fairly intuitive, in our experience, researchers do not often walk through what it takes to publish high-quality research. We attend graduate school, read articles and books, fret over finding new questions, and become so intensely focused on our subject material that, at times, we fail to see the forest for the trees. The process model provides a 30,000-foot view of the process, while also capturing valuable insights gleaned from a wide range of established and emerging scholars. We hope, of course, that it can also serve as a useful organizing framework for discussions with young scholars setting out on their careers.

Concluding Thoughts 14

n this book, we have outlined a comprehensive set of tools that can help readers publish high-quality research. As we close, we consider one final set of factors that play a pivotal role in whether a researcher can convert a great idea into a high-quality paper: namely, persistence and drive.

If you are like many scholars we encounter, you may read a successful paper and think: This paper is flawless; they made it look so easy! As the authors of those papers will usually admit, however, the process is rarely easy. Indeed, making a high-impact contribution is often a real challenge. In this final chapter, we offer some final reflections on meeting that challenge.

Though it may seem obvious, it is important to note that making a contribution is often a social process, with assistance from coauthors. Accordingly, assembling a good team, with complementary skills, can significantly enhance the likelihood that you will succeed. Skilled coauthors who respond in a timely fashion can make the difference between success and failure, frustration and flow. Indeed, science is an

http://dx.doi.org/10.1037/14525-015
How to Publish High-Quality Research, by J. Joireman and P. A. M. Van Lange

inherently social process. Ideas, methods, and data analyses are frequently shared and discussed, and the process of writing and revising typically benefits tremendously from intellectual and social exchanges among coauthors and colleagues, around the corner or on the other side of the world. It is important to communicate and invite help, support, and assistance when you might need it—and to not completely lock yourself up in your study. This not only helps you complete projects but also gives you the tools to pursue perfection in the process.

However, it is also an undeniable fact that if you are the lead author, you are frequently on your own. The lead author is often the one who knows the most about the specific aims of the study, the methods, and the data. He or she is typically the one who begins to think over ideas and methods, and who begins to write. And the lead author is normally the first to see, process, and respond to the editorial letter along with the (frequently) critical reviews. In summary, much of the responsibility for your success rests in your hands.

It is also important to recognize that publishing is a time-consuming and often frustrating process with feedback loops that routinely extend over several months—or, in some cases, years. Inevitably, one must deal with setbacks, delays, frustrations, criticism, rejection, and oftentimes, considerable uncertainty. One may even be convinced that editors and reviewers are out to slam the authors (i.e., stress the limiting aspects of one's manuscript; Van Lange, 1999), and there is some evidence suggesting that reviewers in (social) psychology tend to be quite critical, even more so than editors, who already tend to reject 80% of manuscripts or more. In the face of these challenges it may, at times, be tempting to quit or settle for an easier option. For some, this temptation may, ironically, be especially likely as one nears the completion of a project. Indeed, "sealing the deal" can be the hardest part of the process.

With this in mind, it is helpful to consider a (somewhat shared) personal quote, namely: "One should go for the banana." One of us has often used this saying when there is a natural tendency to not finish what one has started with a lot of conviction and enthusiasm. Quitting is often an inferior (though understandable) option, because most projects will face obstacles, barriers, and strong uncertainties. The saying "Go for the banana" may serve as a reminder that the broad goals with which one began the project are worth pursuing, and can make a difference, but that it takes willpower and a long-term orientation to make the difference.

Indeed, it takes exceptional levels of self-discipline, determination, and willpower—or Grit (see Duckworth, Peterson, Matthews, & Kelley, 2007, as discussed in Chapter 9 of this book)—to convert an idea into a paper that has a real impact on one's field. And as Gladwell (2008) suggested in his book *Outliers*, many people who become truly exceptional have dedicated numerous hours to their craft (i.e., at least

10,000 hours of practice). To succeed, you must believe in what you are doing, have a strong motivation to complete what you have started, and be motivated to improve your skills. You also need to be aware that many people not familiar with the publication process may not appreciate the tremendous skill and effort that went into a scientific contribution, or on hearing of the findings, may express a genuine feeling that they "knew it all along," thanks (in part) to the pervasive hindsight bias.

In the final analysis, it is always important to keep in mind why we do what we do. Science is about producing knowledge that helps us explore uncharted territory, identifying principles needed to understand causal processes and phenomena, and contributing to the development of interventions for effectively resolving the plethora of personal and societal issues we face. Our hope is that the tools and illustrations provided in this book can help you achieve these fulfilling ideals, and ultimately "go for the banana."

References

Aarts, H., Dijksterhuis, A., & De Vries, P. (2001). On the psychology of drinking: Being thirsty and perceptually ready. *British Journal of Psychology, 92*, 631–642. doi:10.1348/000712601162383

Adamopoulos, J., & Lonner, W. J. (2001). Culture and psychology at a crossroad: Historical perspective and theoretical analysis. In D. Matsumoto (Ed.), *The handbook of culture and psychology* (pp. 11–34). New York, NY: Oxford University Press.

Alba, J. W. (2012). In defense of bumbling. *Journal of Consumer Research, 38*, 981–987. doi:10.1086/661230

Albarracín, D., Johnson, B. T., Fishbein, M., & Muellerleile, P. A. (2001). Theories of reasoned action and planned behavior as models of condom use: A meta-analysis. *Psychological Bulletin, 127*, 142–161.

American Psychological Association. (2010). *Ethical principles of psychologists and code of conduct (2002; amended June 1, 2010)*. Retrieved from http://www.apa.org/ethics/code/index.aspx

Anderson, C. A., & Bushman, B. J. (2001). Effects of violent video games on aggressive behavior, aggressive cognition, aggressive affect, physiological arousal, and prosocial behavior: A meta-analytic review of the scientific literature. *Psychological Science, 12*, 353–359. doi:10.1111/1467-9280.00366

Aquino, K., Freeman, D., Reed, A., Lim, V. K. G., & Felps, W. (2009). Testing a social–cognitive model of moral behavior: The interactive influence of situations and moral identity centrality. *Journal of Personality and Social Psychology, 97*, 123–141. doi:10.1037/a0015406

Argo, J. J., Dahl, D. W., & Morales, A. C. (2006). Consumer contamination: How consumers react to products touched by others. *Journal of Marketing, 70*, 81–94. doi:10.1509/jmkg.70.2.81

Argo, J. J., Dahl, D. W., & Morales, A. C. (2008). Positive consumer contagion: Responses to attractive others in a retail context. *Journal of Marketing Research, 45*, 690–701. doi:10.1509/jmkr.45.6.690

Ariely, D., & Levav, J. (2000). Sequential choice in group settings: Taking the road less traveled and less enjoyed. *Journal of Consumer Research, 27*, 279–290. doi:10.1086/317585

Ashton, M. C., Lee, K., Perugini, M., Szarota, P., De Vries, R. E., Di Blas, L., . . . De Raad, B. (2004). A six-factor structure of personality-descriptive adjectives: Solutions from psycholexical studies in seven languages. *Journal of Personality and Social Psychology, 86*, 356–366. doi:10.1037/0022-3514.86.2.356

Asplund, C. L., Fougnie, D., Zughni, S., Martin, J. W., & Marois, R. (2014). The attentional blink reveals the probabilistic nature of discrete conscious perception. *Psychological Science, 25*, 824–831. doi:10.1177/0956797613513810

Axelrod, R. (1984). *The evolution of cooperation.* New York, NY: Basic Books.

Aziz, N. A., & Rozing, M. P. (2013). Profit (*p*)-index: The degree to which authors profit from co-authors. *PLoS ONE, 8*(4), e59814. doi:10.1371/journal.pone.0059814

Ball, A. D., & Tasaki, L. H. (1992). The role and measurement of attachment in consumer behavior. *Journal of Consumer Psychology, 1*, 155–172. doi:10.1207/s15327663jcp0102_04

Balliet, D., & Joireman, J. (2010). Ego depletion reduces proselfs' concern with the well-being of others. *Group Processes & Intergroup Relations, 13*, 227–239. doi:10.1177/1368430209353634

Balliet, D., Li, N., & Joireman, J. (2011). Relating trait self-control and forgiveness within prosocials and proselfs: Compensatory versus synergistic models. *Journal of Personality and Social Psychology, 101*, 1090–1105. doi:10.1037/a0024967

Balliet, D., Mulder, L. B., & Van Lange, P. A. M. (2011). Reward, punishment, and cooperation: A meta-analysis. *Psychological Bulletin, 137*, 594–615. doi:10.1037/a0023489

Barnhart, M., & Peñaloza, L. (2013). Who are you calling old? Negotiating old age identity in the elderly consumption ensemble. *Journal of Consumer Research, 39*, 1133–1153. doi:10.1086/668536

Baron, R. M., & Kenny, D. A. (1986). The moderator-mediator variable distinction in social psychological research: Conceptual, strategic, and statistical considerations. *Journal of Personality and Social Psychology, 51,* 1173–1182. doi:10.1037/0022-3514.51.6.1173

Barrick, M. R., & Mount, M. K. (1991). The Big Five personality dimensions and job performance: A meta-analysis. *Personnel Psychology, 44,* 1–26. doi:10.1111/j.1744-6570.1991.tb00688.x

Bateson, M., Nettle, D., & Roberts, G. (2006). Cues of being watched enhance cooperation in a real-world setting. *Biology Letters, 2,* 412–414.

Baum, M. L., Anish, D. S., Chalmers, T. C., Sacks, H. S., Smith, H., Jr., & Fagerstrom, R. M. (1981). A survey of clinical trials of antibiotic prophylaxis in colon surgery: Evidence against further use of no-treatment controls. *The New England Journal of Medicine, 305,* 795–799. doi:10.1056/NEJM198110013051404

Baumeister, R. F., Bratslavsky, E., Muraven, M., & Tice, D. M. (1998). Ego depletion: Is the active self a limited resource? *Journal of Personality and Social Psychology, 74,* 1252–1265. doi:10.1037/0022-3514.74.5.1252

Bearden, W. O., Netemeyer, R. G., & Haws, K. L. (2011). *Handbook of marketing scales: Multi-item measures for marketing and consumer behavior research.* Thousand Oaks, CA: Sage.

Berger, J. (2011). Arousal increases social transmission of information. *Psychological Science, 22,* 891–893. doi:10.1177/0956797611413294

Berger, J., Bradlow, E. T., Braunstein, A., & Zhang, Y. (2012). From Karen to Katie: Using baby names to understand cultural evolution. *Psychological Science, 23,* 1067–1073. doi:10.1177/0956797612443371

Berger, J., & Rand, L. (2008). Shifting signals to help health: Using identity signaling to reduce risky health behaviors. *Journal of Consumer Research, 35,* 509–518.

Berry, J. W., Poortinga, Y. H., & Pandey, J. (Eds.). (1997). *Handbook of cross-cultural psychology: Theory and method* (2nd ed., Vol. 1). Boston, MA: Allyn & Bacon.

Berry, J. W., Poortinga, Y. H., Segall, M. H., & Dasen, P. R. (1992). *Cross-cultural psychology: Research and applications* (1st ed.). Cambridge, England: Cambridge University Press.

Berry, J. W., Poortinga, Y. H., Segall, M. H., & Dasen, P. R. (2002). *Cross-cultural psychology: Research and applications* (2nd ed.). Cambridge, England: Cambridge University Press.

Bessenoff, G. R. (2006). Can the media affect us? Social comparison, self-discrepancy, and the thin ideal. *Psychology of Women Quarterly, 30,* 239–251. doi:10.1111/j.1471-6402.2006.00292.x

Bowling, N. A., & Beehr, T. A. (2006). Workplace harassment from the victim's perspective: A theoretical model and meta-analysis. *Journal of Applied Psychology, 91,* 998–1012. doi:10.1037/0021-9010.91.5.998

Brennan, K. A., Clark, C. L., & Shaver, P. R. (1998). Self-report measurement of adult romantic attachment: An integrative overview. In

J. A. Simpson & W. S. Rholes (Eds.), *Attachment theory and close relationships* (pp. 46–76). New York, NY: Guilford Press.

Bryan, C. J., Walton, G. M., Rogers, T., & Dweck, C. S. (2011). Motivating voter turnout by invoking the self. *Proceedings of the National Academy of Sciences, USA, 108*, 12653–12656. doi:10.1073/pnas.1103343108

Burke, B. L., Martens, A., & Faucher, E. H. (2010). Two decades of terror management theory: A meta-analysis of mortality salience research. *Personality and Social Psychology Review, 14*, 155–195. doi:10.1177/1088868309352321

Bushman, B. J., & Anderson, C. A. (2009). Comfortably numb: Desensitizing effects of violent media on helping others. *Psychological Science, 20*, 273–277. doi:10.1111/j.1467-9280.2009.02287.x

Buss, D. M. (1989). Sex differences in human mate preferences: Evolutionary hypotheses tested in 37 cultures. *Behavioral and Brain Sciences, 12*, 1–49. doi:10.1017/S0140525X00023992

Cacioppo, J. T., Berntson, G. G., & Decety, J. (2011). A history of social neuroscience. In A. W. Kruglanski & W. Stroebe (Eds.), *Handbook of the history of social psychology* (pp. 123–136). New York, NY: Psychology Press.

Cacioppo, J. T., & Petty, R. E. (1982). The need for cognition. *Journal of Personality and Social Psychology, 42*, 116–131. doi:10.1037/0022-3514.42.1.116

Calogero, R. M. (2013). Objects don't object: Evidence that self-objectification disrupts women's social activism. *Psychological Science, 24*, 312–318. doi:10.1177/0956797612452574

Carlson, K. D., & Ji, F. X. (2011). Citing and building on meta-analytic findings: A review and recommendations. *Organizational Research Methods, 14*, 696–717. doi:10.1177/1094428110384272

Carnagey, N. L., Anderson, C. A., & Bushman, B. J. (2007). The effect of video game violence on physiological desensitization to real-life violence. *Journal of Experimental Social Psychology, 43*, 489–496. doi:10.1016/j.jesp.2006.05.003

Chan, E., & Sengupta, J. (2010). Insincere flattery actually works: A dual attitudes perspective. *Journal of Marketing Research, 47*, 122–133. doi:10.1509/jmkr.47.1.122

Chan, W. K., & Wan, W. E. (2012). How can stressed employees deliver better customer service? The underlying self-regulation depletion mechanism. *Journal of Marketing, 76*, 119–137. doi:10.1509/jm.10.0202

Condon, P., Desbordes, G., Miller, W., & DeSteno, D. (2013). Meditation increases compassionate responses to suffering. *Psychological Science, 24*, 2125–2127. doi:10.1177/0956797613485603

Corley, K. G., & Gioia, D. A. (2011). Building theory about theory building: What constitutes a theoretical contribution? *Academy of Management Review, 36*, 12–32. doi:10.5465/AMR.2011.55662499

Cosmides, L., Barrett, H. C., & Tooby, J. (2010). Adaptive specializations, social exchange, and the evolution of human intelligence. *Proceedings of the National Academy of Sciences, USA, 107*, 9007–9014. doi:10.1073/pnas.0914623107

Cox, E. P., III, Wogalter, M. S., Stokes, S. L., & Tipton Murff, E. J. (1997). Do product warnings increase safe behavior? A meta-analysis. *Journal of Public Policy & Marketing, 16*, 194–204.

Crum, A. J., & Langer, E. J. (2007). Mind-set matters: Exercise and the placebo effect. *Psychological Science, 18*, 165–171. doi:10.1111/j.1467-9280.2007.01867.x

Csikszentmihalyi, M. (1998). *Finding flow: The psychology of engagement with everyday life.* New York, NY: Basic Books.

Dahl, A., Campos, J. J., Anderson, D. I., Uchiyama, I., Witherington, D. C., Ueno, M., . . . Barbu-Roth, M. (2013). The epigenesis of wariness of heights. *Psychological Science, 24*, 1361–1367. doi:10.1177/0956797613476047

Davis, M. (1983). Measuring individual differences in empathy: Evidence for a multidimensional approach. *Journal of Personality and Social Psychology, 44*, 113–126. doi:10.1037/0022-3514.44.1.113

Deci, E. L., & Ryan, R. M. (2012). Self-determination theory. In P. A. M. Van Lange, A. W. Kruglanski, & E. T. Higgins (Eds.), *Handbook of theories of social psychology* (Vol. 1, pp. 416–437). Thousand Oaks, CA: Sage.

De Dreu, C. K. W., Greer, L. L., Handgraaf, M. J. J., Shalvi, S., Van Kleef, G. A., Baas, M., . . . Feith, S. W. W. (2010). The neuropeptide oxytocin regulates parochial altruism in intergroup conflict among humans. *Science, 328*, 1408–1411. doi:10.1126/science.1189047

Dietvorst, R. C., Verbeke, W. J. M., Bagozzi, R. P., Yoon, C., Smits, M., & van der Lugt, A. (2009). A sales force–specific theory-of-mind scale: Tests of its validity by classical methods and functional magnetic resonance imaging. *Journal of Marketing Research, 46*, 653–668. doi:10.1509/jmkr.46.5.653

Duckworth, A. L., Peterson, C., Matthews, M. D., & Kelly, D. R. (2007). Grit: Perseverance and passion for long-term goals. *Journal of Personality and Social Psychology, 92*, 1087–1101.

Dunn, E. W., Aknin, L. B., & Norton, M. I. (2008). Spending money on others promotes happiness. *Science, 319*, 1687–1688. doi:10.1126/science.1150952

Durante, K. M., Griskevicius, V., Hill, S. E., Perilloux, C., & Li, N. P. (2011). Ovulation, female competition, and product choice: Hormonal influences on consumer behavior. *Journal of Consumer Research, 37*, 921–934.

Edwards, J. R., & Lambert, L. S. (2007). Methods for integrating moderation and mediation: A general analytic framework using moderated path analysis. *Psychological Methods, 12*, 1–22. doi:10.1037/1082-989X.12.1.1

Eisend, M. (2011). How humor in advertising works: A meta-analytic test of alternative models. *Marketing Letters, 22,* 115–132. doi:10.1007/s11002-010-9116-z

Eisend, M., & Küster, F. (2011). The effectiveness of publicity versus advertising: A meta-analytic investigation of its moderators. *Journal of the Academy of Marketing Science, 39,* 906–921. doi:10.1007/s11747-010-0224-3

Eisenegger, C., Naef, M., Snozzi, R., Heinrichs, M., & Fehr, E. (2010). Prejudice and truth about the effect of testosterone on human bargaining behavior. *Nature, 463,* 356–359. doi:10.1038/nature08711

Ellis, B. J., Figueredo, A. J., Brumbach, B. H., & Schlomer, G. L. (2009). Fundamental dimensions of environmental risk: The impact of harsh versus unpredictable environments on the evolution and development of life history strategies. *Human Nature, 20,* 204–268. doi:10.1007/s12110-009-9063-7

Escalas, J. E. (2004). Narrative processing: Building consumer connections to brands. *Journal of Consumer Psychology, 14*(1–2), 168–180. doi:10.1207/s15327663jcp1401&2_19

Faber, R. J., & O'Guinn, T. C. (1992). A clinical screener for compulsive buying. *Journal of Consumer Research, 19,* 459–469. doi:10.1086/209315

Fehr, E., & Gächter, S. (2002). Altruistic punishment in humans. *Nature, 415,* 137–140. doi:10.1038/415137a

Festinger, L. (1942). Wish, expectation, and group standards as factors influencing level of aspiration. *Journal of Abnormal and Social Psychology, 37,* 184–200. doi:10.1037/h0060328

Fiedler, K. (2004). Tools, toys, truisms, and theories: Some thoughts on the creative cycle of theory formation. *Personality and Social Psychology Review, 8,* 123–131. doi:10.1207/s15327957pspr0802_5

Fischer, P., Krueger, J. I., Greitemeyer, T., Vogrincic, C., Kastenmüller, A., Frey, D., & Kainbacher, M. (2011). The bystander-effect: A meta-analytic review on bystander intervention in dangerous and non-dangerous emergencies. *Psychological Bulletin, 137,* 517–537. doi:10.1037/a0023304

Fiske, S. T. (2004). Mind the gap: In praise of informal sources of formal theory. *Personality and Social Psychology Review, 8,* 132–137. doi:10.1207/s15327957pspr0802_6

Fiske, S. T., & Taylor, S. E. (1984). *Social cognition.* New York, NY: Random House.

Forgas, J. P. (1995). Mood and judgment: The affect infusion model (AIM). *Psychological Bulletin, 117,* 39–66. doi:10.1037/0033-2909.117.1.39

Frederick, S. (2005). Cognitive reflection and decision making. *The Journal of Economic Perspectives, 19*(4), 25–42. doi:10.1257/089533005775196732

Garlin, F. V., & Owen, K. (2006). Setting the tone with the tune: A meta-analytic review of the effects of background music in retail settings. *Journal of Business Research, 59,* 755–764. doi:10.1016/j.jbusres.2006.01.013

Gholami, M., Lange, D., Luszczynska, A., Knoll, N., & Schwarzer, R. (2013). A dietary planning intervention increases fruit consumption in Iranian women. *Appetite, 63,* 1–6. doi:10.1016/j.appet.2012.12.005

Gilbert, D. T., Pelham, B. W., & Krull, D. S. (1988). On cognitive busyness: When person perceivers meet persons perceived. *Journal of Personality and Social Psychology, 54,* 733–740. doi:10.1037/0022-3514.54.5.733

Gladwell, M. (2008). *Outliers: The story of success.* New York, NY: Little, Brown and Co.

Grant, A. M. (2013). Rethinking the extraverted sales ideal: The ambivert advantage. *Psychological Science, 24,* 1024–1030. doi:10.1177/0956797612463706

Greenfield, P. M. (1997). Culture as process: Empirical methods for cultural psychology. In J. W. Berry, Y. H. Poortinga, & J. Pandey (Eds.), *Handbook of cross-cultural psychology: Theory and method* (2nd ed., Vol. 1, pp. 301–346). Boston, MA: Allyn & Bacon.

Greenwald, A. G., & Banaji, M. R. (1995). Implicit social cognition: Attitudes, self-esteem, and stereotypes. *Psychological Review, 102,* 4–27. doi:10.1037/0033-295X.102.1.4

Greenwald, A. G., Poehlman, T. A., Uhlmann, E. L., & Banaji, M. R. (2009). Understanding and using the Implicit Association Test: III. Meta-analysis of predictive validity. *Journal of Personality and Social Psychology, 97,* 17–41. doi:10.1037/a0015575

Griskevicius, V., Tybur, J. M., & Van den Bergh, B. (2010). Going green to be seen: Status, reputation, and conspicuous conservation. *Journal of Personality and Social Psychology, 98,* 392–404. doi:10.1037/a0017346

Gross, J. J., & John, O. P. (2003). Individual differences in two emotion regulation processes: Implications for affect, relationships, and well-being. *Journal of Personality and Social Psychology, 85,* 348–362. doi:10.1037/0022-3514.85.2.348

Hagger, M. S., Wood, C., Stiff, C., & Chatzisarantis, N. L. D. (2010). Ego depletion and the strength model of self-control: A meta-analysis. *Psychological Bulletin, 136,* 495–525. doi:10.1037/a0019486

Hagtvedt, H., & Patrick, V. M. (2008). Art infusion: The influence of visual art on the perception and evaluation of consumer products. *Journal of Marketing Research, 45,* 379–389. doi:10.1509/jmkr.45.3.379

Haley, K. J., & Fessler, D. M. T. (2005). Nobody's watching? Subtle cues affect generosity in an anonymous economic game. *Evolution and Human Behavior, 26,* 245–256.

Harrison, D. A., Newman, D. A., & Roth, P. L. (2006). How important are job attitudes? Meta-analytic comparisons of integrative behavioral outcomes and time sequences. *Academy of Management Journal, 49,* 305–325. doi:10.5465/AMJ.2006.20786077

Hartwig, M., & Bond, C. F., Jr. (2011). Why do lie-catchers fail? A lens model meta-analysis of human lie judgments. *Psychological Bulletin, 137*, 643–659. doi:10.1037/a0023589

Haugtvedt, C. P., Liu, K., & Min, K. S. (2008). Individual differences: Tools for theory testing and understanding in consumer psychology research. In C. P. Haugtvedt, P. M. Herr, & F. R. Kardes (Eds.), *Handbook of consumer psychology* (pp. 1161–1176). New York, NY: Psychology Press.

Hayes, A. F. (2013). *Introduction to mediation, moderation, and conditional process modeling: A regression-based approach.* New York, NY: Guilford Press.

Hayes, J., Schimel, J., Arndt, J., & Faucher, E. H. (2010). A theoretical and empirical review of the death-thought accessibility concept in terror management research. *Psychological Bulletin, 136*, 699–739. doi:10.1037/a0020524

Hedges, L. V., Laine, R. D., & Greenwald, R. (1994). An exchange: Part I: Does money matter? A meta-analysis of studies of the effects of differential school inputs on student outcomes. *Educational Researcher, 23*(3), 5–14. doi:10.3102/0013189X023003005

Hedges, L. V., & Olkin, I. (1985). *Statistical methods for meta-analysis.* New York, NY: Academic Press.

Henrich, J., Heine, S. J., & Norenzayan, A. (2010). The weirdest people in the world? *Behavioral and Brain Sciences, 33*, 61–83, 111–135. doi:10.1017/S0140525X0999152X

Herrmann, B., Thöni, C., & Gächter, S. (2008). Antisocial punishment across societies. *Science, 319*, 1362–1367.

Higgins, E. T. (2004). Making a theory useful: Lessons handed down. *Personality and Social Psychology Review, 8*, 138–145. doi:10.1207/s15327957pspr0802_7

Hoch, S. J., & Loewenstein, G. F. (1991). Time-inconsistent preferences and consumer self-control. *Journal of Consumer Research, 17*, 492–507. doi:10.1086/208573

Hofstede, G. (1980). *Culture's consequences: International differences in work-related values.* Beverly Hills, CA: Sage.

Hubert, M., & Kenning, P. (2008). A current overview of consumer neuroscience. *Journal of Consumer Behaviour, 7*, 272–292. doi:10.1002/cb.251

Hunt, M. (1997). *How science takes stock: The story of meta-analysis.* New York, NY: Russell Sage Foundation.

Isen, A. M., Nygren, T. E., & Ashby, F. G. (1988). Influence of positive affect on the subjective utility of gains and losses: It is just not worth the risk. *Journal of Personality and Social Psychology, 55*, 710–717. doi:10.1037/0022-3514.55.5.710

Iyengar, S. S., & Lepper, M. R. (2000). When choice is demotivating: Can one desire too much of a good thing? *Journal of Personality and Social Psychology, 79*, 995–1006. doi:10.1037/0022-3514.79.6.995

Jahoda, G., & Krewer, B. (1997). History of cross-cultural and cultural psychology. In J. W. Berry, Y. H. Poortinga, & J. Pandey (Eds.), *Handbook of cross-cultural psychology: Theory and method* (2nd ed., Vol. 1, pp. 1–42). Boston, MA: Allyn & Bacon.

James, W. (1907). The energies of men. *Science, 25,* 321–332. doi:10.1126/science.25.635.321

Jaremka, L. M., Fagundes, C. P., Peng, J., Bennett, J. M., Glaser, R., Malarkey, W. B., & Kiecolt-Glaser, J. K. (2013). Loneliness promotes inflammation during acute stress. *Psychological Science, 24,* 1089–1097. doi:10.1177/0956797612464059

John, O. P., Naumann, L. P., & Soto, C. J. (2008). Paradigm shift to the integrative Big Five trait taxonomy: History, measurement, and conceptual issues. In O. P. John, R. W. Robins, & L. A. Pervin (Eds.), *Handbook of personality: Theory and research* (3rd ed., pp. 114–158). New York, NY: Guilford Press.

Johnson, B. T., & Eagly, A. H. (2000). Quantitative synthesis of social psychological research. In H. T. Reis & C. M. Judd (Eds.), *Handbook of research methods in social and personality psychology* (pp. 496–528). New York, NY: Cambridge University Press.

Johnson, P. O., & Neyman, J. (1936). Tests of certain linear hypotheses and their application to some educational problems. *Statistical Research Memoirs, 1,* 57–93.

Joireman, J., Anderson, J., & Strathman, A. (2003). The aggression paradox: Understanding links among aggression, sensation seeking, and the consideration of future consequences. *Journal of Personality and Social Psychology, 84,* 1287–1302. doi:10.1037/0022-3514.84.6.1287

Joireman, J., Grégoire, Y., Devezer, B., & Tripp, T. (2013). When do customers offer firms a "second chance" following a double deviation? The impact of inferred firm motives on customer revenge and reconciliation. *Journal of Retailing, 89,* 315–337. doi:10.1016/j.jretai.2013.03.002

Joireman, J., Kees, J., & Sprott, D. (2010). Concern with immediate consequences magnifies the impact of compulsive buying tendencies on college students' credit card debt. *Journal of Consumer Affairs, 44,* 155–178. doi:10.1111/j.1745-6606.2010.01161.x

Joireman, J., Lasane, T. P., Bennett, J., Richards, D., & Solaimani, S. (2001). Integrating social value orientation and the consideration of future consequences within the extended norm activation model of proenvironmental behavior. *British Journal of Social Psychology, 40,* 133–155. doi:10.1348/014466601164731

Joireman, J., Strathman, A., & Balliet, D. (2006). Considering future consequences: An integrative model. In L. Sanna & E. Chang (Eds.), *Judgments over time: The interplay of thoughts, feelings, and behaviors* (pp. 82–99). Oxford, England: Oxford University Press.

Joireman, J., Van Lange, P. A. M., & Van Vugt, M. (2004). Who cares about the environmental impact of cars? Those with an eye toward the future. *Environment and Behavior, 36,* 187–206. doi:10.1177/0013916503251476

Joseph, D. L., & Newman, D. A. (2010). Emotional intelligence: An integrative meta-analysis and cascading model. *Journal of Applied Psychology, 95,* 54–78.

Judd, C. M., McClelland, G. H., & Ryan, C. S. (2009). *Data analysis: A model comparison approach* (2nd ed.). New York, NY: Routledge.

Judge, T. A., Cable, D. M., Colbert, A. E., & Rynes, S. L. (2007). What causes a management article to be cited—article, author, or journal? *Academy of Management Journal, 50,* 491–506. doi:10.5465/AMJ.2007.25525577

Karremans, J. C., Stroebe, W., & Claus, J. (2006). Beyond Vicary's fantasies: The impact of subliminal priming and brand choice. *Journal of Experimental Social Psychology, 42,* 792–798.

Keizer, K., Lindenberg, S., & Steg, L. (2008). The spreading of disorder. *Science, 322,* 1681–1685. doi:10.1126/science.1161405

Kelley, H. H., Holmes, J. W., Kerr, N. L., Reis, H. T., Rusbult, C. E., & Van Lange, P. A. M. (2003). *An atlas of interpersonal situations.* New York, NY: Cambridge University Press.

Kelley, H. H., & Thibaut, J. W. (1978). *Interpersonal relations: A theory of interdependence.* New York, NY: Wiley.

Kim, Y.-H., & Cohen, D. (2010). Information, perspective, and judgments about the self in face and dignity cultures. *Personality and Social Psychology Bulletin, 36,* 537–550. doi:10.1177/0146167210362398

Kitayama, S., Markus, H. R., Matsumoto, H., & Norasakkunkit, V. (1997). Individual and collective processes in the construction of the self: Self-enhancement in the United States and self-criticism in Japan. *Journal of Personality and Social Psychology, 72,* 1245–1267. doi:10.1037/0022-3514.72.6.1245

Knutson, B., Rick, S., Wimmer, G. E., Prelec, D., & Loewenstein, G. (2007). Neural predictors of purchases. *Neuron, 53,* 147–156. doi:10.1016/j.neuron.2006.11.010

Kramer, L. A., & Weber, J. M. (2012). This is your portfolio on winter: Seasonal affective disorder and risk aversion in financial decision making. *Social Psychological and Personality Science, 3,* 193–199.

Kronrod, A., Grinstein, A., & Wathieu, L. (2012). Go green! Should environmental messages be so assertive? *Journal of Marketing, 76,* 95–102. doi:10.1509/jm.10.0416

Kruglanski, A. W. (1990). Motivations for judging and knowing: Implications for causal attribution. In A. W. Kruglanski (Ed.), *Handbook of motivation and cognition: Foundations of social behavior* (Vol. 2, pp. 333–368). New York, NY: Guilford Press.

Kruglanski, A. W. (2006). Theories as bridges. In P. A. M. Van Lange (Ed.), *Bridging social psychology: Benefits of transdisciplinary approaches* (pp. 21–34). Mahwah, NJ: Erlbaum.

Kruglanski, A. W., Thompson, E. P., Higgins, E. T., Atash, M. N., Pierro, A., Shah, J. Y., & Speigel, S. (2000). To "do the right thing" or to "just do it": Locomotion and assessment as distinction self-regulatory imperatives. *Journal of Personality and Social Psychology, 79,* 793–815. doi:10.1037/0022-3514.79.5.793

Kuhn, T. S. (1962). *The structure of scientific revolutions.* Chicago, IL: University of Chicago Press.

Leary, M. R., & Hoyle, R. H. (2009). *Handbook of individual differences in social behavior.* New York, NY: Guilford Press.

Lee, L., Amir, O., & Ariely, D. (2009). In search of homo economicus: Cognitive noise and the role of emotion in preference consistency. *Journal of Consumer Research, 36,* 173–187. doi:10.1086/597160

LePine, J. A., & King, A. W. (2010). Editors' comments: Developing novel theoretical insight from reviews of existing theory and research. *Academy of Management Review, 35,* 506–509. doi:10.5465/AMR.2010.53502455

Leung, A. K.-Y., & Cohen, D. (2011). Within- and between-culture variation: Individual differences and the cultural logics of honor, face, and dignity cultures. *Journal of Personality and Social Psychology, 100,* 507–526.

Leung, A. K.-Y. Maddux, W. W., Galinsky, A. D., & Chiu, C. (2008). Multicultural experience enhances creativity: The when and how. *American Psychologist, 63,* 169–181. doi:10.1037/0003-066X.63.3.169

Levav, J., & Zhu, R. J. (2009). Seeking freedom through variety. *Journal of Consumer Research, 36,* 600–610. doi:10.1086/599556

Lewin, K. (1936). *Principles of topological psychology.* New York, NY: McGraw-Hill. doi:10.1037/10019-000

Li, N. P., Bailey, J. M., Kenrick, D. T., & Linsenmeier, J. A. W. (2002). The necessities and luxuries of mate preferences: Testing the tradeoffs. *Journal of Personality and Social Psychology, 82,* 947–955.

Lin, C.-H., Tuan, H.-P., & Chiu, Y.-C. (2010). Medial frontal activity in brand-loyal consumers: A behavior and near-infrared ray study. *Journal of Neuroscience, Psychology, and Economics, 3*(2), 59–73. doi:10.1037/a0015461

Lipsey, M. W., & Wilson, D. B. (1993). The efficacy of psychological, educational, and behavioral treatment: Confirmation from meta-analysis. *American Psychologist, 48,* 1181–1209. doi:10.1037/0003-066X.48.12.1181

Lipsey, M. W., & Wilson, D. B. (2001). *Practical meta-analysis* (Vol. 49). Thousand Oaks, CA: Sage.

Little, K. C., McNulty, J. K., & Russell, V. M. (2010). Sex buffers intimates against the negative implications of attachment insecurity.

Personality and Social Psychology Bulletin, 36, 484–498. doi:10.1177/0146167209352494

Luszczynska, A., Cao, D. S., Mallach, N., Pietron, K., Mazurkiewicz, M., & Schwarzer, R. (2010). Intentions, planning, and self-efficacy predict physical activity in Chinese and Polish adolescents: Two moderated mediation analyses. *International Journal of Clinical and Health Psychology, 10*, 265–278.

MacKinnon, D. P., Fritz, M. S., Williams, J., & Lockwood, C. M. (2007). Distributions of the product confidence limits for the indirect effect: Program PRODCLIN. *Behavior Research Methods, 39*, 384–389. doi:10.3758/BF03193007

Mandler, G., & Kessen, W. (1959). *The language of psychology*. New York, NY: Wiley.

Markus, H. R., & Kitayama, S. (1991). Culture and the self. *Psychological Review, 98*, 224–253. doi:10.1037/0033-295X.98.2.224

Masuda, T., & Nisbett, R. E. (2001). Attending holistically versus analytically: Comparing the context sensitivity of Japanese and Americans. *Journal of Personality and Social Psychology, 81*, 922–934. doi:10.1037/0022-3514.81.5.922

McNulty, J. K., & Russell, V. M. (2010). When "negative" behaviors are positive: A contextual analysis of the long-term effects of problem-solving behaviors on changes in relationship satisfaction. *Journal of Personality and Social Psychology, 98*, 587–604. doi:10.1037/a0017479

Mead, N. L., Baumeister, R. F., Stillman, T. F., Rawn, C. D., & Vohs, K. D. (2011). Social exclusion causes people to spend and consume strategically in the service of affiliation. *Journal of Consumer Research, 37*, 902–919.

Merton, R. K. (1949). *Social theory and social structure*. Glencoe, IL: Free Press.

Meyer, R. D., Dalal, R. S., & Bonaccio, S. (2009). A meta-analytic investigation into the moderating effects of situational strength on the conscientiousness-performance relationship. *Journal of Organizational Behavior, 30*, 1077–1102. doi:10.1002/job.602

Mikulincer, M., & Shaver, P. R. (2003). The attachment behavioral system in adulthood: Activation, psychodynamics, and interpersonal processes. In M. P. Zanna (Ed.), *Advances in experimental social psychology* (Vol. 35, pp. 53–152). San Diego, CA: Elsevier Academic. doi:10.1016/S0065-2601(03)01002-5

Mishra, A., & Mishra, H. (2010). We are what we consume: The influence of food consumption on impulsive choice. *Journal of Marketing Research, 48*, 1129–1137.

Miyamoto, Y., Nisbett, R. E., & Masuda, T. (2006). Culture and the physical environment. *Psychological Science, 17*, 113–119. doi:10.1111/j.1467-9280.2006.01673.x

Mogilner, C. (2010). The pursuit of happiness: Time, money, and social connection. *Psychological Science, 21,* 1348–1354. doi:10.1177/0956797610380696

Monga, A. B., & John, D. R. (2007). Cultural differences in brand extension evaluation: The influence of analytic versus holistic thinking. *Journal of Consumer Research, 33,* 529–536.

Muller, D., Judd, C. M., & Yzerbyt, V. Y. (2005). When moderation is mediated and mediation is moderated. *Journal of Personality and Social Psychology, 89,* 852–863. doi:10.1037/0022-3514.89.6.852

Muraven, M., Tice, D. M., & Baumeister, R. F. (1998). Self-control as a limited resource: Regulatory depletion patterns. *Journal of Personality and Social Psychology, 74,* 774–789. doi:10.1037/0022-3514.74.3.774

Nelson, L. D., & Morrison, E. L. (2005). The symptoms of resource scarcity: Judgments of food and finances influence preferences for potential partners. *Psychological Science, 16,* 167–173. doi:10.1111/j.0956-7976.2005.00798.x

Nelson, S. K., Kushlev, K., English, T., Dunn, E. W., & Lyubomirsky, S. (2013). In defense of parenthood: Children are associated with more joy than misery. *Psychological Science, 24,* 3–10. doi:10.1177/0956797612447798

Newman, J. P., Widom, C. S., & Nathan, S. (1985). Passive avoidance in syndromes of disinhibition: Psychopathy and extraversion. *Journal of Personality and Social Psychology, 48,* 1316–1327. doi:10.1037/0022-3514.48.5.1316

Nisbett, R. E., & Cohen, D. (1996). *Culture of honor: The psychology of violence in the South.* Boulder, CO: Westview Press.

Nisbett, R. E., & Kanouse, D. E. (1969). Obesity, food deprivation, and supermarket shopping behavior. *Journal of Personality and Social Psychology, 12,* 289–294. doi:10.1037/h0027799

Nisbett, R. E., Peng, K., Choi, I., & Norenzayan, A. (2001). Culture and systems of thought: Holistic versus analytic cognition. *Psychological Review, 108,* 291–310. doi:10.1037/0033-295X.108.2.291

Norenzayan, A., & Heine, S. J. (2005). Psychological universals: What are they and how can we know? *Psychological Bulletin, 131,* 763–784. doi:10.1037/0033-2909.131.5.763

Nunnally, J. C., & Bernstein, I. (1994). *Psychometric theory.* New York, NY: McGraw-Hill.

Oishi, S., & Diener, E. (2014). Residents of poor nations have a greater sense of meaning in life than residents of wealthy nations. *Psychological Science, 25,* 422–430. doi:10.1177/0956797613507286

Okimoto, T. G., & Brescoll, V. L. (2010). The price of power: Power seeking and backlash against female politicians. *Personality and Social Psychology Bulletin, 36,* 923–936.

Organ, D. W. (1988). *Organizational citizenship behavior: The good soldier syndrome.* Lexington, MA: Lexington Books.

Paharia, N., Keinan, A., Avery, J., & Schor, J. B. (2011). The underdog effect: The marketing of disadvantage and determination through brand biography. *Journal of Consumer Research, 37*, 775–790.

Palmatier, R. W., Jarvis, C. B., Bechkoff, J. R., & Kardes, F. R. (2009). The role of customer gratitude in relationship marketing. *Journal of Marketing, 73*(5), 1–18. doi:10.1509/jmkg.73.5.1

Park, D. C., Lodi-Smith, J., Drew, L., Haber, S., Hebrank, A., Bischof, G. N., & Aamodt, W. (2014). The impact of sustained engagement on cognitive function in older adults: The synapse project. *Psychological Science, 25*, 103–112. doi:10.1177/0956797613499592

Patall, E. A., Cooper, H., & Robinson, J. C. (2008). The effects of choice on intrinsic motivation and related outcomes: A meta-analysis of research findings. *Psychological Bulletin, 134*, 270–300. doi:10.1037/0033-2909.134.2.270

Peracchio, L. A., & Escalas, J. E. (2008). Tell me a story: Crafting and publishing research in consumer psychology. *Journal of Consumer Psychology, 18*, 197–204. doi:10.1016/j.jcps.2008.04.008

Perilloux, C., Easton, J. A., & Buss, D. M. (2012). The misperception of sexual interest. *Psychological Science, 23*, 146–151. doi:10.1177/0956797611424162

Peterson, R. A. (1994). A meta-analysis of Cronbach's coefficient alpha. *Journal of Consumer Research, 21*, 381–391. doi:10.1086/209405

Pinker, S. (2002). *The blank slate: The modern denial of human nature.* New York, NY: Viking.

Podsakoff, N. P., Whiting, S. W., Podsakoff, P. M., & Blume, B. D. (2009). Individual- and organizational-level consequences of organizational citizenship behaviors: A meta-analysis. *Journal of Applied Psychology, 94*, 122–141. doi:10.1037/a0013079

Podsakoff, P. M., MacKenzie, S. B., Paine, J. B., & Bachrach, D. G. (2000). Organizational citizenship behaviors: A critical review of the theoretical and empirical literature and suggestions for future research. *Journal of Management, 26*, 513–563. doi:10.1177/014920630002600307

Popper, K. R. (1959). *The logic of scientific discovery.* New York, NY: Hutchinson & Co. (Original work published 1935)

Preacher, K. J., & Hayes, A. F. (2008). Asymptotic and resampling strategies for assessing and comparing indirect effects in multiple mediator models. *Behavior Research Methods, 40*, 879–891. doi:10.3758/BRM.40.3.879

Preacher, K. J., Rucker, D. D., & Hayes, A. F. (2007). Addressing moderated mediation hypotheses: Theory, methods, and prescriptions. *Multivariate Behavioral Research, 42*, 185–227. doi:10.1080/00273170701341316

Pruitt, D. G., & Kimmel, M. J. (1977). Twenty years of experimental gaming: Critique, synthesis, and suggestions for the future. *Annual Review of Psychology, 28*, 363–392. doi:10.1146/annurev.ps.28.020177.002051

Reimann, M., Zaichkowsky, J., Neuhaus, C., Bender, T., & Weber, B. (2010). Aesthetic package design: A behavioral, neural, and psychological investigation. *Journal of Consumer Psychology, 20,* 431–441. doi:10.1016/j.jcps.2010.06.009

Richins, M. L. (2004). The material values scale: Measurement properties and development of a short form. *Journal of Consumer Research, 31,* 209–219. doi:10.1086/383436

Richins, M. L., & Dawson, S. (1992). A consumer values orientation for materialism and its measurement: Scale development and validation. *Journal of Consumer Research, 19,* 303–316. doi:10.1086/209304

Rick, S., Cryder, C. E., & Loewenstein, G. (2008). Tightwads and spendthrifts. *Journal of Consumer Research, 34,* 767–782. doi:10.1086/523285

Ridgway, N. M., Kukar-Kinney, M., & Monroe, K. B. (2008). An expanded conceptualization and a new measure of compulsive buying. *Journal of Consumer Research, 35,* 622–639. doi:10.1086/591108

Rindfleisch, A., Burroughs, J. E., & Wong, N. (2009). The safety of objects: Materialism, existential insecurity, and brand connection. *Journal of Consumer Research, 36,* 1–16. doi:10.1086/595718

Roberts, B. W., & DelVecchio, W. F. (2000). The rank-order consistency of personality traits from childhood to old age: A quantitative review of longitudinal studies. *Psychological Bulletin, 126,* 3–25. doi:10.1037/0033-2909.126.1.3

Robinson, J. P., Shaver, P. R., & Wrightsman, L. S. (1991). *Measures of personality and social psychological attitudes.* San Diego, CA: Academic Press.

Rosenthal, R. (1991). *Meta-analytic procedures for social research* (Vol. 6). Beverly Hills, CA: Sage.

Rosenthal, R. (1995). Writing meta-analytic reviews. *Psychological Bulletin, 118,* 183–192. doi:10.1037/0033-2909.118.2.183

Rudolph, U., Roesch, S., Greitemeyer, T., & Weiner, B. (2004). A meta-analytic review of help giving and aggression from an attributional perspective: Contributions to a general theory of motivation. *Cognition and Emotion, 18,* 815–848. doi:10.1080/02699930341000248

Sadava, S. W., & McCreary, D. R. (Eds.). (1997). *Applied social psychology.* Upper Saddle River, NJ: Prentice Hall.

Salganik, M. J., Dodds, P. S., & Watts, D. J. (2006). Experimental study of inequality and unpredictability in an artificial cultural market. *Science, 311,* 854–856. doi:10.1126/science.1121066

Schaller, M., & Murray, D. R. (2008). Pathogens, personality, and culture: Disease prevalence predicts worldwide variability in sociosexuality, extraversion, and openness to experience. *Journal of Personality and Social Psychology, 95,* 212–221. doi:10.1037/0022-3514.95.1.212

Schultz, P. W., & Oskamp, S. (2000). *Social psychology: An applied perspective.* Englewood Cliffs, NJ: Prentice Hall.

Schwartz, S. H. (1992). Universals in the content and structure of values: Theoretical advances and empirical tests in 20 countries.

Advances in Experimental Social Psychology, 25, 1–65. doi:10.1016/S0065-2601(08)60281-6

Sentyrz, S. M., & Bushman, B. J. (1998). Mirror, mirror on the wall, who's the thinnest one of all? Effects of self-awareness on consumption of fatty, reduced-fat, and fat-free products. *Journal of Applied Psychology, 83*, 944–949. doi:10.1037/0021-9010.83.6.944

Shadish, W. R. (1996). Meta-analysis and the exploration of causal mediating processes: A primer of examples, methods, and issues. *Psychological Methods, 1*, 47–65. doi:10.1037/1082-989X.1.1.47

Shadish, W. R., Cook, T. D., & Campbell, D. T. (2002). *Experimental and quasi-experimental designs for generalized causal inference.* Boston, MA: Houghton Mifflin.

Shalev, E., & Morwitz, V. G. (2012). Influence via comparison-driven self-evaluation: The case of the low status influencer. *Journal of Consumer Research, 38*, 964–980. doi:10.1086/661551

Shaw, M. E., & Costanzo, P. R. (1982). *Theories of social psychology.* New York, NY: McGraw-Hill.

Shen, H., Wan, F., & Wyer, R. W. (2011). Cross-cultural differences in the refusal to accept a small gift: The differential influence of reciprocity norms on Asians and North Americans. *Journal of Personality and Social Psychology, 100*, 271–281. doi:10.1037/a0021201

Shiv, B., & Fedorikhin, A. (1999). Heart and mind in conflict: The interplay of affect and cognition in consumer decision making. *Journal of Consumer Research, 26*, 278–292. doi:10.1086/209563

Shrout, P. E., & Bolger, N. (2002). Mediation in experimental and non-experimental studies: New procedures and recommendations. *Psychological Methods, 7*, 422–445. doi:10.1037/1082-989X.7.4.422

Silver, R. C., Holman, E. A., Andersen, J. P., Poulin, M., McIntosh, D. N., & Gil-Rivas, V. (2013). Mental- and physical-health effects of acute exposure to media images of the September 11, 2001, attacks and the Iraq War. *Psychological Science, 24*, 1623–1634. doi:10.1177/0956797612460406

Simmons, J. P., Nelson, L. D., & Simonsohn, U. (2011). False-positive psychology: Undisclosed flexibility in data collection and analysis allows presenting anything as significant. *Psychological Science, 22*, 1359–1366. doi:10.1177/0956797611417632

Singer, T., Seymour, B., O'Doherty, J. P., Stephan, K. E., Dolan, R. J., & Frith, C. D. (2006). Empathic neural responses are modulated by the perceived fairness of others. *Nature, 439*, 466–469. doi:10.1038/nature04271

Smith, M. L., & Glass, G. V. (1977). Meta-analysis of psychotherapy outcome studies. *American Psychologist, 32*, 752–760. doi:10.1037/0003-066X.32.9.752

Sobel, M. E. (1982). Asymptotic confidence intervals for indirect effects in structural models. In S. Leinhardt (Ed.), *Sociological methodology* (pp. 290–312). San Francisco, CA: Jossey-Bass. doi:10.2307/270723

Spencer, S. J., Zanna, M. P., & Fong, G. T. (2005). Establishing a causal chain: Why experiments are often more effective than mediational analyses in examining psychological processes. *Journal of Personality and Social Psychology, 89,* 845–851. doi:10.1037/0022-3514.89.6.845

Sprott, D., Czellar, S., & Spangenberg, E. (2009). The importance of a general measure of brand engagement on market behavior: Development and validation of a scale. *Journal of Marketing Research, 46,* 92–104.

Stallen, M., Smidts, A., Rijpkema, M., Smit, G., Klucharev, V., & Fernández, G. (2010). Celebrities and shoes on the female brain: The neural correlates of product evaluation in the context of fame. *Journal of Economic Psychology, 31,* 802–811. doi:10.1016/j.joep.2010.03.006

Steele, C. M., Spencer, S. J., & Aronson, J. (2002). Contending with group image: The psychology of stereotype and social identity threat. In M. P. Zanna (Ed.), *Advances in experimental social psychology* (Vol. 34, pp. 379–440). San Diego, CA: Academic Press.

Strathman, A., Gleicher, F., Boninger, D. S., & Edwards, C. S. (1994). The consideration of future consequences: Weighing immediate and distant outcomes of behavior. *Journal of Personality and Social Psychology, 66,* 742–752.

Sultan, A., Joireman, J., & Sprott, D. (2012). Building consumer self-control: The effect of self-control exercises on impulse buying urges. *Marketing Letters, 23,* 61–72. doi:10.1007/s11002-011-9135-4

Sundie, J. M., Kenrick, D. T., Griskevicius, V., Tybur, J. M., Vohs, K. D., & Beal, D. J. (2011). Peacocks, Porsches, and Thorstein Veblen: Conspicuous consumption as a sexual signaling system. *Journal of Personality and Social Psychology, 100,* 664–680. doi:10.1037/a0021669

Sutton, R. I., & Staw, B. M. (1995). What theory is not. *Administrative Science Quarterly, 40,* 371–384. doi:10.2307/2393788

Tabachnick, B. G., & Fidell, L. S. (2012). *Using multivariate statistics* (6th ed.). Boston, MA: Allyn and Bacon.

Tangney, J. P., Stuewig, J., & Martinez, A. G. (2014). Two faces of shame: The roles of shame and guilt in predicting recidivism. *Psychological Science, 25,* 799–805. doi:10.1177/0956797613508790

Taylor, S. E., & Brown, J. D. (1988). Illusion and well-being: A social psychological perspective on mental health. *Psychological Bulletin, 103,* 193–210.

Taylor, S. E., Klein, L. C., Lewis, B. P., Gruenewald, T. L., Gurung, R. A. R., & Updegraff, J. A. (2000). Biobehavioral responses to stress in females: Tend-and-befriend, not fight-or-flight. *Psychological Review, 107,* 411–429. doi:10.1037/0033-295X.107.3.411

Taylor, S. E., Seeman, T. E., Eisenberger, N. I., Kozanian, T. A., Moore, A. N., & Moons, W. G. (2010). Effects of a supportive or unsupportive audience on biological and psychological responses to stress. *Journal of Personality and Social Psychology, 98,* 47–56. doi:10.1037/a0016563

Thaler, R. H., & Benartzi, S. (2004). Save More Tomorrow™: Using behavioral economics to increase employee saving. *Journal of Political Economy, 112,* S164–S187. doi:10.1086/380085

Thibaut, J., & Kelley, H. H. (1959). *The social psychology of groups.* New York, NY: Wiley.

Topolinski, S., & Strack, F. (2009). The architecture of intuition: Fluency and affect determine intuitive judgments of semantic and visual coherence, and of grammaticality in artificial grammar learning. *Journal of Experimental Psychology: General, 138,* 39–63. doi:10.1037/a0014678

Torelli, C. J., & Shavitt, S. (2010). Culture and concepts of power. *Journal of Personality and Social Psychology, 99,* 703–723. doi:10.1037/a0019973

Townsend, J. M., & Levy, G. D. (1990). Effects of potential partners' costume and physical attractiveness on sexuality and partner selection. *The Journal of Psychology, 124,* 371–389. doi:10.1080/00223980.1990.10543232

Townsend, S. S. M., Major, B., Gangi, C. E., & Mendes, W. B. (2011). From "in the air" to "under the skin": Cortisol responses to social identity threat. *Personality and Social Psychology Bulletin, 37,* 151–164. doi:10.1177/0146167210392384

Triandis, H. C. (1995). *Individualism and collectivism.* Boulder, CO: Westview Press.

Van Boven, L., Campbell, M. C., & Gilovich, T. (2010). Stigmatizing materialism: On stereotypes and impressions of materialistic and experiential products. *Personality and Social Psychology Bulletin, 36,* 551–563. doi:10.1177/0146167210362790

Van den Bergh, B., Dewitte, S., & Warlop, L. (2008). Bikinis instigate generalized impatience in intertemporal choice. *Journal of Consumer Research, 35,* 85–97.

Van Doesum, N. J., Van Lange, D. A. W., & Van Lange, P. A. M. (2013). Social mindfulness: Skill and will to navigate the social world. *Journal of Personality and Social Psychology, 105,* 86–103.

Van Lange, P. A. M. (1999). Why (authors believe) reviewers stress limiting aspects of manuscripts: The SLAM effect in peer review. *Journal of Applied Social Psychology, 29,* 2550–2566. doi:10.1111/j.1559-1816.1999.tb00125.x

Van Lange, P. A. M. (Ed.). (2006). *Bridging social psychology: Benefits of transdisciplinary approaches.* Mahwah, NJ: Erlbaum.

Van Lange, P. A. M. (2012). A history of interdependence: Theory and research. In P. A. M. Van Lange (Ed.), *Handbook of the history of social psychology* (pp. 341–361). New York, NY: Psychology Press.

Van Lange, P. A. M. (2013). What we should expect from theories in social psychology: Truth, abstraction, progress, and applicability as standards (TAPAS). *Personality and Social Psychology Review, 17,* 40–55. doi:10.1177/1088868312453088

Van Lange, P. A. M., Balliet, D. P., Parks, C. D., & Van Vugt, M. (2014). *Social dilemmas: The psychology of human cooperation.* New York, NY: Oxford University Press.

Van Lange, P. A. M., Kruglanski, A. W., & Higgins, E. T. (Eds.). (2012). *Handbook of theories of social psychology* (Vols. 1 and 2). Thousand Oaks, CA: Sage. doi:10.4135/9781446249222

Van Lange, P. A. M., Otten, W., De Bruin, E., & Joireman, J. A. (1997). Development of prosocial, individualistic, and competitive orientations: Theory and preliminary evidence. *Journal of Personality and Social Psychology, 73,* 733–746. doi:10.1037/0022-3514.73.4.733

Van Lange, P. A. M., Ouwerkerk, J., & Tazelaar, M. (2002). How to overcome the detrimental effects of noise in social interaction: The benefits of generosity. *Journal of Personality and Social Psychology, 82,* 768–780.

Van Lange, P. A. M., Rockenbach, B., & Yamagishi, T. (Eds.). (2014). *Social dilemmas: New perspectives on reward and punishment.* New York, NY: Oxford University Press.

Van Prooijen, J. W., & Van Lange, P. A. M. (Eds.). (2014). *Power, politics, and paranoia: Why people are suspicious of their leaders.* Cambridge, England: Cambridge University Press.

Vohs, K. D., & Faber, R. J. (2007). Spent resources: Self-regulatory resource availability affects impulsive buying. *Journal of Consumer Research, 33,* 537–547. doi:10.1086/510228

Wayne, J. H., Casper, W. J., Matthews, R. A., & Allen, T. D. (2013). Family-supportive organization perceptions and organizational commitment: The mediating role of work–family conflict and enrichment and partner attitudes. *Journal of Applied Psychology, 98,* 606–622. doi:10.1037/a0032491

Webster, D. M., & Kruglanski, A. W. (1994). Individual differences in need for cognitive closure. *Journal of Personality and Social Psychology, 67,* 1049–1062. doi:10.1037/0022-3514.67.6.1049

Weisbuch, M., Pauker, K., & Ambady, N. (2009). The subtle transmission of race bias via televised nonverbal behavior. *Science, 326,* 1711–1714. doi:10.1126/science.1178358

Wicker, A. W. (1969). Attitudes versus actions: The relationship of verbal and overt behavioral responses to attitude objects. *Journal of Social Issues, 25*(4), 41–78. doi:10.1111/j.1540-4560.1969.tb00619.x

Wiedemann, A. U., Schüz, B., Sniehotta, F., Scholz, U., & Schwarzer, R. (2009). Disentangling the relation between intentions, planning, and behaviour: A moderated mediation analysis. *Psychology and Health, 24,* 67–79. doi:10.1080/08870440801958214

Williams, K. D., Cheung, C. K. T., & Choi, W. (2000). Cyberostracism: Effects of being ignored over the Internet. *Journal of Personality and Social Psychology, 79*, 748–762. doi:10.1037/0022-3514.79.5.748

Wilson, T. D., Lindsey, S., & Schooler, T. Y. (2000). A model of dual attitudes. *Psychological Review, 107*, 101–126. doi:10.1037/0033-295X.107.1.101

Wolke, D., Copeland, W. E., Angold, A., & Costello, E. J. (2013). Impact of bullying in childhood on adult health, wealth, crime, and social outcomes. *Psychological Science, 24*, 1958–1970. doi:10.1177/0956797613481608

Zaltman, G., LeMasters, K., & Heffring, M. (1982). *Theory construction in marketing: Some thoughts on thinking.* New York, NY: Wiley.

Zhao, X., Lynch, J. G., & Chen, Q. (2010). Reconsidering Baron and Kenny: Myths and truths about mediation analysis. *Journal of Consumer Research, 37*, 197–206. doi:10.1086/651257

Zimbardo, P. G., & Boyd, J. N. (1999). Putting time in perspective: A valid, reliable individual-differences metric. *Journal of Personality and Social Psychology, 77*, 1271–1288. doi:10.1037/0022-3514.77.6.1271

Zuckerman, M. (1994). *Behavioral expressions and biosocial bases of sensation seeking.* New York, NY: Cambridge University Press.

Zuckerman, M., Kuhlman, D. M., Joireman, J., Teta, P., & Kraft, M. (1993). A comparison of three structural models for personality: The Big Three, the Big Five, and the Alternative Five. *Journal of Personality and Social Psychology, 65*, 757–768. doi:10.1037/0022-3514.65.4.757

Index

About the Authors

Jeff Joireman, PhD, was originally trained in social psychology and has held positions in departments of psychology and marketing. Dr. Joireman is currently an associate professor of marketing at Washington State University, where he teaches consumer behavior and marketing research and serves as the department's PhD coordinator. Dr. Joireman's research has addressed a wide range of topics, and his articles have drawn on many of the paradigms detailed in this book. He has published over 60 articles and book chapters in psychology and marketing, with many of his publications appearing in the fields' leading journals, including the *Journal of Personality and Social Psychology, Personality and Social Psychology Bulletin,* the *Journal of Applied Psychology, Organizational Behavior and Human Decision Processes,* the *Journal of International Business Studies,* the *Journal of Retailing,* and *Marketing Letters.* In 2005, Dr. Joireman coedited a book with Alan Strathman titled, *Understanding Behavior in the Context of Time: Theory, Research, and Application.* He has also reviewed over 200 articles for over 25 different journals, served on the editorial boards for the *Journal of Personality and Social Psychology, Psychological Science,* the *Journal of Environmental Psychology,* and *Group Dynamics,* and has twice been named the *Journal of Environmental Psychology*'s Most Prolific Reviewer. Dr. Joireman has won numerous honors and awards, including a Fulbright Scholarship to the Netherlands, multiple Dean's Excellence Awards, an Outstanding Faculty Service Award, and the Department of Marketing's Professor of the Year Award.

Paul A. M. Van Lange, PhD, is professor of social psychology and chair of the Department of Social and Organizational Psychology at the VU University at Amsterdam, the Netherlands, and holds a position as Distinguished Research Fellow at the University of Oxford in England. Most of his research on human cooperation and trust is grounded in interdependence theory, through which he seeks to understand the functions of forgiveness, generosity, empathy, fairness, retaliation, and competition, as well as general beliefs of human nature in various situations. He has published influential papers that have appeared in journals such as the *Annual Review of Psychology, Psychological Bulletin,* and the *Journal of Personality and Social Psychology.* With various colleagues around the globe, Dr. Van Lange has published several books, including the *Atlas of Interpersonal Situations* (Kelley et al., 2003), *Bridging Social Psychology* (Van Lange, 2006), the *Handbook of Theories of Social Psychology* (Van Lange, Kruglanski, & Higgins, 2012), *Social Dilemmas: The Psychology of Human Cooperation* (Van Lange, Balliet, Parks, & Van Vugt, 2014), and *Power, Politics, and Paranoia* (Van Prooijen & Van Lange, 2014). He has served as associate editor for various journals, including the *European Journal of Social Psychology,* the *Journal of Personality and Social Psychology, and Psychological Science,* and is founding editor of an interdisciplinary series on *Social Dilemmas* (Van Lange, Rockenbach, & Yamagishi, 2013). He has been a director of the Kurt Lewin Institute, has been president of the Society of Experimental Social Psychology, and has supervised more than 20 PhD students and five postdoctoral students. Dr. Van Lange's scientific work has been supported by numerous grants and was recognized by the Kurt Lewin Award from the European Association of Social Psychology (2014).